P9-CPZ-664

AMERICAN
RELIGIOUS
PHILOSOPHY

AMERICAN RELIGIOUS PHILOSOPHY

ROBERT J. ROTH, S.J.

Fordham University

HARCOURT, BRACE & WORLD, INC.
New York / Chicago / San Francisco / Atlanta

Acknowledgments

The author is grateful to the publishers of the following periodicals for permission to reprint his articles in whole or in part.

AMERICA. "Charles Sanders Peirce: 1839–1914," Vol. 111, No. 5 (August 1, 1964).

INTERNATIONAL PHILOSOPHICAL QUARTERLY. "Is Peirce's Pragmatism Anti-Jamesian?" Vol. 5, No. 4 (December, 1965).

THOUGHT. "The Challenge of American Naturalism," Vol. 39, No. 155 (December, 1964). "The Religious Philosophy of William James," Vol. 41, No. 161 (Summer, 1966).

He is also grateful to the following publishers for permission to reprint material in this book.

HARVARD UNIVERSITY PRESS. Charles Hartshorne, Paul Weiss, and Arthur Burks, eds. *The Collected Papers of Charles Sanders Peirce*. Volume I, copyright 1931, © 1959; Volume V, copyright 1934, © 1962; Volume VI, copyright 1935, © 1963 by the President and Fellows of Harvard College.

DAVID MCKAY COMPANY, INC. William James, *Pragmatism*, copyright 1907 by Longmans, Green and Company, Ltd. William James, *The Varieties of Religious Experience*, copyright 1902 by Longmans, Green and Company, Ltd. William James, *The Will to Believe and Other Essays in Popular Philosophy*, copyright 1912 by Longmans, Green and Company, Ltd. Used by permission of David McKay Company, Inc.

PREFACE

The present volume is the result of some ten years of study, lecturing, and writing. During those years I always felt that, though almost every area of American philosophy had been ably handled, the attention given the religious ideas of our leading American philosophers was seriously deficient. It can be argued that religion and theology are best left to theologians. But for all that, philosophers in the course of history have frequently raised problems and offered suggestions that have helped in the development of a religion and a theology relevant to a given age and culture.

In this book, I have tried to show that our foremost American philosophers have produced leading ideas in religion. I have even been presumptuous enough to maintain that Americans have made a contribution to the religious thought not only of America but of the world. Hence the audience I have in mind includes the professional philosopher and the theologian as well as all those who feel that religion plays an important role in the growth of civilization and culture.

Every author feels the need to acknowledge a debt to a host of people who have influenced his thinking: his teachers, his colleagues, his pupils—in addition to the recognized giants in their fields whose works he has read and whose ideas he has assimilated. Among the latter, of course, I would include the five great American philosophers whose thought forms the subject matter of the present study.

Beyond these, I would like to mention several people by name. Professor James M. Somerville, who was Chairman of the Fordham University Philosophy Department while I was writing this book, graciously arranged my teaching schedule to give me sufficient time to complete the manuscript. My friend and colleague, Professor Walter E. Stokes, read the whole work and made several valuable suggestions. Through frequent discussions with him, I have come to understand Alfred North Whitehead better and to share some of his enthusiasm for that great philosopher. However, I am sure that Professor Stokes would not subscribe to everything I have said about Whitehead in Chapter V. Through Lorenzo K. Reed, Dean of Fordham College of Philosophy and Letters, I was able to obtain a grant for research and secretarial assistance. Mrs. Mary Zircher proved to be invaluable in editing and typing the manuscript in its final form.

Fordham University   Robert J. Roth, S. J.

CONTENTS

AMERICAN
RELIGIOUS
PHILOSOPHY

I

AMERICAN
RELIGION AND
NATURALISTIC
PHILOSOPHY

There would seem to be little doubt that we Americans are deeply interested in religion. We follow closely its latest trends as they are reported through mass media and we discuss the leading issues with some degree of understanding. Publicists who are always ready to give their readers what they want make sure to keep religion in the forefront of the news. It is not unusual for a magazine or a newspaper to devote a series of articles to a discussion of the major religious faiths, and ample coverage is given to national and international meetings of religious groups, such as the World Council of Churches. Through the medium of television, a whole nation in October of 1965 followed the Roman Catholic Pontiff, Paul VI, step by step from his arrival at Kennedy Airport in New York City, through his historic appearance before the United Nations, to a closing religious service at Yankee Stadium. These events were later reviewed through stunning color photographs in magazines. We are impressed, too, by the number of books being published on religious questions. The field representative of a leading publishing firm has said that there is a ready market today for anyone with a manuscript on liturgy, scripture, or ecumenism.

Religion in a Modern Age: Niebuhr, Herberg, and Cox

Whether we are a religious nation is another question. Thirty years ago Reinhold Niebuhr took a definite stand on one phase of this question when he wrote a devastating critique of "liberal Christianity," a movement within Protestantism that had reached its peak during the first three decades of this century. Two books especially, *Moral Man and Immoral Society* and *An Interpretation of Christian Ethics*, carried the burden of his message.[1]

In Niebuhr's view liberal Christianity had drained from religion its distinctive contribution, which is the dimension of depth in life. It concentrated on immediate values and deficiencies and no longer looked to God as the ultimate ground and fulfillment of existence. The result of all this was that life no longer had meaning and coherence. Niebuhr felt that the crux of the issue between essential Christianity and modern culture is found in the conflict between an awareness of sin as a fact of human existence and a naive trust in human nature. Though it must be admitted that man has tendencies toward love and generosity, he said, too little attention was given to the "demonic force in human life" that makes ever precarious the hopes of the liberal to achieve a new era of peace and harmony in this world. Evil can result not merely from ignorance, which is gradually eliminated by an increase in knowledge, but also from the free choice of man. For this

[1] R. Niebuhr, *Moral Man and Immoral Society* (New York: Scribner's, 1932); *An Interpretation of Christian Ethics* (New York: Harper and Brothers, 1935).

reason the flux of reality contains the possibilities of chaos as well as harmony. Niebuhr admitted, however, that this conclusion would be completely unacceptable to the modern mind.

On the larger social level, Niebuhr complained that liberal thought had allied itself too closely with the ethos of a brutal commercial civilization. Religion, then, becomes identified with the American dream of a good life. Related to this is too great a confidence in democracy and in the alliances between nations as the solution for national and international ills. In the thirties he could indict liberalism with failure by pointing to the Great Depression, to the difficulties confronting the League of Nations, and to the growing conflicts between foreign countries.

For Niebuhr the problem was more than a theological one, for he felt that liberal Christianity had capitulated to naturalistic philosophy and that at times they were scarcely distinguishable. This fear was not without foundation. In 1933 there appeared the famous "Humanist Manifesto," signed by representatives from the more liberal groups within Christianity and Judaism.[2] The Manifesto called for a radical alteration of religious beliefs, dictated by science and economic change and by increased knowledge and experience. The signers claimed that religion in the traditional sense had lost its significance for human living in the twentieth century. For this reason they hailed the passing of theism and deism and placed the whole purpose of man in the complete realization of personality in this world. Over the years, Niebuhr and the naturalistic philosophers have engaged in frequent polemics through books and articles.

A decade ago, Will Herberg, in his *Protestant, Catholic, Jew*, gave evidence from statistics to show that we Americans were a religious people.[3] No matter what category was selected, the religious level of America was shown to have reached an all-time high—in belief in God, life after death, and prayer; in Church membership and attendance; in material expansion; in the status of religion and religious leaders; in intellectual prestige; and, finally, in interest in religion on our college campuses.

Yet, there were also statistics to mar this impressive record of Amer-

[2] "Humanist Manifesto," *The New Humanist*, Vol. 6 (May–June, 1933), pp. 58–61.
[3] W. Herberg, *Protestant, Catholic, Jew: An Essay in American Religious Sociology*, rev. ed. (New York: Doubleday, 1960).

ica's burgeoning regilious life. These, too, Herberg noted, and they forced him to conclude that the rise of religion is accompanied by a rise in secularism. In other words, there is emerging a strange phenomenon called *secularized religion*, which has lost both the sense of a transcendent, holy God before whom man stands in awareness of his own nothingness and that of his works, and the sense of an almighty God who judges, shatters, and reconstructs life itself. Religion has become Americanized, which means that its primary object is not God but the good life, for it has come to be equated with the American virtues of free enterprise, self-reliance, humanitarianism, and self-improvement. In short, according to the conclusions of Herberg religion in America is man-centered:

> In this kind of religion it is not man who serves God, but God who is mobilized and made to serve man and his purposes—whether these purposes be economic prosperity, free enterprise, social reform, democracy, happiness, security, or "peace of mind." . . . Religion as he understands it is not something that makes for humility or the uneasy conscience; it is something that reassures him about the essential rightness of everything American, his nation, his culture, and himself; something that validates his goals and his ideals instead of calling them into question; something that enhances self-regard instead of challenging it; something that feeds his self-sufficiency instead of shattering it; something that offers him salvation on easy terms instead of demanding repentance and a "broken heart." Because it does all these things, his religion, however sincere and well-meant, is ultimately vitiated by a strong and pervasive idolatrous element.[4]

Not long ago Harvey Cox wrote *The Secular City*,[5] a book that in many respects fits into the pattern of thinking so severely criticized by both Niebuhr and Herberg. The book is one grand plea for recognition of the fact that man can no longer ignore his responsibility for the world and its progress. This laudable intention, however, is connected with the thesis that this process of "man's coming of age" involves his turning away from the world beyond. In fact, the book seems openly to equate religion with naturalistic philosophy, an identification against which Niebuhr warned thirty years ago. For, in emphasizing the role of man in furthering the development of the world, and even in the insistence that man is God's partner, Cox has left little or no

[4] *Ibid.*, pp. 268–69.
[5] H. Cox, *The Secular City* (New York: Macmillan, 1965).

place for God. He has, indeed, stated in a closing chapter that the question of God's existence is "a desperately serious issue" that every man must confront for himself. But in explaining what he means by human maturity, the author seems to believe that man will eventually get along without God, that he will thus become "mature, freed from infantile dependencies, *fully human* [our italics]." [6] Moreover, the book gives the impression that religion in the traditional sense has no place in the secular city.

Harvey Cox professes to find confirmation for his position in a non-religious interpretation of biblical concepts. Thus, "secularization represents an authentic consequence of biblical faith." [7] The Hebrew view of creation was a form of "atheistic propaganda," for it separated God from nature and freed society and culture from religious control and from closed metaphysical world-views. At the same time man was able to face nature and develop natural science, which was so necessary for the emergence of the modern world.

Likewise, the Gospel does not call man back to a state of "dependency, awe, and religiousness," but to mature secularity in assuming responsibility for the world. This is seen in the parable of the steward who is put in charge of affairs in the absence of the master. When Paul exhorts us to put away childish things, he is affirming the fact that we are sons and heirs and, hence, responsible for our father's estate. All this, says Cox, points the way toward a secularization that would remove metaphysical and religious suppositions and encourage men to go out to meet the universe.

The views of religion in America as given by Niebuhr, Herberg, and Cox have commanded a great deal of interest and not a little discussion. They have had their critics, too, and the question regarding the state of religion in America will no doubt be debated for a long time to come. A judicious assessment regarding the validity of their treatments is not easy, but perhaps the following can be offered by way of stimulation to further thought and discussion.

Niebuhr was quite right—one might say prophetic—when, thirty years ago, he expressed fear that religion was fast losing its traditional orientation. The trend has continued, and we approach a leveling of the meaning of religion so that it is no longer different from an open naturalism. The United States Supreme Court gave official recognition

[6] *Ibid.*, p. 258.
[7] *Ibid.*, p. 18.

to this trend when, in *Torcaso v. Watkins* (1961), it declared that secular humanism and ethical culture were "religions."

He was correct, too, when he stated that liberal Christianity and naturalistic philosophy, by not giving sufficient attention to the possibility of human evil, have placed too great a stress on the goodness of man and his ability to achieve a lasting peace and harmony in this life. But he seems to exaggerate when he says that these movements are essentially tied to the institutions of a modern age such as democracy, the League of Nations, and international alliances. The naturalists, at least, would admit that these institutions are tentative and that they may be modified or completely changed according to future conditions.

The central point of the liberal movement is that man must involve himself with the world if he is to be truly human. This, indeed, is a valuable insight; and Niebuhr would seem to accept it, at least in its broad outlines. But one can ask if he has been sufficiently open to the value of man's engagement in the world for his religious development and whether he has clearly acquitted himself of the charge of pessimism regarding human nature. Three decades ago his criticism was of service in warning society against the exaggerations of liberalism, and his criticism has lost none of its timeliness. But we also need to appreciate the insights of liberalism and to integrate them into a new, religious world-view.

Herberg, for his part, rightly criticizes those who are interested not in God but in the good life. If one seeks religion merely to achieve a stage of comfort, security, peace of mind, and social status, his religion is not worthy of the name; and Herberg is right in exposing its shallowness. But I am afraid that in drawing the issue in such bold lines Herberg has missed an important dimension of present religious development in America. He has confused a legitimate interest in the things of this world with a selfish preoccupation with the "good life." He shows this lack of precision when he states that religion in America is a gospel of "adjustment, sociability, and comfort, designed to give one a sense of 'belonging,' of being at home in the society and the universe." [8] Now, I would not find all of these elements equally reprehensible; and one of them, with the proper distinctions, I would not find so at all. Thus, if religion is *merely* a gospel of adjustment, sociability,

[8] Herberg, *op. cit.*, p. 261.

and comfort, it deserves to be condemned; and there is little doubt that there are many in America, and in other countries as well, for whom religion means nothing more than that.

But somehow I cannot bring myself to be unduly alarmed if people look for a sense of belonging, of being at home in society and the universe. Advances in knowledge, especially in science, have given man power over elemental forces of the universe and have enabled him to direct the course of events. This power and ability can be used for the betterment of man, especially for his intellectual and cultural development and for his growth in initiative and creativity.

This, to me, is the crux of the whole problem of religion in America and in the world. Herberg has rightly censured certain aspects of contemporary religion, but he has indiscriminately included what I would call the valid yearning and striving for growth that have stirred to life and consciousness within the American mind. The crucial issue, then, is not whether these tendencies should be ignored or eliminated, but whether religion in the traditional sense has the resources to further them and to integrate them into a religious movement that could be the portent of something new. It is this dimension that I find lacking in Herberg's otherwise brilliant analysis of the religious scene in America.

A quite different appraisal can be made of Cox's book. One can certainly criticize his endeavor to find confirmation in Scripture for his seeming espousal of naturalism. Moreover, though he may have pointed out those shortcomings of traditional Christianity that sometimes make it irrelevant to the contemporary scene, he has overstated Christianity's inability to meet modern problems. In this he has largely criticized "the husk of religious life without penetrating to the core of Christianity," as John Herman Randall once said of John Dewey.[9] Cox himself has admitted that some of his statements in *The Secular City* have led to misunderstandings on the part of his critics, and in recent publications he has tried to clarify his position.[10] He is not opposed to the institutional expression of the church, but only to the claims of some religionists that the church is above all change or criti-

---

[9] J. H. Randall, Book Review, *Thought*, Vol. 39, No. 155 (Winter, 1964), p. 630.
[10] See, for example, H. Cox, *The Secular City*, rev. ed. (New York: Macmillan, 1966), pp. xi–xii; D. Callahan, ed., *The Secular City Debate* (New York: Macmillan, 1966), pp. 186–87, 194–203.

cal reflection. Moreover, Cox did not intend to proclaim the "death of God" in any literal sense, but only to underscore the need of finding new ways to talk about God that would be meaningful to contemporary man. These clarifications should be welcomed by even his severest critics.

In any case, I do think that Cox has gone beyond either Niebuhr or Herberg in his analysis of the conditions that confront religion. Time and again he challenges man to assume responsibility for the world. He maintains that in our present age man has reached a level of maturity at which he can play a crucial role in the continued creation of the world. To refuse this role would be a prolongation of immaturity, an evasion of responsibility, and an excuse for laziness.

Cox emphasizes those situations that cry out for the commitment of individuals in the affairs of the world. There is, for example, a need for leadership in assuming social obligations regarding the plight of the underprivileged. While applauding the zeal of those young people who spend several hours a week in slum areas, he claims that such projects generate a spirit of condescension, while those involved should develop a sense of guilt for allowing such inequities to exist and continue. Their time might better be employed in persuading their fathers to exert pressure for changes in tax structures, zoning laws, and restrictions in home-improvement loans.

Furthermore, Cox complains that religion has overemphasized the onerous character of work so that at best man is conditioned to eke out his salvation by the sweat of his brow and at worst he seeks from his work only a pecuniary reward. In the secular city work should be seen as a human enterprise that has the possibilities of joy and liberation. These are realized when man utilizes his energies so that they "contribute to the enrichment of his life and that of his society." Man, then, approaches his occupation not as something that is thrust upon him but as a task that he freely assumes because it leads to his own fulfillment and that of humanity.

Traditional Religion and Involvement in the World

What has been said so far leads us to the following conclusions: in one sense it can be admitted that America has gone further than any other country in liberalizing religion by eliminating the sources of its depth and richness. But in another sense it has been given to America to discern the serious problem facing contemporary religion. For a considerable period of time now—a period roughly coinciding with, though not limited to, the rise of science from the fifteenth century onward—men have become increasingly concerned with this world. This attitude has been damned by some as naturalistic, which in the present context means having an exclusive interest in the things of this world to the gradual loss of interest in and even denial of anything or anyone beyond this world.

There are others who have hailed the interest in this world as a growth in maturity on the part of man. Advances in knowledge, especially in the natural sciences, have given man considerable power over the universe and have enabled him to control and direct the course of things and events. All this can, of course, be used for man's selfish aims; and it can also lead to the cruelty of man against man. But this should not preclude the possibility that knowledge of the universe and a control of its forces can be used for the elimination of human suffering in the form of poverty and disease. Once these obstacles have been removed, man can move on to interest in his intellectual and cultural development.

This is what is meant by growth in maturity. Man need no longer stand helpless before the forces of nature; he can assume responsibility for their direction. By his intelligence he can to a large extent control the future growth of the world on all levels. What man does now makes a difference; and, in a real sense, the future control of the world and of humanity depends largely on him. Such power has placed on man an awesome responsibility and one he can no longer refuse.

In view of this there has grown in human consciousness a desire, even a demand, to understand more and more the meaning of the world in terms of human growth. In the past man may have been content with a meager knowledge of the universe and its mysteries. What he did not know, he could not control; and what he could not control, he left to the Deity. After all, when this life was over, he could always look to a future one; and, hence, he had no need to interest himself overmuch with the present world. "God's in his heaven—all's right with the world" was undoubtedly a solid religious principle; but like most principles it gives expression to but part of reality. For men knew that in many respects all was *not* right with the world, and they began to realize that it was against good moral and religious principles to avoid a commitment to the good of humanity and to its betterment when the instruments for such a commitment were in their power.

Added to this is the fact that in the minds of many people traditional religion discouraged interest in human affairs or at least limited this interest to what was considered necessary. What men now craved was a religion that would indeed give them a feeling that God was in his heaven but that would also assure them that He was present in the world as well. At first, there was no intention of ignoring God or of denying Him. But consequent upon a growing awareness of the importance of involvement in the things of the world and upon the widening separation from the world that men believed was being induced by traditional religion, many thought that they were being forced into the impossible situation of accepting God and religion while at the same time denying that which helped them to be truly human.

The Task of Christianity: A New Synthesis

This new orientation was expressed in a remarkable way more than fifty years ago by Arthur Cushman McGiffert (1861–1933), who was for ten years President of Union Seminary, New York. In an address, "The Kingdom of God," he outlined the essential features and peculiar needs of the modern age.[11] It is characterized first of all by confidence in the powers of man. What it needs from Christianity is not condemnation for pride and a plea for humility, but the opportunity for service to mankind. Our age has a deep interest in the present world and great faith in the future. Christianity must give not a warning to set one's face against this world but a vision of the worth and meaning of the work to be done in this life. Our age has grown in social consciousness through the notion of the brotherhood of man. What we ask from Christianity is not a narrow concern for personal salvation but a social ideal that will stir our enthusiasm and gain our devotion.

The men whom we have discussed have indicated important elements for religion in a modern age. Men like Niebuhr and Herberg have shown how essential it is that religion retain those elements that have always been a part of its inner life and spirit. McGiffert and Cox

[11] H. S. Smith, R. T. Handy, and L. A. Loetscher, eds., *American Christianity: An Historical Interpretation with Representative Documents* (New York: Scribner's, 1963), Vol. 2, pp. 286–87.

have drawn the shape of the world that religion must face and for whose problems it must provide some answer. It remains for religion to combine these elements into a new synthesis. This, in all likelihood, is its real task.

American Naturalism: Insights for a New Religious View

The following chapters are presented as guides for the fulfilling of this task. They are devoted to a discussion of our leading American philosophers, with attention to what they had to say about theism and religion. Some, of course, may look upon philosophers as dubious guides. We are often told that, after all, it was the philosopher David Hume (1711–76) who established the impossibility of giving rational support to a belief in a revealed religion and even to a belief in God. We are reminded, even by those who never read Immanuel Kant (1724–1804), that he destroyed forever the metaphysical argument for God; it is usually forgotten that he held for such a belief on moral grounds. The German philosopher Friedrich Nietzsche (1844–1900) announced for the benefit of all that "God is dead," and this obituary has spared future generations the trouble of examining the hypothesis of the Deity.

The situation does not appear to be much better on the American scene. At home and abroad, the common opinion is that our contributions to the philosophical world have been pragmatism and naturalism; and quite obviously these movements leave little or no place for God and religion. In fact, these philosophical trends are indicted for causing the total breakdown of theism and religion. They have had their effects in almost every area of American life—in education, in law, in political and social theory, and even in theology. Far from looking to philosophy for religious insights, it is said, it would rather be necessary to go counter to our whole philosophic tradition, to retrace our steps, and to place ourselves at a point prior to the rise of pragmatism and naturalism when people were still imbued with a religious sensitivity.

I do not think that the analysis above of the general attitude toward American philosophy is exaggerated. If anything, it is understated. In our calmer moments, I suppose, we can understand the failure on the part of Europeans to appreciate American philosophy. After all, it is only in the last few decades that we have shed our intellectual colonialism. Furthermore, I am afraid that for a long time to come we will not convince the European that we have achieved some degree of maturity. In his eyes we are a young nation. We point with pride to buildings or traditions that go back to the sixteenth or seventeenth century, while Europe can trace its roots back many centuries earlier. Yet, we cannot fail to become a bit impatient when we realize that our philosophers are better acquainted with European thought than Europeans are with ours.

What is, however, entirely inexcusable is the failure of Americans themselves to give an adequate picture of American philosophy. Those who have written about it in the last three or four decades have stressed only certain dimensions. For example, they emphasize the fact that our philosophy has given full attention to the growth of science. Pragmatism is viewed primarily as a criterion of truth based on empirical verification. Naturalism is hailed for its attempt to apply scientific methodology to every phase of human life. One would think that American philosophy from its very inception has been hostile, or at least indifferent, to religion. Quite the opposite is the case. There is a deep concern for religion on the part of our more important philosophers, and religious themes form a significant part of their writing. On examination their views prove to be valuable source material regarding problems which face religion today, and they can provide leads for the solution of these problems.

In the following pages we shall examine the theories of God and religion proposed by five of our leading American philosophers. One of these, Josiah Royce (1855–1916), represents the school of idealism, which ruled the philosophical world in America roughly between 1875 and 1915. The other four—William James (1842–1910), Charles Sanders Peirce (1839–1914), John Dewey (1859–1952), and Alfred North Whitehead (1861–1947)—represent pragmatism and naturalism, which gained prominence in the early part of the century and which were dominant until the Second World War. These four philosophers we shall call naturalists for reasons that will appear in the course of this book.

Those who are familiar with American philosophy will not be surprised that Josiah Royce has been selected for study in a work on religious philosophy. God and religion are leading ideas in his thought. Perhaps one reason why he was rejected after the rise of naturalism is that he appeared to be too religious in his philosophy, so that he seemed to be proposing idealism as a substitute for theology. I think this judgment is an exaggeration and I also think we can show why he should not be allowed to remain ignored any longer.

It will surprise many, however, to know that men like James, Peirce, and Whitehead developed a theory of theism and that it played an important role in their thought. They lived in an age that was becoming aware of the tremendous possibilities of modern science and they welcomed the importance that was being placed on man's involvement in the world for the development of his personality. But they were equally concerned with the place of God. The fundamental question they asked was: "How can one be a man of science and still be a religious man?" As we shall try to show, it was in the effort to answer this question that James developed his pragmatism.

John Dewey, of course, is a notable example of those who had no place for God in their philosophy. He did, indeed, develop a theory of religion; but it was one which rejected theism. This poses an interesting question: to be an American naturalist, is it necessary to exclude God? In a previously published article on American naturalism, I myself stated that a negation of God was among American naturalism's essential characteristics.[12] I feel now that this appraisal should be clarified, for it gives too narrow a picture, leaving the impression that to be an American naturalist it is necessary to deny God and traditional religion.

Such a view is true only under certain conditions. For example, if one defines the characteristics essential to American naturalism as it is understood by those naturalists who actually deny God, then obviously such a denial must be included in one's definition. Also, one could limit oneself to an examination of those naturalists who actually deny God, and again the classification is accurate. As a matter of fact, these were the guiding principles used when I myself included denial of theism among the characteristics of naturalism. (At the time I was attempting to state the essentials of American naturalism and to indicate that to reject naturalism because of its denial of God would be to lose the valuable insights it can give to religious thought. In other words, my thesis stated that *even though naturalism denies God*, it still can fructify a religious view.)

[12] R. J. Roth, S.J., "The Challenge of American Naturalism," *Thought*, Vol. 39, No. 155 (Winter, 1964), pp. 559–84.

However, this is but one way to view American naturalism. Another approach would be to broaden the scope to embrace all those who, whether theists or not, have raised questions that must be faced by Europe and the world as well as by America in any attempt to work out a theory of religion. We shall then be open to a strong and influential stream of American naturalism, represented by men like James, Peirce, and Whitehead—all of whom attempted to find a place for God in their philosophy. We shall at the same time include the philosophy of John Dewey, which, in spite of its denial of God, can be more instructive than the thought of many theists. In order to appreciate the importance of American naturalism in this broader sense, it would be well at this time to examine its main characteristics. A study of individual naturalists will then help us to understand how a common background and a common experience found expression in the philosophy of individual men.

It would seem curious that to date no attempt has been made to write a definitive history of naturalism in American thought. One American philosopher has suggested that "perhaps naturalism is still too much alive to qualify for an obituary." [13] More than that, trends in American philosophy are difficult to classify. American philosophers, like Americans generally, resent being put into pigeonholes; and while openly owing much to beloved masters, they prefer to be considered innovators rather than imitators. For this reason, naturalists often differ widely among themselves on some issues, even though many are bound together by reason of their common debt to such representatives of naturalism as George Santayana (1863–1952), John Dewey (especially), Frederick J. E. Woodbridge (1867–1940), or Morris R. Cohen (1880–1947). Hence it is difficult, if not impossible, to speak of a "school" of American naturalism. Harold A. Larrabee has said that "the career of naturalism in America is the history of the slow growth of an attitude rather than of a specific philosophical doctrine." [14]

How would one, then, begin to describe a naturalist and how distinguish him from, say, a pragmatist? For example, some might say that William James, a pragmatist, could be called an early naturalist,

[13] J. L. Blau, *Men and Movements in American Philosophy* (Englewood Cliffs, N.J.: Prentice-Hall, 1952), p. 380.
[14] H. A. Larrabee, "Naturalism in America," in Y. H. Krikorian, ed., *Naturalism and the Human Spirit* (New York: Columbia University Press, 1944), p. 319. This essay is one of the best of a fine series on various phases of naturalism.

though his attempt to establish his right to believe in a God makes him anathema among later naturalists, while John Dewey, a thorough-going naturalist, could perhaps be called a pragmatist come to term. Historically, this is an acceptable appraisal of the situation, though I would deny that James inevitably leads to Dewey and I would regret the loss of James's insights at the hands of contemporary naturalists.

In spite of these limitations, however, it is possible to outline areas of agreement common to most, if not all, American naturalists. In the process of doing this, we make no claim to writing a definitive treatment of the movement. Instead, we shall suggest points of view from which naturalism may be better understood and appreciated.

At the outset it would be well to dispel a misconception prevalent in many accounts of naturalism. It would be a mistake to look upon naturalists as men who have formulated their philosophy with the one purpose of corrupting men's souls by leveling the citadels of religion and morality wherever they are found. This approach is as fantastic as it is unfair. It stems from the fact that so often naturalism is given serious consideration only when it openly opposes positions held sacred by organized religions. Then naturalism becomes the object of an all-out attack. That its pronouncements on such issues should be opposed with decision is by no means denied. What is questioned is the wisdom and fairness of the wholesale nature of the attack, which indicts naturalism with everything from juvenile delinquency to Nazism and Communism. What is perhaps even more unfortunate is the failure to consider with calm and unbiased mind the positive contributions that naturalism may be able to make to American and Christian thought and influence.

Basic to this misconception is the opinion that naturalism as a philosophy antedated the rise of irreligion and immorality in America and was, indeed, their cause. This would be difficult to prove historically. On the broader level, a serious study of the history of philosophical ideas would show that philosophers have been primarily formulators of the dominant movements of an age and only secondarily determiners of the movements of subsequent ages. The more important philosophers have often found themselves at the junction of a stubborn past and an insistent future, as John Dewey phrased it.[15] When new ideas are already in ferment in the minds of men, philosophers give articu-

---

[15] J. Dewey, *Philosophy and Civilization* (New York: Putnam's, 1931), p. 7.

late expression to these insights. Once formulated, of course, these ideas have consequences, good or bad, depending on one's viewpoint. But it would seem that philosophic ideas give events an added thrust along directions already taken in the popular mind.

The Course of Naturalism

The period after the Civil War witnessed the convergence of events that occasioned the rise of naturalism. One such event was the triumph of determinism within science in the Western world, for this reached its peak during the second half of the nineteenth century. Determinism had long been an accepted position in physics, for Laplace had given it its classical formulation in the early 1800s. Biology, too, felt the impetus of determinism; and biologists were dedicating themselves to the task of proving that no forces were active in the living organism save the physicochemical ones found in inorganic matter.

More than any other area of scientific interest, evolution, with its acceptance of unpredictable origins and growth, would seem to stand in sharpest opposition to determinism. However, Herbert Spencer (1820–1903), both in his writings and in a personal visit, preached the message of Darwinian evolution in America; and so great was his popularity here that lavish tributes were paid to him by leading figures from all walks of life. Spencer's brand of evolution stressed the passive adaptation of man to outer circumstances and his inability to control the course of future events. Such a position was to have important consequences for the development of American social and economic theory.[16]

Another event was the rise in interest in various forms of idealism. Kant and G. W. F. Hegel (1770–1831) were read and studied enthusiastically by members of the "St. Louis Movement," which was begun before the Civil War and resumed after it. The two leading figures of this movement were Henry Brokmeyer (1826–1906), a businessman who as a youth had left Germany and studied Hegel in this country, and William Torrey Harris (1835–1909), an educator. Under their leadership the group launched *The Journal of Speculative Philosophy* —the first philosophical journal published in the United States—

[16] For a good study of this whole question see R. Hofstadter, *Social Darwinism in American Thought* (Philadelphia: University of Pennsylvania Press, 1945).

which appeared from 1867 to 1893. On the academic level, George Sylvester Morris (1840–1889), as a university professor at Johns Hopkins and Michigan, had considerable influence on John Dewey's early interest in Kant and, especially, Hegel. Idealism in one form or other was to dominate American philosophical thought in our universities and colleges until the early part of the twentieth century, its last great representative in America being Josiah Royce.

Although the precise time and place of the birth of naturalism cannot be fixed, its appearance can be seen largely as a reaction to the two views of the meaning of reality proposed by mechanistic determinism and by idealism. The former attempted to explain the universe in terms of matter and energy, physicochemical laws, and combinations of these. It left little room for the possibility of human aims and purposes or for recognized human values such as religion, morality, and aesthetics. Many already began to foresee that this approach was leading to the depersonalization of man and his reduction to the status of "atoms-in-motion." Human purpose and creative endeavor were excluded in a universe whose every activity was already determined, from the smallest atom, through man himself, to the larger realm of economic, political, and social institutions.

On the other hand, these same individuals were dissatisfied with idealism. In their view all forms of idealism proposed ends and purposes that were entirely of another world, above and beyond nature and human experience, and consequently unattainable by human striving.

On the positive side, American naturalism basically affirmed what both materialism and idealism stood for. With materialism, it saw the essential importance of matter. Within the American conscience there was the conviction that the future development of man's highest aspirations could be achieved only in and through matter. And so the naturalists faced the challenging question: How can one come to terms with matter? Deal with it, they felt, we must; but they were likewise convinced that the answer of the mechanist was not enough. Man is not just another particle of matter whose every movement is rigidly determined according to mechanistic laws. He is a source of freedom and creativity, capable of bringing to fruition the potentialities within the human personality.

With idealism, naturalism affirmed human values, ends, and purposes. Man is superior to all other things because he can see beyond the forces of matter and energy to the aspects of things that evoke appreciation and love, and because he can set for himself goals and purposes to be achieved by human effort. But naturalism strenuously resisted any attempt, however slight, to impose these aspects and goals from above the natural processes of the universe. Such ideals must be found in and through nature or they could not be found at all. Man's hopes and aspirations, values and ideals, goals and purposes must begin in nature, develop in it, and in it find their fulfillment. To separate these from nature is to put them out of reach of human means.

It would be well not to attempt a more detailed analysis of naturalism itself. In the hope of underscoring what has been said by others and of adding a fresh approach to the problem, I would like to characterize naturalism as including an insight and a method. The insight consists in a recognition of the importance of matter and of the involvement in matter for the development of the human person in contemporary civilization; the method is the scientific method.

Emphasis on the Importance of Matter

It can be said, I think, that the insight of naturalism regarding the importance of man's involvement in matter is what is most characteristic of American theological and philosophical development. It is astounding how this has been consistently missed. Herbert W. Schneider, an otherwise competent historian of American philosophy, after indicating the influence of European culture in the development of American ideas, has this to say:

> Have they [American traditions] a central content, a dominant note, or a moral lesson? I think not. The reader of this story will probably be at least as bewildered as I am in trying to tell what American history teaches us or what American philosophy "stands for." [17]

Some years ago John E. Smith wrote a series of essays on five men who form "the golden period of American philosophy"—Peirce, James, Royce, Dewey, and Whitehead. He states: "They shaped and brought to clearest expression what we have called 'the spirit of American philosophy.' " [18] Yet, in spite of this "clear expression," Professor

[17] H. W. Schneider, A History of American Philosophy (New York: Columbia University Press, 1946), pp. viii–ix.
[18] J. E. Smith, The Spirit of American Philosophy (New York: Oxford University Press, 1963), p. 187.

Smith admits to an inability to formulate and communicate that spirit. This makes for a vague and scattered treatment that, after so much promise, is not a little disappointing.

One can sympathize with the reluctance on the part of some to label men and movements; for, as indicated above, such a procedure goes counter to the American temperament. Admittedly, it is hazardous to sum up a whole history of ideas in a single formulation, and it would take an omniscient mind to do this with complete success. Nonetheless, incomplete as it may be, such an attempt is far more fruitful than an attitude of almost complete bewilderment, as though American philosophical development were a crazy quilt of ideas gathered from disconnected materials.

What was central to the development of American thought and experience was the recognition of the importance of involvement in the environment. The American pioneer learned early that in order to carve out a new frontier and a new civilization he had to become involved in temporalities. There were forests to be leveled, fields to be plowed, houses to be built. More figuratively, the new settler had to build institutions—political, social, economic, and, when he had time, cultural. His whole experience was geared to active engagement with his environment, whether physical or social. Certainly, the "Turner thesis," with its emphasis on the importance of the frontier in the development of America, has become slightly shopworn; and one can find both its proponents and opponents.[19]

When the dust of controversy settles, however, and one screens out the extreme positions—one in favor of the absolute newness of the American experience and the other in favor of considering America as a Europe transposed—it must be admitted that it was elements in the frontier experience that gave America's development its uniqueness. One of the most important of these elements was the emphasis on

[19] In a memorable address to the American Historical Association in 1893 entitled "The Significance of the Frontier in American History," Frederick Jackson Turner (1861–1932) proposed the thesis that the uniqueness of American development is explained by the existence of a frontier and its advance westward. Developed by him in subsequent writing, the "Turner thesis" became for some three decades the dominant approach to the interpretation of American history. Thereafter it came under fire of criticism, though there are still those who feel that the main lines of the thesis are sound. For a good series of essays on both sides of the question, see G. R. Taylor, ed., *The Turner Thesis: Concerning the Role of the Frontier in American History*, rev. ed. (Boston: Heath, 1956).

man's involvement in the world of things and of people. I would almost like to call the American approach pragmatic and practical, except that in the eyes of many Americans and almost all Europeans the American bent for the pragmatic and practical reduces him to a tinkerer with gadgets who views things and situations in terms of their "cash-value" and for whom the value of an object depends on whether it "works." These are James's terms, we remember, but so badly misunderstood.

One can concede that in the beginning the American approach was all of these things, at least at a time when the pioneer was fighting for bare survival. But with growth in American experience came growth in breadth and depth of the meaning of involvement in matter for the development of man as a person. The theory of biological evolution had much to do with deepening this insight. It stressed the close connection of the living organism with the environment, the organism and environment being viewed, not as two things, but as two aspects of a single interaction. Separated from the environment, the organism soon withers and dies. But if allowed to interact with it, the living being grows and improves, at the same time improving the environment. Growth, improvement, and development, of both organism and environment, are contingent upon interaction between the two.

In a certain sense the biological organism becomes the model illustrating the law of growth and development. Man, too, though by no means reduced to the level of a vegetable, is subject to the same law. If he is to develop as a human—with his art, science, and social and political institutions—he must interact with his environment, whether it include the world of things or of people. In this respect, naturalism is in agreement with modern approaches to the psychology of personality, for both stress the fact that isolation is fatal to personality development—that personality develops when it becomes involved in the world of things and of people and that egocentricity is the sign of an immature personality.

Several corollaries follow from this approach. First, naturalism stresses man's continuity with nature. For the naturalist, man is the product of evolution; and though he differs profoundly from nonhuman organisms, his dependence on nature is radical. It is a naturalism that holds that man is a part of nature because he takes his origin from it and develops only through interaction with it. From this aspect, man is not an alien in the world. The world is his natural home. Matter does not stand in opposition to man, preventing or hindering his development. It is precisely in and through man's involvement in matter that his personality is to achieve fuller and better development.

It is under this heading that naturalism raises its strongest objections against separations of all forms—spirit and matter, mind or soul and body, man and nature, subject and object, knower and known. Naturalists seem haunted by the ghost of Descartes, for every distinction of the kind just mentioned is seen in terms of the Cartesian separation, that fatal "bifurcation" which ushered in modern idealism. To the naturalist this was one of the most tragic moments in the history of philosophy, and he has resolutely dedicated himself to the task of eliminating separations wherever they may be found.

A second corollary of this view of the need for involvement in matter is the law of progressive growth and development. The living organism does not merely achieve a static equilibrium. Only parasitic forms of life do that. As long as it lives, the organism continues its interaction with the environment; and in the interaction both are improved. When growth and development cease, it means the death of the organism. Here we see the principle of evolution that leaves room for novelties and the entrance into nature of new forms of life. It is the absence of this point that is the basis for one of the main objections of the naturalists to mechanical determinism. The latter has no place for novelties; everything is contained, in germ if you will, in advance; and beings develop according to predictable laws. Evolution as accepted by the naturalist, however, involves a development that is open and progressive, with room for surprises and unpredictable things and events. Similarly in the case of man, his life as a human depends on continuous growth and improvement. Life for him does not mean a war, or even a truce, with the environment. Man can never say that he has reached the end of development; he cannot close off growth. If he does, it means the end of his career not only as an organism but as a human as well.

Thirdly, according to the naturalist, the human personality is open and unfinished; it is always in the process of being shaped and formed. In this sense man is an artist who is forming his personality in new ways and with new materials, just as the artist uses line and color to produce an original work of art. Art grows and develops insofar as the artist expresses an experience proper to the particular age and environment in which he lives. Even here the artist does not merely mirror what he sees. The true artist is endowed with the powers of imagination and vision that enable him not only to express more vividly what everyone else feels but also to anticipate experiences that are still in the process of coming to consciousness in the people of a given age or civilization. When artistic imagination and vision die, art dies with them. So, too, when man ceases to express his personality in new ways according to the corresponding growth and development of the environment in which he lives, it will mean his death as a human being.

The last of these corollaries derives from the fact that the naturalist has a keen sense of community. This should not be surprising, since he views the universe not as a series of isolated objects and individuals but as a continuous and unified series of interactions. On the specifically human level this means interaction with the world of people. The naturalist is convinced that human growth can be achieved only when man functions as a member of a community—in a unity of purpose that is the releasing of human potentialities for the full development of the personality, and in a unity of means shared by all the members of the community. In this way all men will be bound together in the common enterprise of acquiring for all the natural goods everyone cherishes: peace, freedom from tyranny, friendship, loyalty and love, release from sickness and poverty, and cultural, aesthetic, and moral development. In fact, the personality is fulfilled only when each one dedicates himself unselfishly and wholeheartedly to the good of humanity now and for the future. It is this dedication to the task of improving the lot of future generations that constitutes man's highest fulfillment.

The Method of Naturalism

The method proper to the naturalist is the scientific, the experimental, the empirical method. One might even say that this method was native to the American from the beginning. He was continually meeting new situations—physical, social, political, economic, religious—so much so that the unfamiliar became the commonplace. Decisions had to be made and executed; in some cases he could apply time-honored principles, but more often the novel situation demanded a novel solution. Moreover, the solution that was applied was often tentative, subject to test, usually revised, and frequently disearded for a new one.

That procedure which in the past was dictated by necessity becomes for the naturalist a conscious method. The scientific method means that every position adopted concerning reality is a hypothesis to be tested. If the hypothesis gives rise to favorable consequences—such as furthering the growth and development of human experience in keeping with environmental conditions—then the hypothesis is verified and the position should be maintained; otherwise, it should be discarded for another. Applied to the world of fact, then, any proposed solution is a hypothesis subject to empirical test and always apt to be revised in a new set of circumstances. There are no absolute and unchanging answers to factual problems that may arise in the course of human experience. In this context scientific method admits of a wide meaning and is called a *theory of inquiry*.

This method presupposes an open and developing universe where evolution holds the central position. In a changing world there are no fixed categories, no unalterable facts, no ineluctable processes. Uniformities there may be, for natural processes are not chaotic, but uniformity does not give rise to fixity. One must be ready for novelties at every turn. Convinced of this, the naturalist is also convinced that in planning for the future and, more, in directing the course of future events, man must adapt his method to the changing facts. Hence he is always ready to alter his plans according to developing circumstances.

Scientific method has a narrower meaning when, in particular fields, it makes use of specialized instruments and techniques and carries out its research in separation from practical applications. It then goes by the name of *physical science*. Lastly, it is called *technology* when it is applied for useful purposes on a wide scale.

According to the naturalist, the scientific method must be extended to all areas of human life. So far its application has been limited to acquiring material goods, thereby obtaining for man a more comfortable existence. Science will reach its fullest potential only when its method is used to secure higher goals and purposes in education, aesthetics, morals, religion, and political and economic affairs. In all these areas the same procedure is followed: a problem is raised; a solution is proposed and tried. The ultimate criterion of the validity of the solution will be its success or failure in enabling man to make more satisfactory adjustments to his environment.

Of course, since the beginning of the twentieth century, scientific method has become far more complex than the description of it given above. However, more important for our present purpose than the intricacies of scientific method is the basic issue involved. The naturalist is facing the question regarding the place of science in the development of the human person. To him science is expressive of an authentic experience whereby human growth is manifesting itself in new ways. He does not feel that science is a cancer on the human organism. While well aware of its dangers, he believes that it represents the probing of the human spirit in its constant effort to solve the mysteries of the universe. It is the same spirit that prompted Aristotle to observe animals, Columbus to sail uncharted seas, Galileo to construct a telescope, Lindbergh to cross the Atlantic. This spirit has manifested itself in foolhardy attempts; like evolution itself, it has taken blind alleys. But it has also testified to a fundamental and constant direction toward the uncovering of unsolved problems and unknown aspects of reality.

In our own times we have witnessed the interest in space travel, progress toward which has advanced to such a degree that men talk casually about eventually reaching the moon. Can all this be explained merely on the basis of military strategy or propaganda advantage? Undoubtedly these aspects have favored such an interest. Perhaps without them the rate of progress would be slowed; certainly, there would be a decrease in the colossal waste of money through duplication of effort by competing nations. But it is a fair guess that such interest would still continue, motivated by the same inquisitive spirit that has been at work in so many intellectual advances of the past.

Yet there is involved here more than a desire for the intellectual satisfaction that comes with the solution of mysteries. Such an aim is more characteristic of science in the restricted sense of a systematic body of knowledge. The naturalist is also seeking an answer to the meaning of technology, the application of science to practical uses; he realizes that the world is developing largely along technological lines.

Naturalists have attempted to develop a philosophy that will respect shared goals and values. They believe that science and technology are capable of improving the human estate on a scale never before known in the history of mankind. Science has proved what it can do in eliminating or reducing poverty, sickness, and disease and in acquiring the goods of life more easily and plentifully. It has yet to show that it can pursue those ends that are more properly human: the social, aesthetic, moral, and religious. The naturalist is certain that it can, even while he admits that man's use of the means at his disposal has not yet verified this certainty (simply, he says, because the means have not been universally applied).

Such is the ideal the naturalist proposes to achieve through the scientific method. There is no question of a return to the "atoms-in-motion" of the mechanist. Man is not pushed along like a straw before the wind. He is capable of shaping his destiny within certain limits by the strictly human tools of reflective inquiry and scientific method. Neither is man to succumb to the depersonalizing effects of science. The human spirit has the capacity to rise above these effects and to dominate science as long as man keeps before him the human purposes and goals that science is designed to achieve. As John Dewey has said, "Science is made by man for man"; [20] and here he meant for the development of man in his deepest dimensions.

Such are the characteristics that I feel are essential to American naturalism. They are important for any attempt to work out a theory of religion relevant to the modern world because they contain an essential groundwork that must be integrated into religion. As we stated earlier, the question of theism need not be included in our characterization of naturalism. What is important is that the naturalists, as described above, have drawn in detail the shape of the world that confronts religion. As a matter of fact, three of the naturalists whom we shall discuss did make theism an important element in their thought.

Finally, this book does not pretend to be a philosophy of religion in the manner of Edgar Sheffield Brightman (1884–1953), who defined his work as "an attempt to discover by rational interpretation of religion and its relations to other types of experience, the truth of religious beliefs and the value of religious attitudes and practices." [21] In his view, the philosophy of religion attempts to find the truth of all tenets of religion and does not deal with the peculiar tenets of any faith.[22] I am concerned more with what five leading American philosophers have said about God and religion and why they were led to a belief in God or to a rejection of Him. Even more important is their description of the kind of world that confronted them and the nature of the adjust-

[20] J. Dewey, *Experience and Nature* (New York: Norton, 1929), p. 382.
[21] E. S. Brightman, *A Philosophy of Religion* (Englewood Cliffs, N.J.: Prentice-Hall, 1940), p. 22. For a similar approach see P. A. Bertocci, *Introduction to the Philosophy of Religion* (Englewood Cliffs, N.J.: Prentice-Hall, 1951), p. 8.
[22] *Ibid.*, p. viii.

ment to it they thought it necessary to make. Let us turn to American philosophers, then, for what they can teach us about the modern world—to men like Royce, James, Peirce, and Whitehead, who attempted to be religious men in a scientific universe, and to John Dewey, who rejected God because he did not see how theism could make this world meaningful.

II

WILLIAM JAMES

AND THE GOD
OF PRAGMATISM

Williilliam James represents a type of scholar that is rarely met today. This is an age of specialization, when scientists find it more and more difficult to communicate with classicists or philosophers and vice versa. We even seem to be reaching the point where scholars in the same discipline will not be able to understand one another. But James had the advantage of a varied education and a diversified academic career. Born in 1842, he studied in England and on the continent before he was nineteen, laying the foundation for his later facility in French and German. Throughout his life he made occasional trips to

Europe, mainly to restore his ever failing health, but also to keep in touch with the intellectual movements abroad. James graduated from the Lawrence Scientific School at Harvard, where he studied chemistry and biology. He received a degree from Harvard Medical School in 1869, though poor health prevented him from pursuing a medical career.

His first teaching assignment came in 1873, when he was appointed an instructor in anatomy and physiology at Harvard. During this period he taught courses in the evolutionary thought of Herbert Spencer. While abroad, James had become aware of the developments in experimental psychology, or the "new psychology," as it was called, which had taken its rise in Germany. It is not surprising, then, that his interest in physiology soon led him into psychology, and he began lecturing in that subject in 1875. In the same year he organized the first laboratory of psychological experimentation in the United States. Some would like to claim that he thus anticipated by four years the achievement of Wilhelm Wundt (1832–1920) at the University of Leipzig, for the latter is credited with setting up the first laboratory of experimental psychology. But it is clear that the type of work James was doing was not experimental in the real sense. Nonetheless, in 1890, after many years of study and research, he published his two-volume *Principles of Psychology*, a work that still stands as a landmark in that field. James's lasting contribution to psychology has won for him the title of "the father of American psychology."

In 1880, James began to teach philosophy, a subject that had always fascinated him. He remained at Harvard as Professor of Philosophy until his retirement in 1907, when he closed a teaching career that, although interrupted frequently by periods of illness, had been filled with fruitful years of study, teaching, lecturing, writing, and travel. He continued to develop his philosophical ideas in published books until his death in 1910.

The name of William James inevitably calls to mind the word "pragmatism" and with it the hard-bitten, time-serving practicalism that is usually associated with American thought. "Get the job done the best way you can" is the most familiar characterization of our spirit. James himself contributed not a little to this misconception, for he used terms like "practical consequences," "cash-value," and "stubborn facts" to explain his thought. American philosophers after him have not helped the situation, for even though they have attempted to counteract exaggerations, they have emphasized the empirical, objective, scientific aspects of his thought, while ignoring other elements. Hence Americans have come to wear the above epithets like scars of reproach, and there seems to be little likelihood that the situation will change radically in the near future.

In the light of this, the attempt to discuss James's religious philosophy may come as a surprise. Surely he did treat of religious themes, but these are often considered to be out of character with his philosophical thinking, as represented by pragmatism, or with his scientific thinking, as represented by his psychological works. According to this viewpoint, his religious philosophy is badly thought out and proves embarrassing in the light of his other work. It should even be considered outside his philosophy and science; peripheral to his thought, not to say contrary to it; a product of his old age, when he retired from academic life to contemplate the eternal verities and prepare himself for the final day. After all, isn't it true that, when one's days are numbered and the burden of life becomes intolerable, one likes to turn one's mind to Gōd and derive from this thought what consolation it affords?

Yet James's pragmatic philosophy was never an all-out espousal of empiricism, objectivism, and scientism. It included elements that were personal, subjective, and religious. A careful reading of him will show that his hope was to reconcile these two currents, for he felt that, in varying degrees, both were found in the men of his generation. On the one hand, the whole spirit of his age was one of great excitement over the advances made in science. James himself was writing as one thoroughly conscious of the fact that he was standing on the threshold of a new age of science, and he was as convinced as any man could be of the importance of that age. He was conversant especially with the new discoveries that were being made in physiology and psychology and with respect to evolution both in this country and abroad, and he had great hopes in what they could do for the betterment of mankind. He knew, too, that all about him science was in the air as more minds dedicated themselves to the task of scientific research and discovery: "Never were as many men of a decidedly empiricist proclivity in existence as there are at the present day. Our children, one may say, are almost born scientific." [1]

[1] W. James, *Pragmatism* (London: Longmans, Green, 1907), p. 14.

However, men had not completely forgotten religion. But, as a deeply religious man, James shared with others the fear that the new science would rise to submerge the traditional belief in God and all that it has meant for the growth and development of civilization. The common man was of the same mind, pulled two ways, for "He wants facts; he wants science; but he also wants a religion." [2] James knew that on the professional level attempts had been made to work out a religious philosophy. These attempts had taken expression in the rationalistic idealisms of the German, British, Scottish, and American traditions. But all of these, he felt, were so many abstract constructions, entirely divorced from the concrete human situation. Religion must in some way be relevant to man's deepest needs, and the God in whom men would believe must be one who bends down to involve himself in the pressing problems that make up daily existence.

The task of reconciling the scientific and religious currents of his time was something that preoccupied James throughout his scholarly life. Treatments of him have not sufficiently taken into account the fact that the problem of God is central to his thought. His writing on this theme goes back as far as 1879, when he was 37 years old. The ideas expressed then and thereafter had been germinating for years, just as his ideas in psychology were long being shaped and formed even though he did not finish his great work, *The Principles of Psychology*, until 1890, at the age of 48. Once the subject of theism entered his writings, there began a line that ran continuously through all of his important philosophical works: *The Will to Believe*, containing essays dating from 1879 to 1896; *The Varieties of Religious Experience*, in 1902; and *Essays in Radical Empiricism*, published posthumously in 1912, though containing essays from 1904 and 1905.

Let there be no mistake about it: the problem of God is integral to all James's philosophical works, including his *Pragmatism*. All of them must be accepted on this ground or not at all. It is true that he professed to propose pragmatism simply as a method that could lead to absolutism, theism, atheism, or materialism; but, despite this disclaimer, he offered it as a theistic solution to what he deemed were the inadequacies of the materialism of a Spencer and the absolutism of a Bradley or a Royce.

It will be the burden of this chapter to reassess James's thought in

[2] *Ibid.*, p. 15.

the light of his religious orientation. There is value in such an undertaking: for one thing, it should show that the theory of pragmatism, which has been called America's first indigenous philosophy, is not atheistic at its source. In the area peculiarly its own, American philosophical thinking at its origins did not eliminate God. Recognition of this point should also help to counteract the disservice done to James's thought and to American philosophy generally by those who leave out elements that do not fit into their own philosophical presuppositions.

It will be seen, too, that the disagreements between pragmatism and the likewise indigenous naturalism were not ones that concerned the minor issue as to whether one could "go as far as James" in admitting a deity. The break was radical, on this point at least, and concerned an issue that was central to James's thought.

The following pages, then, will attempt to analyze James's main philosophical works, not with the view to giving a complete exposition of his thought, but with the hope of piecing together his religious philosophy. The limitations dictated by the purpose should not give a distorted picture, since the works of James under discussion present the main lines of his thought.

Some preliminary remarks should be made regarding James's style, for this has been his greatest strength as well as his greatest weakness. On the one hand, his writings are often truly literary, with the power to portray dimensions of human experience many others have felt but were unable to bring to articulate expression. One has the feeling that James has walked through the world and has made contact with human experience on all levels, that he can appreciate the grandeur as well as the commonplace of reality, that he has known joy and sorrow, hope and despair. His sensitivity to various shades of experience has enabled him to see life in all its richness and to draw upon that richness for the development of a more meaningful philosophy.

On the other hand, James's style has left him open to serious misinterpretations. Most of his important works were in the form of lectures. Furthermore, he believed that words should speak to the heart as well as to the head. Consequently, his works lack the clarity of finished treatises, and he spent half his time developing his philosophical ideas and the other half trying to correct misunderstandings of them. A judicious discussion must keep this problem in view, for, while his style makes for pleasant reading, it also makes the task of interpretation a difficult one.

"The Will to Believe" and Other Essays

A beginning can best be made with "The Will to Believe," the opening essay of the book of the same title.[3] It was written in 1896 and is frequently the main, if not the only, source used in discussing James's religious philosophy. Since it is a prime example of the stylistic difficulties already noted, one could predict that it would be open to misunderstandings. Though he apologizes for beginning with some technical distinctions, James hopes to make his whole discussion "as little technical as I can."

His thesis is stated three times in the course of the work, and it would be well to quote the texts exactly:

> . . . an essay in justification *of* faith, a defence of our right to adopt a believing attitude in religious matters, in spite of the fact that our merely logical intellect may not have been coerced.[4]

> Our passional nature not only lawfully may, but must, decide an option between propositions, whenever it is a genuine option that cannot by its nature be decided on intellectual grounds; for to say, under such circumstances, "Do not decide, but leave the question open," is itself a passional decision,—just like deciding yes or no,—and is attended with the same risk of losing the truth.[5]

> *In concreto,* the freedom to believe can only cover living options which the intellect of the individual cannot by itself resolve.[6]

At the beginning of the work James states the kind of decision or option he has in mind. It must first of all be *living*—that is, it must make some appeal to the individual. Thus, in modern terms, to be an astronaut would be a dead option for a lawyer, but it would be a living one for an air-force pilot. Second, the option must be *forced*, so that acceptance or rejection must be unavoidable. For example, "either love me or hate me" is avoidable, since one could be indifferent; while "either accept this truth or go without it" is forced, since there is no alternative. Even a state of indifference constitutes a rejection. Lastly, an option must be *momentous*—for example, the choice of a permanent career.

[3] W. James, *The Will to Believe and Other Essays in Popular Philosophy* (New York: Longmans, Green, 1927). The present study will consider four essays from this book: "The Will to Believe," "The Sentiment of Rationality," "Reflex Action and Theism," and "Is Life Worth Living?"
[4] "The Will to Believe," *ibid.*, p. 1.
[5] *Ibid.*, p. 11.
[6] *Ibid.*, p. 29.

In James's terms, belief in religious matters involves an option that is living, forced, and momentous. Though all of the aspects are important, it is the character of being forced that occupies most of his attention; this is the one that seems most crucial to the whole problem. He argues that the resolve to defer judgment in this case is the same as rejecting the point in question, just as the decision to defer taking out insurance on a house for lack of conviction as to its worth is the same as the decision to refuse to do so.

In the case, then, of a living, forced, and momentous option, the right to believe involves two elements: first, that the intellect is not coerced by the evidence; and second, that one's "passional nature" bids one to believe. Each of these requires some amplification.

Regarding evidence, James has used three modes of expression in this essay: "in spite of the fact that our merely *logical intellect* may not have been coerced," "whenever it is a genuine option that cannot by its nature be decided on *intellectual grounds*," and "options which the *intellect* of the individual cannot by itself resolve." To what kind of evidence do these phrases refer? In the essay being discussed they refer mainly to the empirical evidence of the senses, especially that derived from the physical sciences. That this is their meaning seems clear from the fact that James plays the part of an objector to his own position by citing the advances made by the scientific mind, which submerges personal preferences and adheres to the impersonal, objective method of science. It would seem that he is leaving no doubt that he is aware of the main objection to his position and that he is just as clear in going against this tradition.

In the case, then, where empirical evidence does not coerce the mind, our "passional nature not only lawfully may, but must, decide." All sorts of interpretations have been given to the meaning of "passional nature," though the most common one takes it to mean subjective, emotional states. If this interpretation were valid, James would deserve all the criticism he has received in this regard.

But it is evident that James did not mean anything as naive as this. He is trying to make the point that there is another kind of evidence, besides the empirical evidence of the senses, that deserves consideration in any judgment. It is the evidence of the drives, desires, instincts, demands, exigencies of our own nature. He was convinced that these were in the main faithful and would lead to valid judgment and action, just as those of the animals lead them in the main to the choices necessary for their continued survival. He did not, of course, reduce man's life to the level of blind instincts; but he did feel that man's demands, as found in his own nature, should be respected as indicative of external reality. He warns the scientist against "putting your extinguisher upon my nature" [7] and against commanding "that we shall put a stopper on our heart, instincts, and courage." [8]

The challenge raised extends even to the claim of the scientist to pure objectivity in his own field of research. In support of his position, James tries to give examples of cases where both the common man and the scientist allow personal preferences and prejudices to sway their judgment, especially regarding those positions we want to be true. The common man, for example, believes in molecules and the conservation of energy, in democracy and human progress, not because he sees the inner reasons of these beliefs, but because they are backed by authority or are meaningful for everyday life.[9] Likewise, the scientist will sometimes refuse to consider certain hypotheses because they do not quite fit into current scientific theory. James cites the example of a leading biologist who stated that, even if telepathy were true, it should be concealed because it disrupts the uniformity of nature.[10]

By way of rejoinder, of course, one may point out that James has merely proved that the scientist as well as the layman can become careless and allow personal prejudice to weaken his objectivity; then James has merely shown the defect in the scientist and not in his methodology. This answer is valid enough against the treatment of the subjectivity of science as given in this essay. Especially since they were offered at a time when it was looked upon as a betrayal of science to question the validity of the objective method, James's arguments seem naive.

His failure to think this through also led him to propose examples that not only weaken but even discredit the whole thesis of "The Will to Believe." Thus, in order to show the force of subjective aspects, he states that in some cases "faith in a fact can help create the fact." [11] For example, a train robbery would be thwarted if all the passengers could count on one another and would rise up as one man to overcome the few robbers who are holding all at bay. The irrelevance of this example is all too evident, and it is unfortunate that James's eagerness to

[7] *Ibid.*, p. 27.   [10] *Ibid.*, p. 10.
[8] *Ibid*, p. 29.   [11] *Ibid.*, p. 25.
[9] *Ibid.*, p. 9.

show the force of personal faith betrayed him into using it. It is no wonder that his whole position, as given in this essay, has been interpreted to mean a voluntarism of an exaggerated kind, where things are brought into being by human fiat.

From this brief analysis of "The Will to Believe" we may make several observations. The main thesis may be stated as follows: we have the right to believe whenever—in an option that is living, forced, and momentous, such as belief in the existence of God—the empirical evidence of sense data is not sufficient to warrant assent. In that case our "passional nature"—that is, our desires and instincts—may, indeed must, sway our judgment so that we are justified in believing.

The main force of James's argument centers on the fact that in the absence of compelling empirical evidence the option is *forced*. In other words, suspension of choice is equivalent to refusal to believe. In that case one will lose all the advantages that would follow upon belief in theism, though what these advantages are is presumed rather than stated. Beyond this, James does not give more than indications of a positive reason in favor of belief. He does make vague and inconclusive references to "passional nature," or simply nature, which seems to mean desires and instincts. Though these latter reasons appear strong as developed in other works to be discussed later, his failure to amplify them here has undoubtedly been the cause of misinterpretations.

Also in the essay is an attack on the claim of the scientist to pure objectivity in his method. The attack loses its force, however, by reason of the weakness of the examples of faith helping to create the fact. Hence, the argument is less than satisfying.

"The Sentiment of Rationality"

The essay called "The Sentiment of Rationality" is interesting for two reasons: first, though it covers a theme similar to that of "The Will to Believe," it is much more carefully worked out and is a more serious attempt at philosophical discussion. Second, it is a much earlier work than "The Will to Believe," one part having been written in 1879 and the other in 1880. For this reason, it can and should be used in any attempt to interpret "The Will to Believe."

Perhaps the most important aspect of this essay is the reinterpretation James gives to the term "rational." His basic problem is how the philosopher knows when he has fulfilled his task of attaining a rational frame of things. James takes the standpoint of the philosopher himself and cites subjective indicators that constitute the "sentiment of rationality." By this he means "a strong feeling of ease, peace, rest. . . . The transition from a state of puzzle and perplexity to rational comprehension is full of lively relief and pleasure." [12] He then defines it as follows:

> This feeling of the sufficiency of the present moment, of its absoluteness—this absence of all need to explain it, account for it, or justify it,—is what I call the Sentiment of Rationality. As soon, in short, as we are enabled from any cause whatever to think with perfect fluency, the thing we think of seems to us *pro tanto* rational.[13]

There are two ways of attaining this sentiment; one is the theoretic, the other the practical. The first fulfills man's craving both to simplify and to distinguish by classifying things into kinds and by arranging their relations and conduct into extensive laws. This procedure succeeds in some measure in accounting for both the unity and multiplicity of things. Yet, because it is abstract, it is inadequate, "the rest of the living fact being for the time ignored by the classifier." [14] From this we conclude "that the simple classification of things is, on the one hand, the best possible theoretic philosophy, but is, on the other, a most miserable and inadequate substitute for the fullness of the truth. It is a monstrous abridgment of life." [15]

This indicates that there is another road to the free movement of the mind, called the practical aspect of the rational. Other demands besides the theoretic must be considered—cravings, needs, and exigencies without which the universe will in no way appear "rational" in spite of neat classifications and conceptualizations.

Specifically, there is in man, according to James, the "ontological wonder," which is the craving of the mind for further explanation. Man is not satisfied with abstract classifications but presses on to the further question of the ultimate "why": "Why was there anything but nonentity; why just this universal datum and not another?" In James's view the theoretic aspect of the rational leads to unanswered questions, and the free movement of the mind has been blocked.

[12] "The Sentiment of Rationality," *ibid.*, p. 63.
[13] *Ibid.*, p. 64.
[14] *Ibid.*, p. 67.
[15] *Ibid.*, p. 69.

James then tries to spell out the elements of the philosophic conception of the universe that will satisfy this aspect of man and restore to the mind its free movement. This conception must be one that, in a general way at least, banishes uncertainty from the future. In his view no conception of the universe can be considered fully rational that leaves man with a haunting sense of uneasiness, fear, and ultimate doom.

Moreover, to be called rational a philosophy must define the future that is in accord with our spontaneous powers.[16] Without lasting goals to our final purposes and objects for our deepest loves and energies, the world will be completely unintelligible in spite of all the theoretic explanations that one may devise. For this reason James rejects materialism as inadequate, since it "denies reality to the objects of almost all the impulses which we most cherish." [17] James concludes this section of the essay by predicting the failure of any philosophy that is not in accord with the most powerful of our emotional and practical tendencies. On the other hand, he maintains that moral beliefs that speak to these tendencies will be accepted in spite of inconsistency and vagueness.[18]

In these terms, then, James has raised the challenge to any philosophy that would attempt to appeal merely to the theoretic aspect of man while ignoring his practical, or perhaps better, affective side. The universe must make its appeal to the whole man, not merely to the man who tries to reduce the manifold into some sort of order and unity, but also to the man who feels within himself certain exigencies that are so deep-seated that they can never be shaken off. James would challenge any philosophy that did not do both. In his view, it could never be called "rational," for it gives a distorted view of the universe by leaving man's imperious demands unfulfilled.

Had James ended his essay there, he would have given a clear presentation of his position—one that could be examined and evaluated in its own right. In a way that is much clearer than that in "The Will to Believe," he has developed his argument in favor of theism from an analysis of "passional nature," so vaguely alluded to in the latter essay; and he has shown its relation to "rational."

However, he feels that he must further justify the introduction of

[16] *Ibid.*, p. 82.
[17] *Ibid.*, p. 83.
[18] *Ibid.*, p. 88.

subjective elements into the argument. As in "The Will to Believe," he tries to show that all knowledge, scientific as well as philosophic, depends on subjective elements and that in the absence of empirical verification we may, in forced options of a religious nature, take up the position of belief under the impact of subjective tendencies. He even brings in examples where faith creates its own verification. In doing all this, he has, I believe, weakened his case and opened the essay to much the same criticism that we have leveled against "The Will to Believe."

On the other hand, the strength of "The Sentiment of Rationality" lies in the interpretation James has given to the term "rational" and the orderly way in which he has presented it. In this it foreshadows his other philosophical works.

"Reflex Action and Theism"

Two more essays from *The Will to Believe* deserve at least passing consideration. One, "Reflex Action and Theism," is dated 1881, only a year after "The Sentiment of Rationality" to which it bears some similarities even though it is written from a different standpoint. James is speaking particularly as a teacher of physiology, since he was invited to lecture in that capacity; and he relates his talk to theism, since he is addressing a group of Unitarian ministers.

His purpose is to discuss the latest developments in the theory of reflex action and apply them to theism. Reflex action comprises three stages: sensory impressions that come from the outside; reflection, which is the mid-point of the triad and transforms the world of impressions into our world of conception; and action that is outward behavior. The dominant stage is the stage of action, and it commands the sensing and conceiving stage. In fact, one sees the mind as a teleological mechanism:

> I mean by this that the conceiving or theorizing faculty—the mind's middle department—functions *exclusively for the sake of ends* that do not exist at all in the world of impressions we receive by way of our senses, but are set by our emotional and practical subjectivity altogether. . . . Destroy the volitional nature, the definite subjective purposes, preferences, fondnesses for certain effects, forms, orders, and not the slightest motive would remain for the brute order of our experience to be remodelled at all.[10]

[10] "Reflex Action and Theism," *ibid.*, pp. 117–18.

James maintains that for a theory of the universe to be accepted, it must conform to each department of this triad. It must be faithful to the department of sense impessions or the facts of nature, it must eliminate inconsistencies, and it must provide our active and emotional powers with objects worth living for. However, when he applies the theory to theism, he prefers to concentrate on department three, discreetly avoiding the question as to whether theism can satisfy departments one and two. He insists on the importance of the third element, which he calls practical rationality, a phrase reminiscent of "The Sentiment of Rationality." Actually, his whole orientation is much the same, even though he is now approaching it from the standpoint of physiology. In other words, the dominant influence is given to the inner demands and needs of man, for these are to be trusted.

It is here that the strength of theism is seen, for it presents a practically rational solution by appealing to our active nature and releasing the springs of our emotions. The world is changed from a dead *it* to a living *thou*, and this elicits a response from the whole man.[20] By reason of its practical rationality, theism will outlast all other creeds, for it provides an object toward which the active forces of our nature can be most deeply and worthily discharged.

"Is Life Worth Living?"

The last essay of this series to be discussed is the one entitled "Is Life Worth Living?" Since it came only a year earlier than "The Will to Believe," it is not surprising that these two should bear close resemblances. James again takes his starting point from man's inner needs. On the intellectual level, these have been time and again prophetic in leading to new scientific discoveries. Scientists have uncovered harmonies hidden in the world of nature because they felt an inner demand for harmony on the logical and mathematical levels. Laws have been established and facts discovered because they were sought after in order to satisfy an inner need.[21]

James then asks why inner needs cannot be prophetic on the religious level, too:

> But the inner need of believing that this world of nature is a sign of something more spiritual and eternal than itself is just as strong and

[20] *Ibid.*, p. 127.
[21] "Is Life Worth Living?" *ibid.*, p. 55.

authoritative in those who feel it, as the inner need of uniform laws of causation ever can be in a professionally scientific head. The toil of many generations has proved the latter need prophetic. Why *may* not the former one be prophetic, too? And if needs of ours outrun the visible universe, why *may* not that be a sign that an invisible universe is there? [22]

James challenges the right of science to prevent us from trusting our religious demands, for science tells us only what is, not what is not. His conclusion from this is that one has the right to adopt religious belief when scientific evidence does not either prove or disprove it and when one's inner needs demand it. In fact, these inner needs are our most reliable contact with the nature of things, "and compared with these concrete movements of our soul all abstract statement and scientific arguments—the veto, for example, which the strict positivist pronounces upon our faith—sound to us like mere chatterings of the teeth." [23]

James's basic message is that life, with its hopes and ambitions, trials and struggles, cannot be ultimately meaningless and worthless. The affective side of man makes certain demands that, if not fulfilled, cause the universe to appear irrational in spite of our growth in intellectual and scientific understanding.

Such, then, are the early essays of James that center around the question of theism. It can be seen that his interest in this theme extends as far back as 1879, during a period coterminus with his scientific work. It will be the task now to show how the main lines of these works, for the most part poorly expressed and unevenly developed from a technical point of view, bear the seeds of further growth.

The Varieties of Religious Experience

The *Varieties* is important for an understanding of James's position regarding religion. Although he did not write it until the spring of 1901 and 1902 (as two series of Gifford Lectures), he had pondered the question for many years; and the work gives evidence that he had long been collecting material from books, articles, and letters.

James originally intended that the work be metaphysical as well as descriptive. However, so eager was he to complete his examination of

[22] *Ibid.*, p. 56.
[23] *Ibid.*, p. 62.

experience that the descriptive becomes almost the whole of it. It is only at the end that he takes up again a philosophical orientation already evident in his other writings on religion; and though schematic and unsatisfactory, the treatment is continuous with his previous work and gives hints of his later philosophical development. For these reasons the *Varieties* should be read as an introduction to the serious philosophical works he was soon to write, especially his *Pragmatism*, for these in large part do in a philosophical vein what James intended to do in the *Varieties*.

This work can be looked upon as one great protest against the attempt to ignore or explain away religious experience. It seemed incredible to James that such experience should tell us nothing about man and external reality, in spite of the fact that many of its manifestations were in his eyes invalid and even absurd. By reason of its long history, its seriousness, its special characteristics, and its influence upon the conduct of men, there seemed to him to be something intellectually dishonest in refusing to respect the data of religious experience and the imperiousness of its demands.

James would go to religious experience, then, to see what could be learned from it. As he notes early in the first lecture, his standpoint is that of psychology, "the only branch of learning in which I am particularly versed." He delves into personal histories and seeks out examples of religious experience wherever he can find them. He covers a wide range of topics—including the "healthy-minded" and the "sick soul," conversion, saintliness, and mysticism. No example is too trivial, no case too insignificant for examination and evalution, for he is convinced that religious experience forms an independent source of data. At the close of the work he admits that perhaps the cases related have given evidence of exaggerated emotionality, but he feels that as data they were as worthy of examination as the more commonplace for a full elaboration of his topic.

The purpose of these examples is to underscore the importance of man's inner feelings and demands for a full picture of the universe, especially when they seem to tell us of the reality of theism and religion. The work is thus a continuation in more extended form of the theme already developed in "The Sentiment of Rationality," where he took the position that both the theoretic and the practical aspects of man are essential if our view of reality is to be "rational." It is "man's whole mental life" that deserves consideration, for the fruits of the theoretic compared with the practical are "relatively superficial." [24]

In a section that introduces an element not found in the works already treated, James discusses what he calls the "sense of presence." By this he means the pervasion of the inner soul by a sense of reality, of "presence" regarding external objects, that is different from knowledge through abstract conceptualizations about them and different from knowledge through the senses known to psychology. He writes:

> It is as if there were in the human consciousness a *sense of reality, a feeling of objective presence, a perception* of what we may call "*something there,*" more deep and more general than any of the special and particular "senses" by which the current psychology supposes existent realities to be originally revealed. If this were so, we might suppose the senses to waken our attitudes and conduct as they so habitually do, by first exciting this sense of reality; but anything else, any idea, for example, that might similarly excite it, would have that same prerogative of appearing real which objects of sense normally possess.[25]

James gives examples to illustrate the existence of such a sense. He appeals to the example of cases where people have the feeling of the presence of someone in the room with them even though their ordinary senses give no evidence of it. A clearer illustration of what is meant is seen in the sense of the habitual presence of a loved one to the lover: the feeling of the other's presence affects everything that the lover says or does.

For the most part, James draws upon examples of hallucinations and of what was known in his day regarding psychical research. He makes no attempt here to pass judgment on the objective validity of such experiences but merely cites them as data for investigation. In addition, they serve as illustrations leading into the religious sphere. People do at times feel impregnated with the presence of God, with an intimate communion with the divine. Such instances deal mainly with the transient and periodic sense of God's presence, though there are other cases where the felt presence is more lasting. Regarding this sense of presence, James concludes with the conviction that in the sphere of religious experience many people believe in objects not through mere conceptions of the intellect but through the direct apprehension of quasi-sensible realities.[26]

[24] W. James, *The Varieties of Religious Experience* (New York: Longmans, Green, 1902), p. 73.
[25] *Ibid.*, p. 58.
[26] *Ibid.*, p. 64.

It should be noted that as a psychologist James is not so much concerned for the moment with the objective validity of these feelings as with their power to convince the mind. In fact, they are often as convincing as the conclusions drawn from the data of direct sensible experience. He admits, of course, that science has greater prestige; but in the last analysis one's feelings hold the main position:

> . . . [science] can challenge you for proofs, and chop logic, and put you down with words. But it will fail to convince or convert you all the same, if your dumb intuitions are opposed to its conclusions. If you have intuitions at all, they come from a deeper level of your nature than the loquacious level which rationalism inhabits. Your whole subconscious life, your impulses, your faiths, your needs, your divinations, have prepared the premises, of which your consciousness now feels the weight of the result; and something in you absolutely *knows* that that result must be truer than any logic-chopping rationalistic talk, however clever, that may contradict it.[27]

For this reason James is highly critical of reliance merely on logical arguments in favor of religious positions. Unless there is a deep inner conviction based on man's intuitions, rational arguments will be useless: "The unreasoned and immediate assurance is the deep thing in us, the reasoned argument is but a surface exhibition. Instinct leads, intelligence does but follow." [28] James is not making a judgment here as to which type of evidence is better. He is merely pointing out which one "as a matter of fact" is predominant in the religious sphere.

The examples given above are taken from the earlier sections of the *Varieties*. There, as throughout the greater part of the work, James speaks as a psychologist; and, hence, he confines himself to a description of religious experience. Even when he speaks favorably of subjective evidence and critically of rational proofs and arguments, he deals exclusively with their strength or weakness in convincing the mind and not with the objective existence of the objects in question.

It is only in the final pages, all too few and brief, that he begins to develop anything like a religious philosophy, for there he takes up the question of whether religious experience gives evidence of anything objectively true. He admits that "religious philosophy is an enormous subject," and he hopes to give only "that brief glance at it which my limits will allow." [29] He is correct on both counts, and hence the read-

[27] *Ibid.*, p. 73.
[28] *Ibid.*, p. 74.
[29] *Ibid.*, p. 429.

ing of this treatment proves to be somewhat irritating by reason of its brevity and vagueness. For this reason one must keep in mind that his later philosophical works are extensions of leads begun in the *Varieties*.

James returns to positions already stated several times. On the one hand, he is strongly critical of "intellectualism in religion," which for him means the attempt "to construct religious objects out of the resources of logical reason alone, or of logical reason drawing rigorous inference from non-subjective facts" and which includes "a disdain for merely possible or probable truth, and of results that only private assurance can grasp." [30] There follows a criticism and rejection of scholastic proofs that deal with God's existence and His attributes. At the basis of his criticism is the position that, while such proofs lay claim to universal authority, which is valid for everyone, as against feeling, which is valid only for the individual, they actually fail in their claim: "If you have a God already whom you believe in, these arguments confirm you. If you are atheistic, they fail to set you right." [31]

With regard to God's attributes—His aseity, necessity, immateriality, simplicity, and the rest—James asks what connection they make with life, what difference they entail in the daily living of one's concrete existence. This is, as James explicitly points out, an application of the pragmatic principle. But though here, as in his later *Pragmatism*, he persists in using such words as "cash-value" and "practical consequences," he always includes the relevance an idea or object will have for human conduct in terms of the deeper dimensions of human experience. It is in these terms that James has some rather harsh things to say about systematic philosophy and theology:

> What is their deduction of metaphysical attributes but a shuffling and matching of pedantic dictionary-adjectives, aloof from morals, aloof from human needs, something that might be worked out from the mere word "God" by one of those logical machines of wood and brass which recent ingenuity has contrived as well as by a man of flesh and blood. . . . One feels that in the theologians' hands, they are only a set of titles obtained by a mechanical manipulation of synonyms; verbality has stepped into the place of vision, professionalism into that of life. Instead of bread we have a stone; instead of a fish, a serpent. Did such a conglomeration of abstract terms give really the gist of our knowledge of the deity, schools of theology might indeed continue to flourish, but religion, vital religion, would have taken its flight from this world. What keeps religion going is

[30] *Ibid.*, pp. 433–34.
[31] *Ibid.*, p. 437.

something else than abstract definitions and systems of concatenated adjectives, and something different from faculties of theology and their professors.[32]

James is equally critical of idealist proofs as represented by the British, German, and Scottish schools. His criterion for rejection is the same: transcendental idealism could not possibly be objectively and absolutely rational, otherwise it would be universally persuasive. James draws the conclusion that the truths of direct religious experience cannot be demonstrated by purely intellectual arguments.[33]

James's position on this issue is not entirely negative. He is opposing an attempt to validate objects of religious experience by intellectual processes or logical reasons *alone*. On the positive side, man's intellect can prove to be a strong ally of religion by purifying it of the "scientifically absurd and incongruous doctrines" that have incrusted religion throughout its history. Those conceptions that remain can then be treated as hypotheses to be verified or rejected by future experience.

The other element of James's position, to which he returns in this book, is his insistence that one's own experience be respected. He steadfastly refuses to hold that knowledge of reality is restricted to our intellectual part. Our feelings, too, make contact with the world of real things. In fact, we have more genuine contact with reality through these than through abstract conceptualizations:

. . . the recesses of feeling, the darker, blinder strata of character, are the only places in the world in which we catch real fact in the making, and directly perceive events happen, and how work is actually done. Compared with this world of living indivdualized feelings, the world of generalized objects which the intellect contemplates is without solidity or life. As in stereoscopic or kinetoscopic pictures seen outside the instrument, the third dimension, the movement, the vital element, are not there.[34]

To attempt to describe the world while leaving out "the various feelings of the individual pinch of destiny, all the various spiritual attitudes," is to leave the world a hollow and abstract affair.

The whole tenor of the *Varieties* could engender the suspicion that James will go overboard in his praise of subjective evidence for religious truth. He anticipates this feeling on the part of his audience and warns against it. Actually, the position he adopts is relatively mild. For one

[32] *Ibid.*, pp. 446–47.
[33] *Ibid.*, pp. 454–55.
[34] *Ibid.*, pp. 501–02.

thing, personal experience can supply the original material for criticism and refinement by the intellect. More than that, James repeats his position that science cannot rule out of court the evidence of personal experience. The latter can stand in its own right as giving testimony to the objectivity of religious objects. Experience can tell us that "God is real since he produces real effects." Belief in Him fulfills man's demand for a picture of reality that is fully rational—one, namely, that not only can be conceptualized and classified but that also corresponds to the deep inner longing for a final and happy consummation "in spite of the gates of hell and all adverse terrestrial appearances," where "tragedy is only provisional and partial, and shipwreck and dissolution are not the absolutely final things." [35] This is but a restatement of James's position that a view of reality that leaves unfulfilled man's deepest and most serious exigencies will always appear irrational no matter how else it may be classified and systematized.

But even here the evidence of personal experience is not absolutely conclusive; mistakes have been made. This does not mean that we should abandon religion, since respect for personal experience will at least be a beginning toward reality, for it will provide a hypothesis. In the process, of course, we give up hope of compelling another's assent. At most, we can present a position so consonant with the facts that scientific logic will have no reason to reject it.[36]

For his own part, James was satisfied that his hypothesis was worthy of belief and that by this belief "I seem to myself to keep more sane and true." [37] It is still possible to listen to science when it says that all that exists is the world of sensations and scientific laws and objects. But "The total expression of human experience, as I view it objectively, invincibly urges me beyond the narrow 'scientific' bounds." [38]

Pragmatism

Everything that James has said so far can be looked upon as preliminary to his *Pragmatism*. This work gives clearer shape and more definite direction to his whole religious orientation. James proposed pragmatism as a means of reconciling the twofold need that was stirring in

[35] *Ibid.*, p. 517.
[36] *Ibid.*, pp. 510–11.
[37] *Ibid.*, p. 519.
[38] *Ibid.*

the hearts of so many men of his time, the need for science and the need for religion:

> I offer the oddly-named thing pragmatism as a philosophy that can satisfy both kinds of demand. It can remain religious like the rationalisms, but at the same time, like the empiricisms, it can preserve the richest intimacy with facts.[39]

> . . . pragmatism may be a happy harmonizer of empiricist ways of thinking with the more religious demands of human beings.[40]

His purpose was to vindicate the place of religion in a scientific world. He echoes the theme already seen—namely, that a world without God is irrational no matter how much science may attempt to make it understandable.

James's statement that pragmatism is primarily a method would seem to contradict the religious purpose expressed above. It is quite true that, verbally, James proposed pragmatism merely as a method that could lead to atheism, theism, science, idealistic metaphysics, or a denial of metaphysics. Pragmatism would then seem to be coolly detached and completely neutral. Yet it is difficult to see how he ever really separated it from his espousal of theism. It is noteworthy that he says that "*at the outset, at least* [our italics], it stands for no particular results. It has no dogmas, and no doctrine save its method. . . . No particular results then, *so far* [our italics], but only an attitude of orientation, is what the pragmatic method means." [41]

James would by all means allow that through pragmatism someone else might arrive at atheism, science, or any other view of the universe, for the facts are not yet such as to compel assent to any position. Nonetheless, throughout the work it is quite clear that for James pragmatism leads inevitably to belief in God as the only means of making the world rational. In his mind, an honest application of the method reveals a universe in which God and the religious sphere are included, for without these the universe is unintelligible. The only alternative he seriously considers lies between religious pluralism, with a God concerned about human affairs, and religious monism, with a God detached from them. But for James, "our pragmatism, tho originally nothing but a method, has forced us to be friendly to the pluralistic view." [42]

[39] *Pragmatism*, p. 33.
[40] *Ibid.*, p. 69.
[41] *Ibid.*, p. 54.
[42] *Ibid.*, p. 166. See also pp. 161, 300–01.

With this as a background, let us look briefly at the theory of pragmatism. It will not be necessary to engage ourselves in a detailed analysis of it, since this is more than a twice-told tale. Instead, we shall emphasize those elements that are pertinent to the present problem.

What is usually considered to be most essential to pragmatism is the aspect of "practical consequences." James explains this aspect as follows: "What difference would it practically make to any one if this notion rather than that notion were true? If no practical difference whatever can be traced, then the alternatives mean the same thing, and all dispute is idle." [43]

Some instances will illustrate this point. For example, what does it mean to say that an object is hard? It means that the object will be resistant to the touch; and, in the case of a diamond, that it will scratch a pane of glass. Hence, my idea of a hard object is true if it actually results in these sense impressions. Or in slightly different terms, the idea is true if it enables me correctly to anticipate modes of behavior in dealing with the diamond. To use a more elaborate example, suppose that I am lost in a forest. I project an idea, a plan, as to the path to take in order to find my way out. If I test the idea by actually following the projected route and eventually succeed in emerging from the forest, my idea is true.

Several things may be noted about these examples: first, the final test of the validity of the idea is sense experience. Further, the examples bring out what James means when he says that an idea is true "if it works." He is far from intending a relativism where man is the measure of the truth of ideas and the ultimate arbiter as to what reality is. In the case of being lost in the woods, the individual does not dictate what path will lead him out. He projects an idea, a plan, and then attempts to verify it by definite actions. The idea is true not because he made it so but because it has found its verification in the external order.

Moreover, the idea is also subject to other truths past and present. New ideas must be compatible with all the other truths we already possess: "In other words, the greatest enemy of any one of our truths may be the rest of our truths." [44] This has special application in cases where face-to-face verification is impossible, and James states that these comprise the overwhelming majority of our ideas. For example, I wish

[43] *Ibid.*, p. 45.
[44] *Ibid.*, p. 78. See also p. 212.

to determine whether Julius Caesar actually existed. The past is verified indirectly "by present prolongations or effects of what the past harbored. . . . That past time was, is guaranteed by its coherence with everything that's present." [45]

In these terms, then, practical consequences include two elements: first, verifiability in the form of sensible experience; and, second, consistency with other truths.[46] The picture we get from this is that of a thoroughgoing empiricist who coldly submerges personal feelings in the face of the stubborn facts of nature. This would lead one to conclude that pragmatism is cast in the empirical, scientific, objective mold; and there are many texts to substantiate this view.

But another look will considerably modify this picture. The problem can be approached from several angles, but our choice will be dictated by our main line of thought. Let us suppose that the criteria of sense data and consistency with other truths are not sufficient to decide the issue between two positions. In this case our decision rests on the subjective basis of "elegance" or "economy." James cites Clerk Maxwell as saying that it is "poor scientific taste" to choose the more complicated of two conceptions that have equal evidence.[47]

Here James clearly indicates that one's personal experience must sometimes be consulted in the solution of a problem. This is an application of his principle that purely objective truth is nonexistent:

> Purely objective truth, truth in whose establishment the function of giving human satisfaction in marrying previous parts of experience with newer parts played no role whatever, is nowhere to be found. . . . Truth independent; truth that we *find* merely; truth no longer malleable to human need; truth incorrigible, in a word; such truth exists indeed super-abundantly—or is supposed to exist by rationalistically minded thinkers; but then it means only the dead heart of the living tree, and its being there means only that truth also has its paleontology, and its "prescription," and may grow stiff with years of veteran service and petrified in men's regard by sheer antiquity.[48]

There are times, then, when pragmatism widens the scope of evidence, for it considers even the humblest and most personal experiences.[49] In the case of probable truths, the only test is "what fits every

[45] *Ibid.*, p. 215.
[46] *Ibid.*, pp. 216–17.
[47] *Ibid.*, p. 217.

[48] *Ibid.*, pp. 64–65.
[49] *Ibid.*, p. 80.

part of life best and combines with the collectivity of experience's demands, nothing being omitted." [50] Though these statements are applied specifically to the search for God, it is clear from the whole context of *Pragmatism* that it is a principle applicable to any search for truth under similar conditions.

It is these aspects of pragmatism that manifest definite links with the works already examined.[51] It is true that James presented his ideas in more orderly fashion here (though his lecture style still leaves him open to misunderstanding) and that he has gradually dropped some of the extreme subjective forms under which his thought had previously been expressed. But he has lost none of his insistence on the importance of personal experience as a source of evidence for informing us regarding the external universe and, more particularly, regarding the truth of theism. An analysis of his arguments for the existence of God will make this clearer.

Evidence for Theism

When James said, "I myself believe that the evidence for God lies primarily in inner personal experiences," [52] what kind of experiences did he mean? One could, for example, make a great deal of the crises of his younger days. We know that from about 1866 until 1872 his health was very poor and he was subject to "insomnia, digestive disorders, eye-troubles, weakness of the back, and sometimes deep depression of spirits." [53] At about the same period, he seems also to have passed through a spiritual crisis caused by his lack of an over-all philosophy of life and manifested in his absence of motivation and incentive for action.

Yet it would be straining the evidence to look upon his religious interest as a refuge in time of spiritual and physical difficulty. Though this period lasted for about five years, and though James thereafter was to be plagued by periods of physical weakness and low levels of energy, the active life that he led—with teaching, lecturing, and writing—belies any attempt to describe him as an invalid who turned to religion in a state of panic.

[50] *Ibid.*
[51] Especially "Reflex Action and Theism."
[52] *Pragmatism*, p. 109.
[53] R. B. Perry, *The Thought and Character of William James* (Boston: Little, Brown, 1935), I, p. 233, n. 7.

These incidents should rather be looked upon as links in a chain of experiences extending over his whole life. It is true that at these critical junctures he knew sorrow, discouragement, and possibly even despair; but these were merely manifestations in more extreme forms of his general sensitivity to the contingent character of man in an unstable universe. Though his searching mind was ever excited by new problems, it could not be satisfied with riddles concerning the ultimate questions of man's purpose and destiny. He could not believe that human needs and demands, hopes and desires, reaching out for the final resolution of sorrow, death, and destruction, were doomed to disappointment and frustration.

It was this reason that ultimately led James to turn away from the materialism of Herbert Spencer (1820–1903) in spite of an early attraction toward the evolutionary aspects of his thought. Though critical of Spencer for other reasons as well, he passes a final judgment on him when he says: "This utter final wreck and tragedy is of the essence of scientific materialism as presently understood." [54] In the *Varieties* he makes the same point. "This sadness lies at the heart of every positivistic, agnostic, or naturalistic scheme of philosophy." [55] In an eloquent and highly imaginative passage, he enlarges upon his theme:

> For naturalism, fed on recent cosmological speculations, mankind is in a position similar to that of a set of people living on a frozen lake, surrounded by cliffs over which there is no escape, yet knowing that little by little the ice is melting, and the inevitable day drawing near when the last film of it will disappear, and to be drowned ignominiously will be the human creature's portion. The merrier the skating, the warmer and more sparkling the sun by day, and the ruddier the bonfires at night, the more poignant the sadness with which one must take in the meaning of the total situation. [56]

James knew that others, too, had criticized the cold, cheerless picture of the universe as presented by scientific materialism, which had substituted a quantitative for a qualitative world, had drained reality of its esthetic qualities, and had reduced human creativity to determined processes. Such critics, while not willing to accept God as the consummation of human hopes and desires, proposed the ideal of striving for the betterment of future generations. This was to become a fundamental tenent of Dewey and the naturalistic school of philosophy in Amer-

[54] *Pragmatism*, p. 105.
[55] *Varieties*, p. 140.
[56] *Ibid.*, pp. 141–42.

ica. According to this position, experience is "religious" when human energies and activities are focused on

> . . . conserving, transmitting, rectifying, and expanding the heritage of values we have received that those who come after us may receive it more solid and secure, more widely accessible and more generously shared than we have received it.[57]

From the naturalist point of view, such an ideal is capable of unifying all man's hopes and activities and of thus providing a religious philosophy that will satisfy the deepest longings of the human personality. James was aware of the possibility of such a proposal, but he completely rejects the suggestion that it can ever attain the high hopes envisioned by it. He does not feel that our love for future nameless and faceless generations would be vital and powerful enough to provide a lasting ideal of action, especially when we realize that their material and cultural advantages will far outweigh our own. Such an ideal, then, is too limited and its weakness is evident.[58]

Since James was a psychologist, it would be easy to assume that he views the need for God as a psychological drive or appetite, especially since his terminology is frequently slanted that way. But this would be a most inadequate interpretation of what James intends. It is not a question of a single organic appetite seeking a single satisfaction, but of the whole human personality reaching out for universal being:

> As through the cracks and crannies of caverns those waters exude from the earth's bosom which then form the fountainheads of springs, so in these crepuscular depths of personality the sources of all our outer deeds and decisions take their rise. Here is our deepest organ of communication with the nature of things.[59]

Here we see a desire for God that is not "psychological" in the narrow sense. James himself calls it a "religious melancholy." [60] As early as "The Sentiment of Rationality" he had spoken about the "ontological wonder," which was the craving for fuller intelligibility of the universe in terms of ultimate questions. He had pointed out the difference between "the ethics of infinite and mysterious obligation from on

---

[57] J. Dewey, A Common Faith (New Haven: Yale University Press, 1934), p. 87.
[58] "The Moral Philosopher and the Moral Life," The Will to Believe, p. 212.
[59] "Is Life Worth Living?" ibid., p. 62.
[60] Pragmatism, p. 108.

high, and those of prudence and the satisfaction of merely finite need." [61]

Ralph Barton Perry has said that James was haunted by "a cosmic nostalgia—by those deeper doubts and hopes which are the perpetual spring of religion." [62] May we not even call it a metaphysical exigence, rooted in the total personality, for plenitude, expansion, and liberation? It is a demand flowing from the whole person that can find completion only in another person, "so that, where he is, tragedy is only provisional and partial, and shipwreck and dissolution are not the absolutely final things. This need of an eternal moral order is one of the deepest needs of our breast." [63]

Perhaps it could be argued that James concluded to God's existence because he felt the need of Him in order to preserve the zest for action. Without God, engagement in life's activities would have no value; hence, James postulated God so that human action would be worthwhile. While this explanation has much to support it and is consequently inviting, it is again too facile. For James, a world without God was a *scandale de l'intelligence,* a phrase used by Henri de Lubac in a similar context,[64] for it would mean absolute death for man and the frustration not merely of this or that sensible desire but of the deepest stirrings of the human personality.

There is one element of James's religious philosophy that may seem to militate against the evidence he brings forward as justification for his belief in God. For, in spite of his affirmation that God's existence is needed to make the world rational, he admits that the evidence is not completely compelling and that, as a consequence, the existence of God is only probable. Several considerations may serve to resolve this difficulty.

First of all, this position is consistent with his empiricism, which is "contented to regard its most assured conclusions concerning matters of fact as hypotheses liable to modification in the course of future experience." [65] From this point of view, all judgments concerning matters of fact are tentative and subject to further test. In some cases we may have to modify completely our position, while in others we may,

[61] "The Moral Philosopher and the Moral Life," *The Will to Believe,* p. 213.
[62] Perry, *op. cit.,* I, p. 450.
[63] *Pragmatism,* pp. 106–07.
[64] H. de Lubac, S.J., *La Pensée religieuse du Père Pierre Teilhard de Chardin* (Paris: Aubier, 1962), p. 256.
[65] "The Will to Believe," *The Will to Believe,* p. vii.

in the course of experience, come ever closer to the real state of things.[66] In this sense, "most, perhaps all, of our laws are only approximations." [67] By further research, we may come closer and closer to the ultimate limit, moving right up "next to" the object without ever really "melting together" with it.[68]

The situation regarding God's existence is the same. Like every statement of fact, it is only probable, even though the degree of probability may be high. Pragmatism, which was proposed as a means of reconciling the place of God in a scientific world, does not have dogmatic answers in this matter any more than in others.[69] But James has rested his case on the pragmatic principle that belief in God "works" —that is, it is a hypothesis that satisfies man's intellectual craving for a rational universe wherein human exigencies are respected. The task now is to extend this hypothesis further through experience "so that it will combine satisfactorily with all the other working truths." [70] This verification will require the experience of the entire human race and will not be completed until the end of time.[71]

But there is another and perhaps more important reason why James was willing to settle for probability concerning God's existence. He preferred a response to God that was free and not compelled by logical argument. There was something too mechanical about the click of logical proof that reduced human assent to the spring of a trap. The choice James would make would have to come after much searching and suffering. It would have to be challenged and renewed each day lest it fall back into a meaningless gesture and become the necessary assent of a fossilized mind rather than the free commitment of a living person. Such an approach means greater risks, perhaps, where salvation hangs in the balance. But again James favored a position that placed the accent on personal responsibility, in which individual salvation and that of mankind depended on the free commitment of human persons.[72] For this reason, James defined faith as:

[66] Ibid., p. 17.
[67] Pragmatism, pp. 56–57.
[68] W. James, The Meaning of Truth (New York: Longmans, Green, 1909), p. 157.
[69] "The Will to Believe," The Will to Believe, p. xii. See also Pragmatism, pp. 300–01.
[70] Pragmatism, p. 299. See also p. 109.
[71] "The Sentiment of Rationality," The Will to Believe, p. 90.
[72] Pragmatism, Lecture VIII.

. . . belief in something concerning which doubt is still theoretically possible; and as the test of belief is willingness to act, one may
say that faith is the readiness to act in a cause the prosperous issue
of which is not certified to us in advance. It is in fact the same
moral quality which we call courage in practical affairs.[73]

This analysis serves to bring out what is characteristic of James's
faith. Perry says that there are two kinds evident in James's works, the
"fighting faith" and the "comforting faith." This is an admirable description, though I would prefer to speak of two aspects of the same
faith rather than of two kinds of faith. The former springs from
strength and is characteristic of *The Will to Believe* and, I might add,
of *Pragmatism*. The moral man fights for the triumph of good over
evil with confidence, courage, and joy even in the face of danger and
uncertainty.[74] The second is the faith arising from weakness that asks
for refuge and security. This is evident in the *Varieties*. Here the sense
of uncertainty is no longer present, and one has the assurance that his
efforts will certainly reach a successful conclusion. James felt the need
for this kind of faith from his own experience of sickness and weariness
and from the tragedies that beset so many of his fellow men.[75]

There is actually no inconsistency in such an account of James's
faith. It is in agreement with his position that every aspect of man
must be taken into account. The God in whom James believes is one
who can give courage in the face of danger as well as consolation in
time of overwhelming adversity. In fact, James would say that everyone
needs both, though the emphasis may vary with the temperament of
each individual.

The Nature of God

A religious philosophy would not be complete without a theory of
God's nature. Hence, it is not out of place to ask in what kind of God
William James believed. What has already been said should serve to
give some indications of his view on the matter, but the question deserves treatment in its own right.

[73] "The Sentiment of Rationality," *The Will to Believe*, p. 90.
[74] Perry, *op. cit.*, II, p. 324.
[75] *Ibid.*, p. 324.

In some respects James's position seems presumptuous, even blasphemous. He appears to be dictating the terms according to which he will believe in God, and even to be stating what the nature of God must be. This is so because he is consciously reacting against the rationalist religious philosophies of his day and focusing his attention upon inner, personal experience. As we have amply seen, he rejects the attempt to establish God's existence and nature by logical arguments. These do not touch life; they are remote from man's deepest aspirations. No matter how probative they may be intellectually, they will never convince because they do not touch the deeper well-springs of human sensitivity.

This theme is especially developed in A *Pluralistic Universe*—a collection of the 1908 Hibbert Lectures at Manchester College, Oxford, with which James carried the battle against absolute idealism into the enemy camp. But nowhere is his whole approach better expressed than in a passage from *The Meaning of Truth*, published a year later in order to clarify misunderstandings consequent upon his *Pragmatism:*

> We have a lively vision of what a certain view of the universe would mean for us. We kindle or we shudder at the thought, and our feeling runs through our whole logical nature and animates its workings. It *can't* be that, we feel; it *must* be this. It must be what it *ought* to be, and it *ought* to be this; and then we seek for every reason, good or bad, to make this which so deeply ought to be, seem objectively the probable thing. We show the arguments against it to be insufficient, so that it *may* be true; we represent its appeal to be to our whole nature's loyalty and not to any emaciated faculty of syllogistic proof. We reinforce it by remembering the enlargement of our world by music, by thinking of the promises of sunsets, the impulses from vernal woods. And the essence of the whole experience, when the individual swept through it says finally "I believe," is the intense concreteness of his vision, the individuality of the hypothesis before him, and the complexity of the various concrete motives and perceptions that issue in his final state.[76]

Time and again he rises to the attack against the God of idealism, the "absolute all-experiencer." [77] More than anything else, he objected to a theory of God that left little place for sympathy with the concrete human condition. In a classic passage, he criticizes the attempt of Gottfried Wilhelm Leibniz (1646–1716) to "justify the ways of God to man," and to prove that ours is the best possible world,

[76] *The Meaning of Truth*, pp. 257–58.
[77] *Ibid.*, p. 125.

where even damned souls are almost as nothing in comparison with the goods of the universe. In James's eyes, "Leibnitz's [sic] feeble grasp of reality is too obvious to need comment from me," for "even hell-fire does not warm" his cold pages.[78] Against this, he contrasts the newspaper account of one unfortunate laborer, too ill to work, who commits suicide rather than face the prospect of seeing his wife and six children without food and shelter.

James, then, originates a "Copernican Revolution" of his own and takes the standpoint of human wants, for these are to be trusted. He lets experience speak to him, and he listens to its voice as it tells him what kind of God it must be that is the object of man's searching and longing.

First of all, God must be "organic and intimate"—that is, internal to the world.[79] A God that was an external creator was in his eyes no longer relevant to human experience. Though He may remain in church formulas, "the sincere heart of us is elsewhere." [80] He was opposed to such formulas not so much because they made God a creator but because they made Him external, and hence irrelevant to the world. For a time, he was strongly attracted to pantheism and to Gustav Fechner's (1801–1887) world-soul, though he finally rejected them both on other grounds.

For similar reasons, he never gave his allegiance to any church or creed. In critiques that were admittedly sketchy and even superficial, he maintained that "Protestantism has been too pessimistic as regards the natural man, Catholicism has been too legalistic and moralistic" to make an appeal,[81] while the God of Calvinism, which "gives so little scope to love" and refuses an object to our most cherished powers, is irrational.[82]

James's insistence that God be internal to the world led him to hold for a finite God. He realized that one of the aspects most traditionally associated with the Deity was being sacrificed, but he felt this view to be dictated by experience. Moreover, he felt that it was a satisfactory compromise between the extreme positions of the "reason" of the rationalists and the "experience" of the empiricists. In this way, "em-

---

[78] *Pragmatism*, p. 27.
[79] W. James, *A Pluralistic Universe* (New York: Longmans, Green, 1909), p. 30.
[80] *Ibid.*, p. 30.
[81] *Varieties*, p. 114.
[82] "Reflex Action and Theism," *The Will to Believe*, p. 126.

piricism and rationalism might strike hands in a lasting treaty of peace." [83]

Lastly, in answer to the question: "Ought all men to have the same religion?" James answered an emphatic, "No." This, too, follows from the emphasis he gave to personal experience. Each individual has different needs and faces different problems. In James's terms, then, each one must keep within his own experience and choose the religion that best answers the experience.[84]

The Naturalism of James

William James can be called a naturalist in the sense in which we used that term in the preceding chapter. A strong scientific background gave him a keen appreciation for the "stubborn facts" of nature, and it is from this source that his empiricism was derived. His pragmatic theory of truth, with its principle of verification in terms of sense experience, gave lasting shape to the methodology of subsequent American philosophy; and so influential did his pragmatism become that there is hardly an aspect of American thought that has not felt its effects. He consistently challenged broad generalizations and abstractions by bringing them down to the touchstone of empirical fact. He was utterly opposed to dogmatism, whether it came from philosophy or religion. Standing at the period when American philosophy was dominantly idealistic, he carried on a polemic against the British version of idealism as represented by Bradley and against the similar orientation of Josiah Royce, his friend and colleague at Harvard.

But James was just as strongly opposed to dogmatism in science, and therefore he impressed upon empiricism the stamp of his own temperament. He followed science wherever its empirical method led him, but he parted company with it when it tried to close off the road to inquiry by dogmatically asserting that there was only one way to truth. This enabled him to pursue his scientific interests while he remained free to accept theism.

James placed man at the very heart of the universe, for he believed that all of us have the universe as our source and that we are its children.[85] He maintained that all men basically crave to feel at home in

[83] *A Pluralistic Universe*, p. 312.
[84] *Varieties*, pp. 487–88.
[85] *A Pluralistic Universe*, p. 31.

the world,[86] and that in some way all problems faced by man have a human motive at their source and all answers are to be judged in terms of human satisfaction.[87] By this he meant that men strive for growth of personality through activity in the world.

What are the conditions for such development? There is, first of all, the world itself. Against determinism and rationalism, he contended that all is not ultimately decided or explained. The world is plastic,[88] malleable,[89] and still in the making.[90] It is a world that is unfinished,[91] with possibilities for novelty waiting to be realized. But there is also man, whose dignity and responsibility as a thinking being [92] consist precisely in his ability to enter into the world and direct its development. The future that opens before man is an uncertain one, fraught with possibilities of failure and frustration as well as of success and fulfillment. But with the cooperation of all, we can hope that the future will be brighter than the past. The important thing is that man must be loyal to his own human nature [93] and must do what he can to cooperate with others in building the universe.

As we have seen in the preceding pages, James's naturalism was extended by his theism. But his is a theism that does not separate man from the world. For this reason, James saw no contradiction between his belief in God and a healthy commitment to this world. While including the essential cooperation of all men, he also believed that God has a hand in the work and that human experience will some day be raised to fulfillment by a higher power.[94] As he stated in the *Varieties*, "Shipwreck and dissolution are not the absolutely final things." James himself knew that the precise nature of the cooperation between the human and divine constituted an aspect of theology that needed further elaboration, though he seemed to feel his own inadequacy to work it out. He thought that he had made a contribution by opening the way to a reconciliation between rationalism and empiricism and between transcendental absolutism and a crude naturalism.[95] At the very least, we can say that he anticipated, with an almost intuitive sense, the problem facing the contemporary man who wants to be religious and still remain faithful to the craving to feel at home in the world.

[86] *Ibid.*, p. 12.
[87] *Ibid.*, p. 159.
[88] *Ibid.*, p. 159.
[89] *Ibid.*, p. 167.
[90] *Ibid.*, p. 167.
[91] *Ibid.*, p. 168.
[92] *Ibid.*, p. 167.
[93] *Pragmatism.* p. 180.
[94] *Ibid.*, p. 192.
[95] *Ibid.*, p. 192.

He clarified the issues and made a start toward the solution of this problem.

Conclusions

Such is the religious philosophy of William James. The picture it presents is an odd mixture of sharp lines and blurred backgrounds. It will never satisfy the demand for a technical and sophisticated treatment of the subject. Nor did James intend that it should. It is even questionable whether he would be entirely happy with the term "religious philosophy," for he very rarely uses it.

What precisely has James accomplished? His sharp criticism of traditional forms of religion will hardly send the theologians running in panic to see what devastation has been wrought on their age-old positions by the power of his arguments. His criticisms are often superficial, and one is not overwhelmed by the depth of his knowledge of theology or of religious philosophy.

William James was not a religious man in the traditional sense—that is, he adhered strongly to no religious denomination and attended regularly no religious services. But he had the basic attitudes of religion. It was just that religion, as he knew it, failed to touch his deeper sensibilities. But what he has to say should make both the philosopher and the theologian seriously reconsider their own approach. James himself had felt the new breezes that were already beginning to stir in the philosophic world: "the loosening of old landmarks, a softening of oppositions, a mutual borrowing from one another on the part of systems anciently closed, and an interest in new suggestions." [96] He was aware of the dissatisfaction of the younger generation with abstract academic systems, and he felt that it craved "more of the temperament of life in its philosophy, even though it were at some cost of logical rigor and of formal purity." [97] What the younger generation was seeking was *relevance*, a word that can be used too easily but that has profound implications if rightly understood. At the very least, James would hope that the philosopher and theologian would adopt a more sympathetic attitude toward the human person who, while bowing low

[96] W. James, *Essays in Radical Empiricism* (New York: Longmans, Green, 1912), p. 38.
[97] *Ibid.*, p. 38.

before the power and majesty of the Almighty, also comes to Him with pain, sorrow, and love.

This insight is the heart and soul of James's philosophy. The human subject was for him the starting point. In this respect—and in many others, too—his thought has similarities with European existentialism. William Barrett has shown himself aware of this, for he says that "We may very well wonder if it would be more accurate to call James an Existentialist than a Pragmatist." [98] This statement has all sorts of interesting implications, discussion of which will have to be postponed to another time.

Neither are the empirically minded likely to feel a resurgence of religious fervor after reading James's glowing pages. In his own day scientists took a dim view of his attempt to justify belief in a God, while later naturalistic philosophers accepted the main lines of his pragmatic method and completely rejected his religious orientation. For this reason, James never founded a "school" in the real sense of the word, nor was he followed by disciples.

There are signs today that there could well be a renaissance of some of James's key ideas. Here and there one comes across a book or article written by a scientist who raises again the question regarding the possibility of subjectivity, intuition, and insight in scientific method.[99] Not all American philosophers are convinced that a satisfactory theory of the human person can be developed by considering him purely in transaction with the environment. On this point, John E. Smith has suggested that "the problematic situation might fall between a man and himself or between a man and the loss of God." [100] Milton Mayeroff has noted in the theories of the later naturalists the absence of the personal side, which he calls the "quiet dimension." [101] The private is as important as the social in appreciating the dignity of the individual, for it concerns the "core of our being." The terms "soli-

[98] W. Barrett, *Irrational Man* (New York: Doubleday, 1958), p. 16. See also R. May, ed., *Existential Psychology* (New York: Random House, 1961), pp. 12–16.
[99] For example, M. Polanyi, *Personal Knowledge* (Chicago: University of Chicago Press, 1958); P. A. M. Dirac, "The Evolution of the Physicist's Picture of Nature," *Scientific American*, Vol. 208, No. 5 (May, 1963), pp. 45–53.
[100] J. E. Smith, Book Review, *The New Scholasticism*, Vol. 36, No. 3 (July, 1962), p. 400.
[101] M. Mayeroff, "A Neglected Aspect of Experience in Dewey's Philosophy," *The Journal of Philosophy*, Vol. 60, No. 6 (March 14, 1963), pp. 146–53.

tude," "stillness," "alone," should be emphasized as much as "community," "joint participation," and "social experience."

If these criticisms are valid, James may still have a message for twentieth-century America. Perhaps he can teach us once again the importance of quiet reflection and the need of a deep interior life. In the specific area of theology and religious philosophy, we may learn the lesson that God will never be found by one who stands apart and challenges Him to prove His existence. Americans may even come to understand the basic attitudes necessary for the solution of the frightening perplexities consequent upon the loss of God.

III

CHARLES SANDERS PEIRCE

MAN OF SCIENCE AND RELIGION

When Charles Sanders Peirce died, a little more than fifty years ago, few would have predicted that some day he would be hailed as one of America's greatest philosophers. It would scarcely be an exaggeration to say that this man, whose work significantly influenced such outstanding American thinkers as William James, Josiah Royce, and John Dewey, has been until recently one of our most neglected philosophers. And this despite the fact that it was he who originated the word "pragmatism," as James himself acknowledged.[1]

[1] W. James, *Pragmatism* (London: Longmans, Green, 1907), p. 46.

Born in 1839, Peirce graduated from Harvard College at the age of twenty and studied chemistry at the Lawrence Scientific School at Harvard. For many years thereafter he worked with the U.S. Coast and Geodetic Survey, winning wide recognition for his work. His far-ranging mind interested itself not only in geodesy and meteorology but also in mathematical logic, psychophysics, photometry, and even philology.

It is ironic that this brilliant man should not have been able to secure a permanent position in one of the important universities. It is true that in 1879 he succeeded in obtaining an appointment at Johns Hopkins University, where he lectured on philosophic logic until January, 1884. But the appointment was abruptly terminated by the university, apparently without explanation. The mystery surrounding his dismissal remains unresolved; thus far, Johns Hopkins' president, Daniel Gilman, appears to be the villain in the piece. Later, through the intercession of William James, one of his few close friends, Peirce managed to obtain occasional invitations for lectures. He gave two series of lectures before the Lowell Institute in Boston, and in 1903 he delivered a series at Harvard on pragmatism.

It is sometimes hinted that Peirce's inability to secure a regular academic position was due to heavy drinking and to a divorce and remarriage, all of which were professionally embarrassing. These explanations, however, are usually thought to be exaggerated. It would seem, in the last analysis, that the chief contributing factors were the failure of those in responsible positions to assess his abilities accurately and their reluctance to risk engaging a man little noted for observing the social amenities.

Peirce was, indeed, a maverick from the start. In recommending him to Charles Eliot, president of Harvard, for a teaching post, William James admitted his widely known "personal uncomfortableness" but held that, in view of his genius, this would have to be accepted by a president as "part of the disagreeableness of the day's work." [2] Among the less engaging of his characteristics was his habit of speaking his mind regardless of consequences. In assessing the ability of students to grasp his ideas, for instance, he decidedly preferred the "coarse, strong, laboring brains" of "New York plebeians" to the students of Harvard, an institution "established to the end that the elite of her youths may

[2] R. B. Perry, *The Thought and Character of William James* (Boston: Little, Brown, 1935), II, pp. 416–17.

be aided to earning comfortable incomes and living softly cultured lives." [3]

Peirce spent the last decade of his life in poverty and eremitic obscurity. He once noted in a letter that his room was so cold he could hardly write. It has been said that few of the inhabitants of Milford, Pennsylvania, where he then lived, knew his name, and that those who did know it mispronounced it. (It is pronounced "purse.") He died of cancer on April 19, 1914, frustrated and alone.

Peirce is not an easy man to read. This is due partly to his style but mainly to his keen, restless mind, which embraced a wide variety of topics and which carried him far beyond most of the men of his generation. He himself called his ideas "a very snarl of twine," [4] while William James once referred to a course of his lectures as "flashes of brilliant light relieved against Cimmerian darkness." [5] Recent interest in Peirce has centered around his truly original work in the fields of mathematical analysis, symbolic logic, and the philosophy of science. Since World War II American philosophy has turned more and more in this direction, as is evidenced by the orientation of philosophy departments and of the programs for the annual conventions of the American Philosophical Association.

There is one aspect of his thought, however, that has received very little attention, and that is his work on religion. Murray Murphey maintains that the religious spirit was always present in Peirce's work, either explicitly or implicitly, and that it was an important element in giving shape to his philosophy.[6] However, this suggestion is not developed; and for the most part scholars either do not see any connection between Peirce's religious thought and the remainder of his system or, if they sense that the religious element is important, do not seem to know quite what to do with it.[7]

Yet in reading Peirce's work on religion, we meet the same challenging, seminal mind that is evident in his technical writings. Painfully aware of his own limitations—a crabbed personality, a tortured style,

[3] 1. 650. All reference to Peirce's works are taken from *Collected Papers of Charles Sanders Peirce*, ed. by A. Burks, C. Hartshorne, and P. Weiss (Cambridge, Mass.: Harvard University Press, 1931–58), 8 vols. References are by volume and paragraph.
[4] 6. 184.
[5] *Pragmatism*, p. 5.
[6] M. G. Murphey, *The Development of Peirce's Philosophy* (Cambridge, Mass.: Harvard University Press, 1961), p. 16.
[7] 6. v. Editorial note.

and a subtlety of ideas that few could understand—alone and isolated, he shows that the inner dimensions of his personality were remarkably open to the stirrings of concrete, human experience. He seems to be telling us the reason he remained largely closed in upon himself. Just as the sharp edge of his mind seldom found any flint from which to strike sparks, so his deep need to experience a God in meaningful ways somehow found no responsive chord in religion as he knew it.

Peirce seems to have been deeply affected by his boyhood experiences within his own family. His father, Benjamin Peirce, was a staunch Unitarian; but Charles himself, though he had great respect and admiration for his father, never followed him in his Unitarian belief. The younger Peirce was repelled by the "angry squabbles" between Unitarians and Calvinists until he came to feel that Unitarianism was based purely on negation. Charles became a member of the Episcopal Church but accepted only its "general essence and spirit." [8]

Man's Relation to Nature

Peirce's ascent to God and religion begins with his view of man's relation to the world. He looked upon man as situated in the world and sensitive to what is stirring within and without him in the environment. One statement of his is especially revealing in this regard. He maintained that man's highest duty and vocation is to complete his personality "by melting it into the neighboring parts of the universal cosmos." [9] This is not an "avocation," a task to be assumed when one has time to spare from his real vocation. It is to be his very life, and it means a total dedication.

This task of uniting oneself with the universal cosmos for the completion of one's personality explains Peirce's commitment to the life of a scientist. On his own testimony, he was literally raised in the scientific laboratory; and he maintained that he was "saturated, through and through, with the spirit of the physical sciences." [10] He was more than superficially excited by the newness of the scientific interest and discovery that broke like a gigantic wave over America's intellectual life at the end of the nineteenth century. The craving to explore the

[8] Murphey, op. cit., p. 15.
[9] 1. 673.
[10] 1. 3.

mysteries of the universe went down to the very roots of his personality because he felt that nature was his home and he delighted in exploring every corner of it.

For Peirce, a scientist is a man with a single purpose, "possessed by a passion to learn" [11] and by an intense love of truth.[12] These are the real scientific men who alone do any progressive work in scientific research.[13] His insistence on the selfless dedication of the scientist to truth caused Peirce to adopt a critical view of those who, in his eyes, demean the life of science by applying their talents to other interests. Among such interests he mentions science when "degraded to pot-boiling arts." [14] Others he includes under the heading of "Americanism," which is the worship of business.[15] He shows a definite disdain for those who engage in science and investigate truth in order to make money,[16] and he notes that scientific inquiry will decline when it is in the hands of "academic professors who are provided with good incomes and looked up to as gentlemen." [17] Peirce also takes to task those whose orientation he includes under the heading of "monasticism" or "sleepwalking," where one's interest in a future life blinds him to concern for this world.[18]

In opposition to these Peirce stresses the need for pure research. In his mind, research not only will prevent the evils of Americanism and monasticism but also will enable science itself to advance and to bear the rich fruits it is capable of producing. The very survival of science depends on it. Once science becomes preoccupied with the merely useful, the "divine spark" (we note the word "divine") will go out; science will be reduced to a mere utensil; and it will, in fact, cease to be scientific. To employ scientific men on useful things "is like running a steam engine by burning diamonds." [19] These are ideas full of meaning and, in the light of more recent clamors on the part of some for increased interest in research, not a little prophetic.

In a sense, man's interest in science presupposes that he is already adapted to nature and in tune with it. When speaking of the ease with which the mind perceives certain aspects of external reality—such as time, space, and force—Peirce took it as incontestable that the human mind is adapted to understanding the world, at least to the extent that

[11] 1. 43. [16] 1. 44.
[12] 1. 49. [17] 1. 51.
[13] 1. 43. [18] 1. 673.
[14] 1. 670. [19] 1. 76.
[15] 1. 673.

certain conceptions arise naturally in the mind. Without this adaptation, the mind would never be able to develop.[20]

Something similar is true in the way man makes discoveries in science. When a physicist comes upon some new phenomenon in his laboratory work, how does he arrive at an explanation of it? "Trillions of trillions of hypotheses" are possible to account for the phenomenon. And yet, after relatively few guesses, the physicist hits upon a hypothesis that comes pretty close to the solution of his problem. Peirce calls this a "certain insight" that is correct often enough to make us marvel at the wonderful harmony between ourselves and nature.[21] Peirce concludes that this harmony can be explained by the fact that both man and nature have developed according to the same laws and that, consequently, there exists in man a "natural light, or light of nature, or instinctive insight, or genius" leading him to make reasonably accurate judgments.[22]

Peirce seeks confirmation for his position in what is observed in the animal kingdom. By instinct, animals quite naturally carry out activities that are necessary for their existence and well-being. A chicken, for example, has an "innate idea" of how to peck at food. If it had to go through a long process of learning, it would not survive. Peirce thus sees no difficulty about accepting in man a natural facility for arriving at correct hypotheses: "Nature fecundates the mind of man with ideas which, when these ideas grow up, will resemble their father, Nature." [23] Man, of course, must subject his hypotheses to the test of facts.[24] His original hypotheses are not as accurate as the instincts of animals, and they demand further verification; but the harmony between man's mind and nature is evident. On the human level, Peirce calls this ability to imagine hypotheses *il lume naturale,* and it is this that great scientists—like Galileo, Kepler, Harvey, and Copernicus—relied on in attempting to solve the mysteries of the universe.[25]

It should be made clear that the context in which the above-mentioned harmony between man and nature is described is a scientific one. It is true that instinct or insight serves as a kind of guiding light enabling man to make reasonably accurate guesses. But the important element in the process is reason, by which man carefully tests a

[20] 6. 417. [23] 5. 591.
[21] 5. 173. [24] 5. 591.
[22] 5. 604. [25] 1. 80.

hypothesis to see if it is valid. In the light of the facts the hypothesis is accepted, modified, or entirely rejected in favor of another. When engaging in scientific research, the emphasis is placed on verification, though insight plays an important role.

In spite of his emphasis on scientific verification, however, it was an intuitive sense that led Peirce to place the development of human personality firmly upon involvement in the world. For him personally, this involvement took the form of a passionate interest in scientific research. But he also recognized that human experience must break through the boundaries of technical science and must concern itself with a larger relationship to the world of people. For Peirce, man is by nature not an individual but a member of society, and he can never achieve the wholeness of his personality in isolation. It is not "my" experience but "our" experience that is important, and man can fulfill his personality only by immersing himself in the social organism of which he is a part.

Peirce had no illusions regarding the contribution each one may be able to make to the social organism. In some instances it may be slight indeed—as in the case of those, constituting the great bulk of mankind, who can do no more than provide the necessities of life for themselves and their families. And yet it is by the collective effort of all men that the continued growth of civilization is achieved through the course of history.[26]

It is here that Peirce exalts insight or instinct, which he variously calls sentiment, conservatism, true conservatism, and sentimental conservatism. It is this that discerns the first command, the highest business and duty of melting one's personality into the total cosmos and of committing oneself to the progressive development of the social whole. Man grasps his relationship with the whole not by reasoning but by instinct or sentiment, which comprises the substance of the human soul and the deepest emotional springs of man's life.[27]

This insight into the necessity of involvement with other people stands in strange contrast with Peirce's isolation throughout most of his life. He appears always to have been a lonely man, but his was not a loneliness that gave him peace. It was precisely his insight into the need of each man for human companionship that made him painfully

[26] 1. 647, 673; 5. 403, n. 2.
[27] 1. 628, 673.

aware of his own inability to open himself fully to other people and that heightened the sense of his own limitations. Surely, in setting down the requirements of human fulfillment, he must have realized that he was confronting himself with the source of his own frustration. But I am sure that at the same time he took some small consolation in the hope that he could assist others in finding the human happiness he so keenly missed.

The Reality of God

Peirce's effort to fulfill his personality by melting it into the universal cosmos made of him a scientific man. But, curiously enough, it also fashioned him into a contemplative and religious man. The reason is that he did not confine his view to science but opened himself to all dimensions of human experience. He adopted what he called "the law of liberty," which breaks through the blocks to inquiry. He felt that for too long the "Sir Oracles" of science had put limits in the way of inquiry by invoking one maxim after another. For example, at one moment we are told that no science may borrow the methods of another science; again, we are forbidden to search for the origins of things. Peirce manifests a scorn for such prohibitions and indicates that each of them has been shown to be false and detrimental to progress. Consequently, he advocates a rejection of maxims that prevent free inquiry and calls for a return to the data of concrete experience, untrammeled by the dictates of science. He asks man to open his eyes, and also his heart—for it, too, is a perceptive organ—and to be awake to what is within and without.

The scientific man is invited to enter more deeply and more reflectively into the universe by opening his mind and heart to the beauty and wonder of nature that surrounds him. In spite of long hours dedicated to laboratory research, Peirce enjoyed a walk out into the countryside at dusk or evening through open fields.[28] During these moments of calm meditation he gave free rein to the flow of his thoughts, which included "aesthetic contemplation" or even "distant castle-building." His artistic sense was drawn to the beauty of nature as seen

[28] 6. 464, 501.

in the colorful array of flowers, butterflies, trees, and sunsets.[29] He
gazed heavenward and admired the vast vault of stars and planets that
met his gaze, and he liked to speculate as to how many more heavenly
bodies were still to be discovered. He was sure that many of these were
inhabited with beings who had reached a level of intelligence far more
advanced than our own.

His interest in the macrocosm was matched by his fascination with
the fact that science was penetrating down to the most minute level of
atomic particles. His ear was attuned to the buzzing and chirping of
insects in the evening air, and he marveled that such primitive crea-
tures could be endowed by nature with fantastic abilities to carry out
their cycle of birth, life, growth, and decay. In man, he saw the culmi-
nation of the animal world, for he believed that we share with animals
a harmony with nature and that we have perfected it, since our minds
can learn what is necessary for our physical and intellectual lives. And
unifying all these elements of nature is the process of evolution, which
accounts for progressive growth from inorganic matter right up to
man.[30] From a consideration of all this, Peirce concludes:

> . . . the idea of God's reality will be sure sooner or later to be
> found an attractive fancy, which the Muser will develop in various
> ways. The more he ponders it, the more it will find response in every
> part of his mind, for its beauty, for its supplying an ideal of life,
> and for its thoroughly satisfactory explanation of his whole threefold
> environment.[31]

The significance of this conclusion can be appreciated only in the
light of the supposition underlying it. For at the basis of Peirce's whole
argument is instinct, which he calls its "substance" or "bedrock." [32]
The strength of the argument consists in the fact that there is in man
a latent tendency toward belief in God founded on universal human
nature, and this belief is the natural result of contemplating the universe.[33] Belief in God, then, is "a fundamental ingredient of the soul"
and not "a vicious or superstitious ingredient."

When man ponders all these things, the belief in God will touch a
responsive chord in every part of his mind—that is, it will satisfy the
human desires for esthetic appreciation, for growth in conduct, and for

[29] 6. 462. [32] 6. 503.
[30] 6. 464, 501. [33] 6. 487.
[31] 6. 465.

intelligibility. The drive for esthetic appreciation is fulfilled by the beauty of God as cause of all beautiful things in nature. The drive for intelligibility is fulfilled because belief in God gives a satisfactory explanation of the universe. This point presupposes Peirce's rejection of mechanistic philosophy, with its attempt to explain all reality in terms of necessary physical laws alone.[34] In his mind, without God the world would be ultimately unintelligible. At the basis of this phase of the argument is Peirce's conviction that there is a harmony between external reality and the inner demands of the human person, just as there is a correspondence between reality and the instincts of animals.

The description above of the mind's journey to God seems at first glance to be nothing but pure fantasy and idle daydreaming, which would open it to all kinds of absurd conclusions. But in Peirce's view it is much more sophisticated than that. It is true that he has advocated a complete freedom of the mind to wander where it would as it contemplates the marvels of nature. Here he would be in complete agreement with William James in his respect for every type of experience. But, with James, he realized that a belief in God, like any hypothesis, must be subjected to test. This belief, resulting from a latent tendency in man consequent upon a consideration of nature, is only the first stage of scientific inquiry.[35] The next step is to verify that belief.

It would seem that at this point we will be brought back to the Peirce with whom most people are familiar—namely, the scientific man who will demand careful and exact reasoning before he admits any hypothesis to be worthy of belief. Though confidence in common sense and in instinct is important, these must be subjected to careful criticism.[36] But here we notice an interesting turn of events, for such criticism means that the ultimate test of the hypothesis of God "must lie in its value in the self-controlled growth of man's conduct of life." We find that the searching criticism to which the hypothesis of God is to be subjected consists not in carefully reasoned analyses of logic, nor in the planned experiments of the laboratory, but in examinations into "the self-controlled growth of man's conduct of life" following upon confidence in common sense and instinct. Peirce's approach to God never loses sight of man's contact with his concrete human condition as seen in his relation to the whole cosmos. An argument for God's

[34] 6. 553–56.
[35] 6. 488.
[36] 6. 480.

reality "should present its conclusion, not as a proposition of metaphysical theology, but in a form directly applicable to the conduct of life, and full of nutrition for man's highest growth." [37] We see here Peirce's deep concern for the development of man's personality, just as it had been evident in his discussion of man's relation to the cosmos and to the social organism. Seen in this context, religion for Peirce is an extension of man's awareness, grasped through instinct or sentiment, of his relationship, first to the universal cosmos in general, then to the social organism, and finally, in a more complete manner, to God. In this awareness there is an appreciation of man's finite duty in this world and of his highest growth, as also of his destiny.[38]

This is the same point Peirce made in the conclusion following upon his contemplation of nature. There he had said that the muser assents to the reality of God "for its supplying an ideal of life." In both instances, Peirce supposes that there is in man an innate tendency to believe in God and that this belief is precipitated by the ideal of life it supplies—or, in other words, by the growth and development that follow upon this belief.

So firm is Peirce in his position that he is willing to propose a possible objection. One could admit, for example, that the plausibility of the existence of God is far beyond that of other hypotheses. So difficult is it to doubt it that one may be tempted to stop at the first stage of inquiry without showing its validity. But one should not stop there. Since an explanatory hypothesis has for its purpose the development of a clear idea of the object in question, an attempt must be made to predict various experiential consequences following upon that idea. But against this attempt there is the disturbing fact that tends to render the argument suspect: the reality of God does not lend itself to clear formulation. God is an omniscient being with no experiences, desires, purposes, or even consciousness, such as we humans have. How then would it be possible to predict His conduct and thus validate the hypothesis of God?

Against this, Peirce opposes the commanding influence this belief has over the whole conduct of life.[39] Thus we again reach the same conclusion, one that is surprising in the sense that it is out of character with the image of Peirce usually presented. We find that with all his

[37] 6. 457.
[38] 1. 675.
[39] 6. 490.

demand for exact thinking and verification as a test for the validity of a hypothesis, his ultimate criterion for belief in the reality of God is its influence on the conduct of life and on man's highest growth.

Pulling together the threads of Peirce's argument for the reality of God, we may state his position as follows. There is in man a latent tendency, founded on human nature, to believe in God, and this tendency is precipitated by a consideration of nature. That this tendency is nothing more than instinct is the substance or bedrock of the argument. The mind moves so readily to belief in God because such belief fulfills a threefold drive in man: the drive for esthetic appreciation, the drive for human growth and fulfillment, and the drive for intelligibility.

It is in the area of instinct for human growth and fulfillment that Peirce finds the ultimate test for the hypothesis of God. A man believes in God because he sees that it is the only hypothesis that fulfills the instinct for continued growth and fulfillment on ever widening levels, not only when this instinct bids man to melt his personality into the neighboring parts of the universal cosmos, not only when it inspires him to commit himself to the progress of the social organism, but also when it liberates him to lift his eyes beyond the huge mountain of our present existence and "enables us to descry a silvery peak rising into the calm air of eternity." [40] At that moment man achieves the complete generalization, the complete regeneration of sentiment that gives meaning and fulfillment to his life and conduct.

Religion

It was only in relatively rare moments that Peirce poured out his soul and expressed the kind of religion he craved. When he did, he foreshadowed some of the ideas that we see coming to expression today in religious men of all faiths. For Peirce, religion was fundamentally a way of life that gave meaning to man in all his aspects. The emphasis he placed on this unifying characteristic should not be surprising in view of his intellectual bent to see things as wholes. He spent much time in classifying the sciences in elaborate schemes and in outlining on a grand scale chapters of books that he never wrote. He had great admiration for the medieval summas because of their unity and organization.

[40] 1. 675.

But this desire for a way of life was not merely the urge to satisfy an intellectual craving. Religion must seep down into human experience in all its dimensions. Peirce saw God everywhere—in the beauty of dawn and sunset, of trees and flowers. It was God who ultimately explained the origin and meaning of natural phenomena, both within and without the human individual, and it was He who supplied for man an ideal that could be the guide for all his thoughts and actions.

For Peirce, the whole universe is one great symbol of God's purpose working out its conclusions in living realities. Man himself has a share in this work, for, by his intelligence and responsible activity, he enters into the process of evolution so that God's purpose may be the more abundantly realized. Even if a man can scarcely do more than provide the necessities of life for himself and his family, yet for all his "miserable littlenesses" he takes on more and more "the Spirit of God, in which Nature and History are rife." [41]

In all aspects of life, man must seek to come into meaningful contact with the living personality of God. It is at prayer especially that man enters into deepest communion with the divine. But Peirce felt that at these most precious moments such union was often impeded by mere outward show, as seen in the exaggerated solemnity of religious ceremony. Hence he asks: "Why observe manners toward the Heavenly Father that an earthly father would resent as priggish?" [42]

In attempting to express the meaning of God and religion, Peirce reminds us that growth of the human person comes only from love. For this reason he appeals to the Johannine formula "God is love" [43] and concludes that religion itself as a way of life is love—primarily, of course, love of God, whose beauty and goodness one sees reflected in the universe and who becomes the focal point and fulfillment of all his aspirations.

But there is also love of neighbor. It is central to Peirce's whole theory of human personality that man is essentially ordained to be a member of society. For him, individualism and falsity are one, for man cannot reach fulfillment in isolation. It is love that binds men together in harmony, while at the same time it enriches the individual even as he sacrifices his own perfection for that of his neighbor.

What is true on the level of nature is true also on the level of religion. Beginning in personal experience, religion can come to maturity

[41] 5. 402, n. *a.*
[42] 6. 437.
[43] 6. 287.

only "in a great church coextensive with a civilization." [44] Peirce envisioned the whole world united in the common bond of love of God and of neighbor. For the accomplishment of this ideal "A great catholic church is wanted." [45] This is why it pained him to witness the schisms that split the churches into so many different sects. He could not reconcile himself to the idea that those who were one in their love of God and neighbor should be separated by doctrinal beliefs.

It was because Peirce saw so clearly the unifying strength of love and felt so deeply the results of divisions that he was critical, sometimes harshly so, of creed and doctrine. Love is essential; everything else is secondary. Once the primacy of love is forgotten, religion becomes a test of belief and salvation depends on a correct metaphysics. When this stage is reached, theology takes the place of the stirrings of the spirit, logic replaces experience, and "the vital spark of inspiration becomes finally quite extinct." [46] Hence Peirce pleaded that religionists once more make of love the focal point of religion, that they not exaggerate differences, and that they not substitute "the rule of angry and bullying insistence" for the law of love.[47]

From his criticism of doctrine, one should not draw the conclusion that Peirce was an anti-intellectual. His polemic can be understood only against the background of his deep conviction regarding the primacy of love. More than that, as a man possessed of superior intellectual ability, he was trying to find the place of the intellectual in religion and in the church. He was aware of the enmity that had developed between science and religion, though he refrained from placing the blame entirely on either side. Science, on the one hand, was guilty in attempting to explain the universe in purely mechanistic terms. Though he recognized that science was well within its rights in excluding considerations of God, teleology, and the like, he resented its attempt to deny their existence.

On the other hand, Peirce chided religion for its failure to open itself wide to the advances of science. He exhorted the religious man to cast aside his timidity and to follow the Lord of history as He leads men's minds into new paths, for in so doing religion will manifest "a bolder confidence in herself and in her own destiny." [48] Then men will not fall away from religion as soon as they become better edu-

[44] 6. 443.   [47] 6. 446.
[45] *Ibid.*   [48] 6. 433.
[46] 6. 438.

cated, and the day will come when the church will number great scholars as well as great saints among its members.[49]

In all this Peirce preserved a genuine admiration for the medieval Christian church. He felt that to it we owed in large measure our science and philosophy, our language and literature, our intellectual framework, and the law of love, as little as this may sometimes be observed.[50] Hence Peirce is not advocating a desertion of the churches. He acknowledges that their stones may have been stained with the grime of its imperfections; but these can be washed clean not by one who leaves the church, but only by one "willing to get down on his knees to his work inside the church." [51]

Such is the paradox of Charles Sanders Peirce: a man largely closed to human friendship and affection, yet open to love of God and of neighbor; literally raised in the scientific laboratory, yet longing to be at home, too, in the atmosphere of religious sensitivities. In some respects he stands at a critical period of America's intellectual development, a period still warm with the life of religious aspirations but already beginning to feel the pangs of a childbirth that was to bring forth America's scientific age.

Peirce reflects in his life the unsettled conditions of the times, for he attempted, not always successfully it would seem, to bring into fruitful harmony all that was best in both science and religion. By far the most substantial part of his writings has to do with science, but what he had to say about religion is far from insignificant. At the very least, the latter represents the effort of an intellectual to find his place in the world, both as a religious man and as a man of science. For those to whom such a task is still a problem, Charles Sanders Peirce, after fifty years, may still be relevant.

Peirce and James

So little do we know about the personal life of Peirce that there seems almost to have been a conspiracy of silence among those who knew him. Undoubtedly, our meager knowledge can be explained in large part by his personality, which rendered him little disposed to forming

[49] 6. 446.
[50] 6. 449.
[51] 6. 447.

many close friendships. Murray Murphey has presented the best biographical account of Peirce that has appeared so far, and the growing interest in Peirce is sure to uncover more details about his life. We do know that Peirce formed a close friendship with William James, for Peirce stated that he "knew and loved him for forty-nine or fifty years." [52] As we have already seen, James did his best to help Peirce's professional career when the latter needed it most.

The close and lasting friendship between the two men is striking in view of their marked differences. Never have two personalities been more unlike. James was outgoing and made friends easily and naturally. He was always kind, patient, and understanding, even when he found it necessary to differ with others in their philosophic views. Peirce, on the other hand, could at times be a very uncongenial companion. Henry James, William's brother, once wrote about Peirce: "He is a very good fellow—when he is not in ill-humour; then he is intolerable." [53] Peirce often gave the impression that he esteemed honesty above tact, even when it wounded sensibilities, for he could be very cutting in his criticisms.

Peirce and James carried on a friendly battle over their philosophical differences. With the growing interest in the philosophy of Peirce during the past few decades, a trend is developing that is not likely to elicit a great deal of enthusiasm on the part of the admirers of James. These have been accustomed to the rejection of his theory of man's right to believe in God and to the criticisms that have been leveled against The Will to Believe ever since it was first published. But now Peirce is being invoked as added justification for such criticism. For, after all, even though the two were close friends, was not Peirce forced to criticize elements of James's thought and even to break completely with the latter's brand of pragmatism? Hence we see that Peirce is becoming the champion of a sizeable anti-James segment of American philosophers, and this seems to be giving added reason for downgrading James's thought even more.

Differences

One can easily find reasons for emphasizing the break between Peirce and James on the matter of pragmatism. Ralph Barton Perry

[52] 6. 182.
[53] Perry, op. cit., I, p. 536.

long ago made the statement, quoted many times since, that "the modern movement known as pragmatism is largely the result of James's misunderstanding of Peirce." [54] In the light of Perry's vast erudition in the area of James's thought, no one, to my knowledge, has seriously challenged this judgment.

And surely, it may be said, one has only to turn to Peirce's own statements to see clearly the break that developed between himself and James on the matter of pragmatism. For example, Peirce affirmed an essential difference between his pragmatism and that of James.[55] And yet, the places where he spells out these differences are not without their difficulties. When he kisses pragmatism good-bye and announces the birth of "pragmaticism," a word safe from kidnappers, he is not talking exclusively about James's pragmatism. He also has in mind the uses made of the term by Ferdinand Schiller (1864–1937) and Giovanni Papini (1881–1956), its abuse in "literary journals," and the criticism to which it had been subjected by "the manners of the British." [56]

In several places Peirce singles out specific aspects of James's pragmatism for discussion and criticism.[57] Thus he maintains that James stresses "conduct to be recommended or experience to be expected." Hence there is "no slight theoretical divergence" between the two forms of pragmatism. But even so, Peirce is willing to admit that the differences disappear in practice, though he adds in vague terms that James emphasizes considerations "not at all pragmatic," and that he and James differ "in other than the pragmatic ingredients of our thought."

Perhaps the first criticism Peirce raised against James's *Pragmatism*, one he mentioned several times in the course of their correspondence over many years, was expressed in "one lingering wish, for your sake and that of countless minds that, directly or indirectly, you influence." [58] His wish was that James would think with more exactitude. This was certainly valid; and if it had been heeded, James might have prevented the many misunderstandings regarding practically everything he wrote.

Had James been less kind, of course, he could have countered with

[54] *Ibid.*, p. 409.
[55] *Ibid.*, p. 409.
[56] 5. 414, 494–95.
[57] 5. 466, 494.
[58] Perry, *op. cit.*, II, p. 437.

the charge that Peirce was the last one to talk about exactitude—to which anyone who has struggled with the latter's style would add a fervent "amen." But more than that, Peirce seems not to have fully realized that James's style was often obscured by his insatiable desire to give expression to dimensions of experience for which he did not have an adequate vocabulary. This was part of his constant polemic against what he took to be the arid abstractionisms of the contemporary idealist philosophies. He was attempting in every way possible to express the delicate shades of concrete human experience and its place as a source of knowledge about reality. James, at one point, twitted Peirce for being in the world of logic, "where every item is changeless to eternity, but the real world is incongruent." [59]

Much attention has been given to Peirce's criticism of *The Will to Believe*. Peirce called it "a very exaggerated utterance," injurious to a serious man, and stated that what James had to say in his *Pluralistic Universe* regarding the "axiom of skipped intermediaries and transferred relations" was "far more suicidal," it being implied, of course, that *The Will to Believe* was itself "suicidal." [60] In support of this Peirce returns to his criticism that James is careless in what he says and that he does not use terms with strict accuracy. This stems from Peirce's position "that philosophy is either a science or is balderdash." Peirce calls "ruinous in practice" an understanding of faith that would mean that consistency in conduct prevents one from changing one's actions when further evidence demanded it.[61]

Agreements

Undoubtedly, a careful reading of the massive eight volumes of *Collected Papers* would reveal other objections Peirce voiced against Jamesian pragmatism. But at this time it would be proper to raise the question as to whether Peirce always understood what James was driving at. That he did seems to be assumed when differences between the two men are brought forward. Actually, it is an infallibility Peirce himself did not claim; neither did James, for that matter. Each honestly admitted that there were aspects of the other's thought he did not understand. Besides James's statement that Peirce's lectures on prag-

[59] *Ibid.*, p. 439.
[60] *Ibid.*, p. 438.
[61] *Ibid.*, p. 222.

matism were like "flashes of brilliant light relieved against Cimmerian darkness,"[62] their letters reveal a constant search for more understanding of each other's meaning.[63]

In addition, Peirce himself conceded that his criticisms were sometimes harsh. We know that in a manuscript passed around in Cambridge he had sharply criticized both James and Josiah Royce. In a beautiful and touching letter, he writes to Mrs. James to assure her of his admiration for William and apologizes for his excessive criticism of him. He pleads that his hermit's life made him lose perspective so that his attempt to express a mild divergence of views sometimes gave the impression of open hostility.[64]

The divergencies in the philosophical positions of Peirce and James are many—it would be futile to deny it. But on several very crucial questions we find that they are in close agreement. A good starting point would be the nature of their empiricisms. James, as we know, stressed the "stubborn facts" of experience. In this he was reacting against the rationalism of his day, which, in his view, had departed from empirical evidence in favor of abstract systems where everything was in its place and where concrete experience had to be forced into a system whether it agreed with that system or not. Although trained in science, James was not particularly attracted to laboratory procedure and so his empiricism was one that conformed not only to scientific evidence in the strict sense but also to the data of ordinary sense experience.

But James's notion of evidence was not limited to this. Just as he refused to be handcuffed by rationalism, so also he refused to be restricted within the narrow confines of empirical evidence as it was ordinarily understood. His appeal to experience was total. This meant experience in the widest sense, not only that which is classified as objective but also that which is personal. In his deep conviction that no maxim should block the road to inquiry, he felt that one's personal experience should be considered as a datum for our knowledge of external reality.

As we have seen, James's plea for an examination of personal experience is not a subjectivism gone wild. He did not mean that each one was to be his own judge regarding external reality. In his *Pragmatism*

[62] *Pragmatism*, p. 5.
[63] Perry, *op. cit.*, II, pp. 422–40.
[64] *Ibid.*, pp. 422–23.

he insists that the conclusions drawn from the data of experience must stand the test of consistency with our other experiences. Nor did "passional nature" mean sheer "emotionalism." It was the "ontological wonder" that goes beyond abstract classifications and scientific laws to the ultimate meaning of reality. James felt that the human mind would not stop until it had asked the ultimate question and had received a satisfactory answer. He could no more conceive that such a question must be judged unanswerable than he could believe that the mind must be held incapable of uncovering the scientific mysteries of nature.

James also recognized in man a drive for the consummation of his highest aspirations. The human being seeks for final goals that are lasting, for peace and security beyond the present sense of ultimate destruction, for objects to complete the human capacity for the fullness of love. He calls absurd the materialist's attempt to answer these needs by a "fatalism, whose solving word in all crises of behaviour is 'all striving is vain,' " and he predicts the collapse of all such philosophies.[65] He openly laughs at the attempt to seek fulfillment in sacrifice for the good of future generations whom we do not know and who by all calculations will be better off materially than we are. It is not that he fails to see the value of such an ideal, for he has spoken of it in stirring terms.[66] But, in the last analysis, "This is all too finite, we say; we see too well the vacuum beyond. It lacks the note of infinitude and mystery." [67]

The evidence James brings forward is not evidence of an empirical kind, at least not as it is ordinarily understood, but James felt that it constituted data that must be respected. Confident that human needs were reliable in this regard, as they are in so many others, and confident, too, that there was something or someone in the order of reality to satisfy one's inner need for personal fulfillment on the highest human level, James could say that he had a "right" to believe in God and that it was eminently "reasonable" to do so. A world that failed to fulfill these needs could in no sense be called rational, no matter how intelligible it might otherwise seem.

Turning now to Peirce, we find striking parallels between his thought and that of James. Peirce's empiricism is surely of a more

[65] W. James, "The Sentiment of Rationality," *The Will to Believe and Other Essays in Popular Philosophy* (New York: Longmans, Green, 1927), p. 88.
[66] *Pragmatism*, pp. 290–98.
[67] "The Moral Philosopher and the Moral Life," *The Will to Believe*, p. 212.

technical kind. He is much more the scientist and experimentalist, the logician and mathematical analyst. Yet, as we have seen from Peirce's treatment of the reality of God, he has also emphasized the role of the personal and subjective. Peirce has no hesitation about using the term "instinct" nor about making explicit its relation to animals—although he also calls it sentiment, a term less applicable to the animal kingdom. He makes clearer the distinction between the areas controlled by reason and instinct: in science, reason is supreme; in vitally important matters, instinct.

His emphasis on personal experience is very similar to James's position. He advocated this viewpoint because he refused to allow scientific maxims to block the way to inquiry. The argument for the reality of God begins with instinct and moves on to the contemplation of nature: "If he allows instinct to speak, and searches his own heart, he will at length find that he cannot help believing it." [68] Not only is this the way a man must think in order to "think straight about such things," but this is the way he must think *if he is a pragmatist.*[69]

When we come to Peirce's position on verification, we again see similarities with James. He, too, has set up conduct as the norm for the validity of an idea. For the most part, it is conduct in the narrow sense of experimental test. Yet we see an entirely different atmosphere when we come to matters of vital importance. Peirce still holds verbally for a careful test before accepting a hypothesis. But, as we have seen, the test in terms of conduct suddenly becomes much wider than an experimental one. Although his position is merely sketched in outline, he argues to the reality of God from a natural tendency to believe, activated by the fact that such belief satisfies man's threefold desire for esthetic appreciation, for intelligibility, and especially for an ideal of life leading to man's highest growth. This last comprises the test of pragmatism or pragmaticism.

It is clear, too, in spite of the use of the word instinct and its application in an analogous sense both to man and to animals, that Peirce no less than James excluded a narrow meaning of the term. He speaks of it in relation to self-controlled growth in the conduct of life; to fulfillment of human personality; and to man's highest duty, which consists in completing one's personality by melting it into the cosmic whole.

[68] 6. 501.
[69] *Ibid.*, p. 501.

Though never stating it openly, Peirce gives indications that he, too, holds for the right to believe in God when empirical evidence does not decide the issue. As a matter of fact, James shows himself to be more the empiricist on this point because he states that we should always continue the attempt to test empirically the hypothesis of God and that it will be so verified even though the process will continue until the end of time.[70] Peirce seems to exclude this possibility,[71] and yet he is ready to believe in the hypothesis where belief means the willingness in vital affairs "to be deliberately and thoroughly prepared to shape one's conduct into conformity with a proposition." [72] In some instances this may mean a commitment involving "superhuman courage," as is witnessed in the lives of men who, for the love of God, will spend their energies in the service of lepers.[73]

Conclusion

In all this we seem to see two Peirces just as we seem to see two Jameses—or perhaps we should speak rather of two dimensions. Both belonged to the scientific tradition and had adopted scientific ways of thinking. But they also felt that there was a level of evidence outside the traditional scientific mold that gives a hearing to concrete human experience in all its aspects. Peirce gives greater emphasis to reason over instinct, and he is more precise regarding the areas covered by each. James places the emphasis on personal experience, though he does not stray far from the guidelines of his empiricism in spite of the exaggerations into which he was sometimes led by the popular style of his lectures and by his eagerness to counteract the abstractions of rationalism. In some ways we see at work in these men two different temperaments; and, in a sense, they are concrete examples of James's own position, stated throughout his *Pragmatism*, that one's philosophy is dictated largely by one's temperament. For all that, they were in agreement in their conviction that one could be both a scientific man and a religious man. In fact, it was their deep and rich contact with nature that brought them more fully into contact with God.

[70] *Pragmatism*, pp. 109, 299; "The Sentiment of Rationality," *The Will to Believe*, p. 107.
[71] 6. 489.
[72] 6. 467.
[73] 6. 503.

IV

JOHN
DEWEY

AND RELIGIOUS
EXPERIENCE

Several years ago the education page of the Sunday *New York Times* carried an article entitled "Dewey's Missing Years." [1] It seems that a national committee had been formed to shed some light on the details of two years of his life when, fresh from college, he was teaching in the public schools of Oil City, Pennsylvania.[2] The mys-

[1] *The New York Times*, July 28, 1963, Sec. IV, p. 7.
[2] *The New York Times* gives the dates as 1880–82. The actual dates seem rather to be 1879–81. *See* M. H. Thomas, *John Dewey: A Centennial Bibliography* (Chicago: University of Chicago Press, 1962), p. xi.

tery surrounding these years is curious in view of the fact that Dewey is "one of the country's most thoroughly documented educators." The committee was formed in the hope of adding the "Oil City Story" to his biography.

The interest on the part of scholars in tracing every bit of information on the life of John Dewey is itself testimony to the stature of the man. Yet, according to his close friends and disciples, his external appearance was more likely to consign him to obscurity. Of medium height, with thin, unruly hair, broad mustache, and a shy look mounted by rimless glasses, he was the perfect example of the absent-minded professor. His lectures, delivered in a soft voice and at a leisurely pace, gave the impression that he was thinking out loud rather than lecturing. For the most part, his written style is colorless and even exceedingly dull, though on rare occasions he can rise to a high pitch of eloquence. It has been said of him that the unwary listener or reader could easily be lulled to sleep, only to miss a brilliant insight that comes as a dramatic climax to a whole chain of thought.

Dewey was born in Burlington, Vermont, on October 20, 1859. He attended the University of Vermont and graduated Phi Beta Kappa with a class of eighteen in 1879. Following the two years of high-school teaching in Oil City, Pennsylvania, he spent one year in the village school of Charlotte, Vermont. With the encouragement of W. T. Harris, his former philosophy teacher at the university, Dewey began two years of graduate work in philosophy at Johns Hopkins University and received the doctorate in 1884.

Dewey taught for the next ten years at the University of Michigan, with the exception of one year at the University of Minnesota. In 1894 he was invited to the University of Chicago as chairman of the department of philosophy, psychology, and pedagogy, and there he set up "The Laboratory School," or "The Dewey School," as it was also called. In 1904 he left Chicago because of differences between himself and the university president, William R. Harper, regarding the future direction to be taken by the Laboratory School. He then began his long teaching career as professor of philosophy at Columbia University, where he remained until his retirement in 1930. He continued to be associated with the university as professor emeritus until 1939. Dewey remained active as writer, lecturer, and champion of unpopular causes until his death in New York City in 1952. He left behind him a staggering record of three dozen books, hundreds of articles and reviews, and a reputation as America's best known philosopher and educator.

In spite of his harmless appearance, Dewey's revolutionary ideas and his involvement in the pressing problems of the day often made him a topic of discussion and even of heated controversy. As early as 1896 he set up an elementary school for the purpose of putting into practice his novel ideas in education. The fact that it was called "The Laboratory School" added to the alarm of those who felt that one should not "experiment" on children. These days, when discussion of academic freedom has become almost a national pastime, it is interesting to note that Dewey was a founder and first president of the American Association of University Professors and a charter member of the first teachers' union in New York City. Dewey spent the years 1919–21 in China, lecturing at the national universities of Peking and Nanking and in the capitals of many of the provinces. Inevitably, of course, the eventual conversion of China to communism has been attributed to his influence.[3]

In 1928 he visited Russia to study the educational situation there, and on his return he published a favorable report on conditions under the Soviet regime. The fact that later developments made him highly critical of the revolution never fully absolved him from the charge of being a "red" and a "Bolshevik." [4] On the other hand, in 1937 he drew upon himself the wrath of the *Daily Worker* and the communist world generally when he served as chairman of a committee that inquired into, and absolved Leon Trotsky of, charges that he had plotted against the life of Joseph Stalin and attempted to incite Germany and Japan to attack the Soviet Union.

In 1941 Dewey went to the defense of Bertrand Russell, who had been barred from teaching at City College of New York because of his views on love, marriage, and divorce. According to Sidney Hook's version of the incident, Dewey did this in spite of personal and doctrinal disagreements between the two.[5]

[3] This widespread opinion has been ably challenged by T. Berry, C.P., in his essay "Dewey's Influence in China," in J. Blewett, S.J., ed., *John Dewey: His Thought and Influence* (New York: Fordham University Press, 1960), Chap. VIII, pp. 199–232.
[4] For a sharp criticism of Dewey for his alleged partiality to communist Russia, see N. D. Roodkowsky, "Marxism's Appeal for American Intellectuals," *The Catholic World*, Vol. 192, No. 1147 (October, 1959), pp. 137–38.
[5] S. Hook, "Some Memories of John Dewey," *Commentary*, Vol. 14 (September, 1952), pp. 248–49.

To Americans, Dewey's name is synonymous with education. His admirers credit him with freeing our students from the straight-jacket control of rigid discipline and passive receptivity and shower upon him their gratitude for enabling young people to develop their intelligence, initiative, and responsibility. His critics charge him with inflicting irreparable harm on the cause of education.

Dewey has long been considered the founder, architect, and father-protector of "progressive education." Most people, however, seem unaware that progressive education may be spelled in either large or small letters and, thus, means different things. In either case, the claim made on Dewey's behalf is highly exaggerated. Progressive education began in the 1890s and was a far more complex movement than it is usually thought to have been. It drew upon many people and upon varied currents of thought, including those affecting social, economic, and political as well as educational factors.[6] The Progressive Education Association, which included only a small part of the teaching profession in spite of its great influence, was founded in the winter of 1917–18 and numbered eighty-five members in 1919. Dewey declined the invitation to become its honorary president and, in fact, did not join it until 1927. He later became critical of what he felt to be the excesses of progressivism in education. Nonetheless, his name has been linked with the movement in both its broad and narrow senses, and he has borne the brunt of criticism for its deficiencies.

Be that as it may, Dewey seems to have suffered a relative decline in popularity after the demise of the Progressive Education Association in 1955. I myself attempted to register for a course on the philosophy of John Dewey at Columbia in the fall of 1959, the centennial of his birth, but the university where he had been professor of philosophy for twenty-six years and professor emeritus for another nine years offered no such course.

Speaking from an admittedly biased position, I am convinced that Dewey should be called a philosopher rather than an educator, in spite of the fact that his work and writing in education preceded the full articulation of his philosophy in written form. He himself maintained that education was the laboratory for his philosophical ideas. It is un-

---

[6] L. A. Cremin has given two excellent treatments of this question: "The Progressive Movement in American Education," *Harvard Educational Review*, Vol. 27, No. 4 (Fall, 1957), pp. 251–70, and *The Transformation of the School: Progressivism in American Education, 1876–1957* (New York: Knopf, 1961).

fortunate that teachers come to Dewey's thought only through his works on education and that few read his philosophy. The reading of books like *Experience and Nature* and *Essays in Experimental Logic* can be a painful experience, for they are prime examples of Dewey's dull and heavy style; his *Art as Experience* and *A Common Faith* are far more engaging. But all these works shed needed light not only on his theory of education but on his social and political theory as well.

Religious Background

As a young boy, John Dewey followed the religious beliefs of his mother and became a member of the Congregational Church. Apparently Mrs. Dewey's strict set of beliefs and rigid code of moral conduct, both of which were heavily Calvinistic, affected her treatment of her children. Dewey himself relates that she closely questioned him and his brother, even in the presence of others, whether they were "right" with Jesus and whether they had asked God for forgiveness. The obvious result for both of them was a sense of guilt as well as of annoyance.[7]

The nature of these incidents could easily lead one to draw all kinds of Freudian conclusions and to see in a mother's excessive concern the ultimate reason for Dewey's later disenchantment with religion. Such a conclusion is not altogether impossible, but a harsh judgment of Mrs. Dewey can be tempered by the fact that she won the love and admiration of the Burlington community for her charitable work on behalf of the poor. Burlington, like every commercial city, had its slums, and Mrs. Dewey dedicated her time and energy on behalf of the people who suffered in them. She personally visited their homes and organized agencies to do the work more efficiently. These acts of love and devotion were appreciated by the townspeople, and she received a tribute in *The Burlington Free Press*.[8]

Yet it must be admitted that Dewey's acceptance of the religious teaching in which he was raised was quite nominal. He made a valiant attempt to believe in the doctrines of the Congregational Church and

[7] Hook, *op. cit.*, p. 246.
[8] G. Dykhuizen, "An Early Chapter in the Life of John Dewey," *Journal of the History of Ideas*, Vol. 13, No. 4 (October, 1952), pp. 568–69.

was regular in his attendance at services and Sunday school. The atmosphere at the University of Vermont was theologically liberal, with Congregationalist leanings; [9] undoubtedly, this served to keep alive his adherence to his religion. As a college student, he even served as Sunday school instructor for a time, and, in 1881, he was active enough in parish affairs to have himself elected first president of the newly formed Young People's Society.[10] But, apparently, he never accepted his religion with any deep conviction of commitment, and he gave up the practice of his Congregational faith three years after graduation, when he left Burlington for graduate studies at Johns Hopkins.[11]

Drift from Traditional Religion: The Unity of Life

Why did Dewey drift away from institutionalized religion? Was it that religion came into conflict with his intellectual ideas? This would be a nice, neat explanation, for, as a matter of fact, the break Dewey made from the religion of his youth dates from the time he left home to study philosophy on the graduate level. Such a thesis would also fit in with the frequent practice of blaming philosophy for the loss of religion by many college and university students.

But, actually, the answer is a bit more complex. Dewey has maintained that philosophy as such never came into real conflict with his religion.[12] The development of his philosophical positions came only after he realized that religion, as he knew it, did not satisfy the needs stirring within his own personality. During his years in Burlington, Dewey felt a deep "inward laceration" that came from a sense of the divisions and separations induced by his New England culture, "divisions by way of isolation of self from the world, of soul from body, of nature from God," which oppressed him like a heavy weight.[13] He could not overcome a sense of alienation—first of all, from God, who somehow was a stranger to him, continually looking down upon him

[9] J. Dewey, "From Absolutism to Experimentalism," in G. P. Adams and W. P. Montague, eds., Contemporary American Philosophy (New York: Macmillan, 1930), II, p. 114.
[10] Dykhuizen, op. cit., p. 556.
[11] Ibid., p. 568.
[12] Dewey, op. cit., p. 19.
[13] Ibid., p. 19.

with displeasure or suspicion. Undoubtedly, the darker shadows of his Calvinistic background had much to do with this. They also made him feel that he was a stranger to the world. As his later interests were to show, Dewey was eager to live fully in the world because a deep commitment to it released his energies and developed his human potentialities. This is why a key point of his later educational theory was that the child should not look upon his years in school as merely a preparation for something to come; school then becoming a drudgery and a bore. Dewey saw these years as opportunities for growth, development, and even for fulfillment here and now. These ideas broadened until he saw man's whole life in the world in the same light. The human person grows not through a constant battle with the world but through fruitful communication with it. This natural feeling of wanting to be at home in the world went counter to all that he understood religion to be, and it goes a long way toward explaining his opposition to traditional religion.

A study in his junior year at college of Thomas Huxley's (1825–95) work on physiology gave Dewey an intellectual basis for this craving for unity, which had become a part of his personal experience. Physiology helped him to see that biological organisms, especially man, are marvelously coordinated in the interdependent action of their diversified parts. Why could not the whole world, and life itself, be as coordinated and as unified as the human organism? Dewey saw no reason why they could not be and, subconsciously, he began searching for a world-view that would accomplish this unification. Physiology thus impressed him more than anything he had yet studied. Though he had no particular desire to continue his work in this subject, he dates his interest in philosophy from this period.

Studies in his senior year broadened his general tendency toward the unification of experience. Courses offered in the history of civilization, political and economic theory, international law, and the Constitution of the United States [14] served to concentrate his interest on the city of man and upon those institutions concerned with enabling men to live in community. In private reading he became acquainted with the social theory of Auguste Comte (1798–1857). He was impressed by Comte's attempts to confront the disorganization of Western culture brought about by the disintegrative forces of individualism and to unify social life through a scientific methodology. Dewey's mother's

[14] Dykhuizen, *op. cit.*, p. 564.

social-mindedness and love for humanity had meanwhile stimulated him to a concern for those social evils that stand in the way of a human and satisfying life in the community.

During his college days, Dewey was certainly not explicitly aware of these currents stirring within himself. Looking back years later, he could analyze more objectively the causes of this "trying personal crisis." The need for unification of experience on the personal and social levels, which he describes as "an intense emotional craving," came into direct conflict with the divisions he thought were essential to the traditional religious beliefs that were part of his New England background. He was still searching for a satisfactory world-view when he made his way to Johns Hopkins to embark upon a career in philosophy.

Influence of Hegelian Idealism

Dewey found in Hegel's thought the unification he sought, for it healed the divisions that had so disturbed him. Hegelianism came as "an immense relief, a liberation." [15] It brought together subject and object, matter and spirit, the human and the divine. A tremendous weight was lifted from his mind, and he seemed to breathe a new atmosphere of freedom and expansion.

Curiously enough, if we did not have his autobiographical accounts, which came fairly late in his life, we probably would never have guessed that his spirit had been the arena of a deep interior struggle. Phrases like "trying personal crisis," "painful oppression," "inward laceration," "intense emotional craving," "immense release, a liberation," help us to catch a glimpse of what went on within his soul. Apparently Hegelian idealism supplied for him the underpinning and even the substitute for religious beliefs with which to resist the inroads of materialism in biology, evolution, and the "new psychology." George Sylvester Morris, who was Dewey's mentor in graduate school and who turned Dewey in the direction of Hegelianism, held philosophy—and, by this, he meant Hegelianism—to be the "true bulwark" of religion, and Dewey occasionally wrote articles adopting the same position.[16] The elements of Hegel's idealism that appealed to these men were the notions of an absolute mind or consciousness unit-

[15] Dewey, *op. cit.*, p. 19.
[16] M. G. White, *The Origin of Dewey's Instrumentalism* (New York: Columbia University Press, 1943), pp. 5–6.

ing all reality, of which individual minds and beings are particular realizations. Furthermore, idealism preserved the notions of a spiritual soul in man and of an Absolute as the ultimate explanation of the universe. Years later, Dewey the experimentalist seemed to realize that many would be surprised at the appeal "an intellectualized subject-matter" had for him, for he admits that his natural inclination made him partial to the theoretical and systematic, even while his personal experience, maturing through acquaintance with the empirical and experimental, made him more open to concrete material and thus modified the technical rigor of his systematic thinking.[17]

Dewey spent the next decade, from 1884 to 1894, at the University of Michigan, with the exception of one year spent at the University of Minnesota. For most of that period, his romance with Hegelian thought was an ardent and happy one. He immersed himself in the academic life of a professor of philosophy and developed his ideas along idealistic lines in his lectures and books. In logic and epistemology, he roundly criticized the British empiricists for their atomistic theory of ideas and passivity of mind, and in psychology, he held to the unique character of the human soul and of consciousness and the union of knower and known. He stressed the need of relationships with other selves for the development of personality, and he saw the need of a total surrender to "the perfect personality, God," in the realization that "whatever we have and are is not of our particular selves, but from God." [18]

His religious orientation is indicated in several articles and lectures that show he had worked out what one writer has called a "Hegelianized Christianity." [19] He could still speak about the Bible as witnessing to the reality of God and to the commands He imposes on man. He shows a respect for loving adherence to Christ and to meditation on the things of God as characteristic of the true believer.[20] In his criticism of the evolutionary theory of Herbert Spencer, he holds fast to a "spiritual" philosophy that coincides rather closely with Christianity.[21] He protests against the evolutionists' attempt to sub-

[17] Dewey, op. cit., pp. 16–17.
[18] J. Dewey, Psychology, 3rd ed. rev. (New York: Harper and Brothers, 1895), p. 339.
[19] J. Blewett, S.J., "Democracy as Religion: Unity in Human Relations," in J. Blewett, op. cit., p. 37.
[20] Ibid., p. 35.
[21] Ibid., p. 35.

ordinate the good of individual men to the final goal of the state, and he proposes that the universal spirit gives meaning and purpose to mankind throughout the course of its history.

Drift from Hegelianism

In describing his eventual break with Hegelianism, Dewey uses the word "drifting" because it indicates that it was a gradual process of which he himself was not fully aware.[22] The forces at work in undermining his confidence in Hegelianism had several sources. As far back as his undergraduate days, he had become familiar with the work being done in biology, evolutionary theory, and experimental psychology. All of these had stressed the natural interaction of all living things, from simple biological organisms to man. A living being cannot be separated from its environment, either conceptually or physically. Life goes on and develops only inasmuch as the living being interacts with the environment, and biological processes, such as digestion and growth, are meaningless once we separate the organism from its surroundings. Psychology made him aware that man, by nature, is a social being and that, for the development of his personality, he needs the world of people. Dewey came to view these relationships as natural, with no need for the all-embracing context of a universal consciousness or Absolute.

At the same time, there grew in his consciousness a realization of the importance of democracy as the political milieu in which the human person is to grow.[23] A democratic way of life places the emphasis on human initiative and responsibility to work out those conditions necessary for the development of the human personality. It can also help to develop a moral man—for democracy can be the atmosphere in which righteousness, peace, and good will can flourish as the "ultimate, ethical ideal of humanity." There is no longer a distinction between the spiritual and secular, the church and state, the human and divine. At this point, Dewey was still under the influence of his "Hegelianized Christianity," though the emphasis was already beginning to shift from the traditional Christian view of man and society

[22] "From Absolutism to Experimentalism," pp. 19–20.
[23] Blewett, op. cit., pp. 36–37.

to a naturalistic one. As a matter of fact, if we did not know that his philosophical orientation was still Hegelian, we could read his treatment of man's relation to society and the world in purely naturalistic terms.

Influence of the Rise of Science

Another important element in his drift from Hegelianism, and indeed from traditional Christianity, was the influence of the rise of science. The scientific temper stressed the freedom of the mind to pursue truth unimpaired by presuppositions of any kind—whether these came from philosophy, religion, or from existing social structures. The prospect of what the human mind could accomplish by the method of free inquiry was an exciting one. It simply had to clash with what he conceived traditional Christianity to be—namely, a religious structure that, though important in its day, was no longer viable because it was closed to or at least suspicious of complete freedom in the pursuit of truth.

The publication of his book *The Outlines of a Critical Theory of Ethics* in 1891 marked the close of Dewey's Hegelian period in philosophy. From then on his criticism of idealism grew; and, though he continued to speak in the terms of idealism, it is quite evident that the content had gone and that the move to naturalism was a steady one.[24] Once the philosophical underpinning had collapsed, it was inevitable that the last remnants of his Christianity would dissolve as well.

Move Toward Naturalism

Just as Dewey's drift from Hegelianism was gradual, so, too, was his shift away from traditional religion to naturalism. In 1894, he left Michigan for the University of Chicago, and for the rest of his life he was absorbed in other problems. His many books and articles rarely deal at any length with religious questions. When he does treat them, it is usually to contrast some aspect of religion with the ideas he was working out. Hence it is difficult to trace step by step his move away from religion.

[24] White, *op. cit.*, p. xiv.

"Religion and Our Schools"

There is one article that can serve as a landmark in the journey, however; it is "Religion and Our Schools," written in 1908.[25] We see that at least by this time Dewey's position is more or less formulated. His thesis is that religion should not be taught in our schools, but he maintains that his opposition to religious instruction did not come from any indifference or hostility to Christianity but from his view of America as an emerging society. Our nation was engaged in absorbing and consolidating peoples of various countries, cultures, and backgrounds, and in developing its industrial, political, and economic life. The democratic form of government in which this enterprise was being achieved needed the unified effort of all concerned so that it might flower in a sharing of goods and opportunities.

In view of this Dewey felt that America's social consciousness should not be disrupted by "divisive ecclesiastical divisions." [26] He looked upon the various denominations and churches as so many rivals vying for the allegiance of our young students, and he thought that the effort did much to discredit the cause of religion. Far better would it be to engage in the "infinitely significant religious work" of uniting our citizens by helping them to achieve an awareness of common goods and by putting at their disposal the tools for achieving them. Hence he adopted a laissez faire attitude toward the teaching of religion and strongly proposed that it be excluded from the curriculum.

This article is interesting for what it tells us about Dewey's view of religion and about the actual state of religion in America in the early part of the century. His own experience had apparently given him the impression that the various religious denominations were at swords points, and we hear an echo of Peirce's complaint against the "angry squabbles" between Calvinists and Unitarians. One could fault Dewey for his sweeping generalization, voiced in his conviction that the denominations had reached an irreconcilable disagreement, making harmony and cooperation an impossibility. And yet he was writing at a pre-ecumenical period of our religious development, and it would be difficult to deny that "angry squabbles" were frequent enough to make the cause of religion seem less than attractive and more than a little divisive. However valid or invalid we may judge Dewey's criticism to be

[25] J. Dewey, "Religion and Our Schools," in J. Ratner, ed., *Characters and Events* (New York: Henry Holt, 1929), II, pp. 504–16.
[26] *Ibid.*, p. 508.

for his own time, it would seem that today, at any rate, the growing eagerness on the part of people of all faiths to accept one another in mutual understanding and charity has rendered Dewey's criticism no longer relevant. For all that, he did put his finger on a serious problem that existed in his own day and that, only in our own times, seems on the way to a happy solution.

Dewey also raised an interesting pedagogical problem regarding the teaching of religion: what precisely is religious instruction? Is it theology, or history of religion, or information like grammar and arithmetic, or memorized formulae and facts? For Dewey, religion is "personal insight, the development of fundamental mood and the formation of permanent attitudes" that take hold of the whole personality and give direction to all areas of human life.[27] But if this is so, can religion be "taught"? Dewey did not think so. He was certainly no anti-intellectual who would drain all content from religious belief. But again, like Peirce, he was more interested in a "way of life" that absorbs one's attitudes and conduct than in a set of beliefs or points of doctrine "gotten up" for class recitation. We are still grappling with the problem Dewey saw sixty years ago.

"Religion and Our Schools" also reveals Dewey's growing concern for the place of science in contemporary civilization. Its growth and influence in all phases of American life could not be ignored. He felt that the transformation it had made in our thinking, our attitudes, and our whole outlook toward life gave science priority over other considerations. He was fully prepared to face the consequences, even when it meant the exclusion of religion from the school curriculum. In the spirit of the age, he believed that knowledge in all fields was still expanding and that every point of doctrine was a hypothesis open to further investigation. All knowledge was public and therefore subject to question, challenge, and new tests. Would religious instructors be willing to present religion in the same way? Would the student be permitted to raise difficulties, explore new areas, even alter points of doctrine in the light of new evidence? Dewey conceived traditional religion as a set of beliefs that are forever unchanged and unchangeable, closed to the scientific method that governed every other subject in the school curriculum. To Dewey, this would conflict with a fundamental pedagogical principle and would raise insuperable difficulties for the teacher and student. Hence religion should be excluded. The reason

[27] Ibid., p. 511.

was a pedagogical one, but it quite clearly had roots in Dewey's own attitude toward both religion and science.

Accommodation to the "Scientific Revolution"

The subsequent development of Dewey's naturalism and his increasing opposition to religion should be understood for what they really were. I do not think that his works ever reveal a spirit of blind prejudice, bitter ranting, or negative hostility. I do not even think that his intellectual journey can be classified mainly as a rejection of religion. By far the most important factor was his growing insight into the relationship of man to the world for the full development of his personality. It was a problem that included much wider perspectives than those of science. James and Peirce had been bothered about the question as to how they could be both religious men and men of science. For them the latter term certainly embraced more than science in the narrow sense, and perhaps could better be described by the term "scientific age." Even so, neither James nor Peirce saw as fully as Dewey did what a scientific age meant. Neither did they give as much attention to the meaning of the development of human personality in such an age.

Dewey gives the impression of a man who stood in awe and reverence before the prospects opened up for man by science. Basically, he had a profound regard for the worth of the human person, and that is why he turned to education as the process by which the infant personality is given room to expand. He also had a genuine respect for matter, which meant a regard for those conditions that can further the maturity of the person and that should be utilized, developed, or altered according to need.[28]

To Dewey, the effect of science has been nothing less than revolutionary. This does not refer principally to the tremendous advances made in actual knowledge and improved technique, as significant as these may be. Neither did he concern himself with the so-called "warfare" between science and religion, which he considered to be vastly exaggerated. These interests, for the most part, concern the experts in both science and theology, but Dewey was more disturbed by the profound change made in the lives of men generally. Science has entered the scene "like a thief in the night":

[28] J. Dewey, *Reconstruction in Philosophy*, 2nd ed. rev. (Boston: Beacon Press, 1948), p. 72.

. . . science affects disturbingly every aspect of contemporary life, from the state of the family and the position of women and children, through the conduct and problems of education, through the fine as well as the industrial arts, into political and economic relations of association that are national and international in scope.[29]

This situation must be met with more than piecemeal solutions. It demands a whole new outlook, a "reconstruction" in our way of thinking. Man must seriously look on the contemporary scene and attempt to integrate into a world-view the varied factors that go to make up the "scientific revolution."

Dualism: the "Secular" and the "Spiritual"

The central issue is the dualism that has penetrated into the depths of the human personality. Contemporary man is a divided man who has been split between two different and competing interests. One part of him tries to preserve a sense of traditional value that cherishes a belief in God, a respect for the human individual, and high ideals of virtue. The other dimension is strongly attracted to technical science and all the areas affected by it. Yet these areas are labeled "secular" and hence are unredeemed and unredeemable. If one is to operate in such a world, he must somehow achieve a state of truce whereby he agrees to involve himself in the secular as long as it does not encroach upon the "spiritual." But even as the terms are drawn up and areas of division carefully outlined, the individual knows in his heart that it is an uneasy truce that threatens to break out into open warfare. Where peace and harmony continue, it is only at the cost of surrendering more and more of one's daily life to the "secular" sphere, with all the self-reproach that goes with such a surrender.

Religious life is profoundly affected, and that is why Dewey maintained that traditional religion was undergoing the greatest revolution that had occurred in the long history of mankind.[30] Never has man

[29] Ibid., p. xx.
[30] J. Dewey, A Common Faith (New Haven: Yale University Press, 1934), p. 65. It has been stated [R. Bernstein, Book Review, International Philosophical Quarterly, Vol. 4, No. 3 (September, 1964), pp. 484–87] that Dewey's explicit treatment of religious issues is relatively sketchy and that A Common Faith (which is only eighty-seven pages long) cannot be considered a detailed treatment. I feel that A Common Faith not only sums up everything that Dewey said on religion but places it firmly within the sweep of his whole philosophy.

66843

become so absorbed in interests and values that are divorced from all connections with any church. It may be true that such interests began under the control of religion, but once launched they have gone their own way. The result is that, under the influence of religion, a great many people look with distrust upon values that emerge in social life: "Natural relations, of husband and wife, of parent and child, friend and friend, neighbor and neighbor, of fellow workers in industry, science, and art, are neglected, passed over, not developed for all that is in them." [31] In many cases such relations are considered to be positively dangerous to religious values.

Dewey admits that, under the influence of liberal tendencies within Christianity, religious men have attempted a compromise by delineating two spheres of values, one supernatural and the other natural, that are considered to be complementary. As long as the two areas do not become confused, it is hoped that all will be well. But Dewey looks upon this as little better than the former position; it is only a "softened version" of the more radical dualism, for it is but a feeble attempt to deck out current changes with the trappings of the supernatural.[32]

In his analysis of the dualism confronting contemporary man, either in its radical or softened form, Dewey echoed the "lacerations" that were characteristic of his earlier period, only now he gave them more developed expression. At the heart of his analysis is his thesis that belief in the supernatural is no longer a viable outlook on life. Too much had happened to man and to the society in which he lives to perpetuate a belief that, in his view, blocks the involvement of man in his surroundings. Supernaturalism stands in the way of any fruitful dealing with natural events, and without this involvement man will remain a stunted thing, incapable of becoming a fully developed person or a religious one in any traditional sense of the word.

But Dewey still retained a conviction that the dualism could be healed and that man could still be religious. It meant, however, that a whole new meaning be given to the term religious. We find that Dewey expresses the high opinion he had of relations with the world by speaking of a respect for matter in terms of the conditions for the growth of man as human, and that he advocates a "natural piety" towards the world and all those social institutions that go to make up

[31] *Reconstruction in Philosophy*, p. 71.
[32] *A Common Faith*, p. 80.

man's relations with other people. His principal aim is to emphasize the fact that these relationships are valuable and lead to the enrichment of human life. He wishes to break down the distrust of them that he thinks has been engendered by traditional religion. Man should not be haunted by a sense of foreboding when he immerses himself in the pursuit of science, in a concern for political and economic institutions, or in a zeal for the alleviation of social ills that make human development difficult or impossible. These interests are valuable, for they intimately affect the human person.

Such an approach inevitably brought man into Dewey's interest to such an extent that all other interests became secondary. We enter the very center of his naturalism, which has gone further than that of either James or Peirce in the exclusive manner in which it is expressed. Dewey was determined to go the full way toward removing every obstacle to those relationships without which man can never become fully human. But in doing so he maintained that he was "religious" in the only authentic meaning of the term because he remained faithful to human experience.

The New Meaning of "Religious"

This brings us to the new meaning Dewey gave to the term "religious." First of all, it does not mean any special category of things or relationships that distinguishes them from the "secular." All relationships can be religious to the extent in which they enrich man— whether this means the fundamental task of removing social ills or the more advanced stages of developing intellectual potentialities or of allowing for the possibility of expansion in science, art, political, social, or economic institutions. In this view nothing is "secular" or "irreligious" if it contributes to the enrichment of the human organism.

Such an approach will also remove the separation between ordinary and religious experience. Dewey rejects a special category of experience that we term religious and that it is the function of traditional religion to foster. A man is religious as much when he is engaged in those natural relationships that are part of his daily life as when he devotes himself to communion with a deity in prayer or to the rites and ceremonies of liturgical worship. In this sense, Dewey feels, the religious has not been cheapened or diluted but enlarged and enriched.

For an experience to be religious, then, it must include a relationship of man to his environment, for only then does it entail the growth of the human person. Drawing upon his knowledge of biology, Dewey maintains that any living organism must retain its interaction with surrounding conditions to live and grow. When separated from the environment, the organism dies. This is true on the human level as well. As far back as his *Psychology*, which was written during the height of his Hegelian period, Dewey developed the thesis that the human being becomes truly a person and matures as a person only when he is in relationships with other people. Though his Hegelianism gradually faded, he accepted the findings of experimental psychology that confirmed a position he had held for philosophical reasons. The insight became a dominating force in the development of his social and political theories. The cardinal point was that only as a member of a social whole can man truly develop as a person.

This idea became for Dewey a high form of altruism, for it meant that the peak of human fulfillment is reached when the individual commits himself to the good of humanity and when he sees that every act he performs will somehow benefit his fellow men. Isolation of man from his fellows only draws one in upon oneself, making one stunted and discontented. On the other hand, an individual will reach a high degree of satisfaction and fulfillment when he devotes his labors to the enrichment of those with whom he is associated in community life. But the important point to note is that Dewey does not make personal fulfillment the aim of action, for that would make the commitment to the good of mankind merely subservient to selfish ends, thus continuing a form of selfishness and self-love he is trying to eliminate. The fulfillment one achieves in action for others comes as a consequence of a response to a value that, in this case, consists in the good of others and that draws the free response of the individual. A person thus gives himself unreservedly for the good of others and, in the very process, achieves fulfillment.[33]

These ideas are implicitly contained in most of Dewey's writings after his final break with Hegelianism. They are expressed in different ways and in varied contexts. They must be understood as background for his thinking when he took up the religious question in *A Common Faith*, the only book he wrote dealing explicitly with religion. Since it

[33] J. Dewey and J. H. Tufts, *Ethics*, 2nd ed. rev. (New York: Henry Holt, 1908), p. 336.

was written fairly late in his life, it gave him the opportunity to look back over the progress of his thought during more than forty years and to trace, in a more ordered way, the direction it had taken. When Dewey undertook to explain what he meant by religious experience, he expressed it in terms of self-sacrificing effort for all men, those who are living in the present and those who will come after us. In the awareness of solidarity with all mankind and in the exertion of effort on its behalf, man reaches religious experience. It takes concrete form in every action that one performs in daily life. It will include engaging in the technical work of science, in developing art, in building up a business enterprise, in social work for the poor and underprivileged, in teaching, in forming and maintaining friendships, in caring for a family. None of these is excluded from the possibilities of religious experience; all are, or can be, "religious" in the only meaning of the term Dewey will accept. In this way, he believed that he had closed the gap between the secular and the religious. Man, secure in the knowledge that whatever he does has the potential to benefit other individuals, need no longer be afraid to commit himself wholeheartedly to his daily tasks. In this sense, all activities and all aspects of the universe are sacred and worthy of profound respect because they converge upon the truly worthwhile goal of enriching human persons. "Whether or no we are, save in some metaphorical sense, all brothers, we are at least all in the same boat traversing the same turbulent ocean. The potential religious significance of this fact is infinite." [34]

As might be expected, the new interpretation Dewey gave to the category of the religious has been praised by his admirers and condemned by his critics. His use of the word "God" has likewise been the cause of discussion and debate.[35] Some concluded that, despite all his attacks on supernaturalism, he ended up by accepting a personal God anyway, at least as some power beyond nature. Others thought that he rejected God but held for some kind of impersonal process in nature. Still others saw no modification of the thoroughgoing naturalism that had characterized his thinking for many years. And so the opinions went.

Though a theist would like very much to see in the use of the word

[34] A Common Faith, p. 82.
[35] On this point, see the excellent article of C. Lamont, "New Light on Dewey's Common Faith," The Journal of Philosophy, Vol. 58, No. 1 (January 5, 1961), pp. 21–28.

God a return on Dewey's part to a belief in a deity, a much more sober judgment would have to be made. It is quite clear that in A *Common Faith* God stands for the ideal unification, projected by the imagination, of all those values that can be achieved for mankind through the cooperative effort of all individuals. Included in this ideal is the power of human intelligence, employing all the resources of science, to achieve a richer and fuller life for man now and for the future. In this definition of God we see no point of contact with the Deity of traditional theologians and philosophers. On the face of it, the surprising thing is that anyone could have read his description in terms of theism. The main reason this happened is that Dewey, for the first time, gave the word God explicit treatment and formulation, and theists found it difficult to interpret this as other than a fundamental change in his position or, better, as a return to a position he once held. And so they enthusiastically welcomed him into their ranks.

Why did Dewey bring the term God into the discussion at all? Sidney Hook states that he himself advised Dewey not to use it. But Dewey answered that the term has no fixed meaning and that his own use would not cause confusion. Moreover, he felt that many people would feel bewildered and hurt if they were barred from using the term God, even if, with Dewey, they rejected the supernatural meaning of God and religion. And so, in deference to these, he introduced God into the discussion.[36] But it is a strange twist of fate that one of the rare instances of his adherence to tradition should have been met with so much misunderstanding.

But there were still the existing churches. What room did Dewey leave for them? Surprisingly enough, he did not advocate that they be disbanded. Of course, they could never be what they had been: their basic outlook and spirit would have to be different, for supernaturalism as Dewey understood it would be eliminated. The central place was to be given to human values, and it would be the task of the churches to cherish and enlarge them. Traditional rites and symbols could be preserved, but only if they respect and reinforce human values. "In that way the churches would indeed become catholic" because they would become universal by unifying the attitudes and activities of all our citizens in a common enterprise.[37]

The meaning Dewey gave to the religious was, in reality, a basic out-

[36] Hook, *op. cit.*, p. 253.
[37] A *Common Faith*, p. 82.

look on life. It did not suddenly emerge with the writing of A *Common Faith*, for its origin can be traced back even as far as his Hegelian period. At that time, for him, it was a universal mind that united all things and all people into one reality. Dewey never lost the sense of unity, and his most admirable manifestation of it was the feeling that all men were his brothers and that their concerns were his. He himself found his deepest satisfaction in involving himself with the affairs of others and in cooperating with others for the enrichment of all. He took this to be a common experience and in no way did he think it peculiar to himself. His own observation and the teaching of psychology told him that individuals become truly fulfilled and satisfied when their interests break out of the narrow confines of self-centeredness and extend to all mankind.

Dewey thought that a failure to realize this was the reason so many people in America are discontented and dissatisfied. The goals they set for themselves are centered upon themselves, for the only things they are interested in are the money they can make and the material advantages they can buy. Dewey was by no means blind to the importance of making one's way in life; he was not so idealistic as to counsel a complete unconcern for material goods so that we would develop a nation of parasites. But he felt that unless a man's interest extends beyond the material to the contribution he can make to the good of all the citizens, his life will remain forever stunted. This does not apply only to the ordinary workman who comes to his job each day, spends his eight hours at a machine or a desk, and returns home; it applies also to the so-called "captain of industry." In a sense, the influence the latter has may seem to be far more extensive because the decisions he makes and the policies he sets may affect hundreds of people. To all appearances, he has the potential to be more social-minded because he can affect so many lives. Yet his interests are as narrow as the ordinary workman's, for he has as his goal not what he can contribute to the good of others but what advantages will accrue to himself.

The analysis Dewey makes here is analogous to the distinction he made between "religious" and "secular," for by their failure to open their minds to the social consequences of their acts, both the workman and the captain of industry have drained value and importance from a great many actions of their daily lives. The actions they perform are valuable only insofar as they contribute to the selfish aims of the agent. They have no value in themselves. Dewey would again wish to heal the division between the valuable and the indifferent by helping the individual to see the relationship of everything he does to the common good. The action performed partakes of the good of the goal and shares in its importance. In religious terms, Dewey would say that all actions by a man in the fulfillment of his job are sacred, and the experience one can have in the performance is truly religious.

For this reason, Dewey was interested in social questions. He had seen enough of American cities both large and small to realize that even in a modern age there were still many people who were living under conditions of extreme poverty. The poor, the sick, the aged, those suffering under racial prejudice—all these drew from him a sympathetic response. To him, work on behalf of such people should not be looked upon as a work of supererogation but as the normal response of a human being who is aware of his solidarity with all mankind. It is also a religious response in the sense of his redefinition of the religious. He thought, too, that such an outlook removed the artificiality he seemed to detect in the lives of traditionally religious people who, when they engage in such social work, somehow feel they are really only "baptizing" something that is mundane and secular. Dewey considered such work to be inherently religious and worthy of our highest respect and esteem.

As described earlier in this chapter, Dewey was interested and extensively involved in national and international affairs. His college course in United States government and law instilled in him an admiration and love for democracy. It is the political milieu in which personal responsibility and inventiveness can be exercised and in which the citizens can assume the task of working in a cooperative manner for the improvement of man's condition.

Since Dewey considered political and social institutions to be vehicles for social life, he took them seriously and thought deeply about them. Problems of liberalism and conservatism, collectivism and individualism, socialism and capitalism, labor and management, civil liberties and academic freedom were discussed in lectures, articles, and books. He was equally interested in international affairs and wrote many articles related to this subject.

When we consider that, in addition to all these activities, Dewey wrote on logic, education, psychology, science, morals, humanism, and esthetics, the breadth of his vision becomes truly fantastic. It is all the more inspiring when we consider that the dynamism of such varied interests and activities was the ideal of assisting humanity to achieve a richer life. For him, the ideal had a particular attraction because it was religious and the task he set before himself was sacred. The religious and sacred character of his vocation enabled him to look upon himself as a creator who exercised his creative ability for the formation of a new world. Man did not have to stand by as a spectator watching the course of events as they emerged in time. He could enter nature to make changes and assume the divine role of directing the activities of finite beings on all levels.

In the exercise of his creativity man also becomes mature. He can step into the universe and assume responsibility, exercise initiative, and accept the consequences. Science, of course, put into man's hands the tools for working changes that could not have been accomplished before. There is no longer any excuse for the individual not to assume responsibility for the improvement of the human estate. He can now bring all his intellectual powers and physical resources to bear upon shaping the direction the universe will take in the course of its evolution. This means, too, that the enrichment of human experience is largely in our own hands, and it opens to all of us the exciting prospect of seeing our efforts rewarded. In the process man creates a universe that will provide the surroundings best suited for the development of the person on the highest level.

Conclusion

Throughout his long life, Dewey alarmed and angered theists and religionists of the traditional type. There was good reason, of course: the more his naturalism developed, the more it clashed with traditional beliefs and practices. Dewey never made any attempt to disguise his opposition, just as he did not go out of his way to manifest it. Whenever the direction of his thought led him into the area of religion, he pointed out precisely where he stood. Those who maintained that A Common Faith marked a softening of his opposition were certainly ill advised, for in it he gave to the terms God and religious experience meanings entirely different from the traditional ones. We can find no clearer indication that his position had not changed than his statement that there is no bridge between religious values, as he understood them, and traditional religions. So important did he consider it to foster these values that he saw no alternative but to separate them once and for all from the creeds and cults of religions.[38] Moreover, the influence of his naturalistic outlook has been strongly felt in morals, law, politics, and social theory. In all these areas, he maintained that the goal of man is the complete realization of the human personality.

The passing of time has given us the opportunity to look more calmly and objectively at the thought of John Dewey. Within the ranks of religionists themselves voices have been raised that echo some of Dewey's themes. These are the voices of men who have experienced in their own lives the dualism of trying to be religious in contemporary society. They long to find meaning in activities that are considered secular and, hence, nonreligious. They vaguely sense that human values need not be divorced from religion and that religious experience should embrace more activities of their daily lives. Religionists have been prompted to reconsider their own outlook in order to see if their lives can be integrated into the one religious experience. It has suddenly become apparent that men like Dewey have raised real problems regarding religion and that these problems can no longer be ignored.

The cause of religion may have received a staggering blow from the impact of naturalism during the last three or four decades, but the blow has not been fatal. Religionists can face the future more confidently because, by heeding the voice of the naturalist, they can see more clearly the problem facing them. They can also feel secure in knowing that Dewey has done a service in pointing out the values inherent in human relationships. When carefully examined, they can be seen to present no obstacle to integration into religion in its traditional sense. To be fully human does not necessarily conflict with being truly religious and theistic. All the difficulties surrounding this enterprise have not been solved, but a confident step was taken once it became apparent that interest in the growth of human personality through involvement in the world was worthy of being prized and cherished. Religionists have begun to take seriously something to which they have paid little more than lip service for centuries: "Grace does not destroy nature but perfects it." We can apply to this dictum the words with which Dewey spoke of his naturalistic faith in the closing lines of his book on religion: "Such a faith has always been implicitly the common faith of mankind. It remains to make it explicit and militant." [39]

[38] *A Common Faith*, p. 28.
[39] *Ibid.*, p. 87.

V

ALFRED
NORTH
WHITEHEAD
AND THE GOD
OF PROCESS

The reading of Alfred North Whitehead's works can be an exciting as well as a confusing experience. Most people make first contact with his thought through a reading of *Science and the Modern World*. The first half-dozen chapters, on the rise of science, are stimulating, even though the wide sweep of ideas seems too great even for six chapters, and many details demand further analysis. The second half of the book is quite difficult to follow. Whitehead was working through a philosophy of natural science and setting the guidelines of his metaphysics, and there seems little connection between the two halves of the book. This is simply because, in this work, Whitehead was feeling his way and groping for words to express ideas that were still taking shape.

I think the best way to approach Whitehead is to read the books of his philosophical period in the order in which they were published. *Science and the Modern World* is only a preliminary statement of his position, and his ideas are developed in his subsequent works. It soon becomes clear that there is a relationship between his metaphysics—as seen in *Science and the Modern World* (second half), *Process and Reality*, *Religion in the Making*, and *Modes of Thought*—and his analysis of cultural history—as seen in *Science and the Modern World* (first half), *Aims of Education*, *Adventures of Ideas*, and *Science and Philosophy*. Whitehead's work then appears as a complete picture and not as a heap of unrelated pieces.

The sources for an account of Whitehead's life are rather meager. We have some charming glimpses of his early life and of his academic career, written by himself,[1] and a few brief sketches of him given by those who knew him well.[2] There are also some good discussions of the growth of his thought.[3] But there is no work that gives us a picture of his personal life, with its struggles, gropings, triumphs, and failures—after the manner of Ralph Barton Perry's work on William James or that of Ernest Jones on Sigmund Freud. This will have to be done by someone who had a close friendship with Whitehead and who has also mastered the intricacies of his science and metaphysics. The chances of such a work ever being produced grow slimmer each year. Nonetheless, we shall have to do with what we have in piecing together the details of his life, confining ourselves to those facts that bear upon the present study.

In view of the current interest in Whitehead and the contemporary nature of his ideas, it is difficult to believe that he was born during the opening years of the American Civil War—February 15, 1861, to be

[1] A. N. Whitehead, "Autobiographical Notes," in *Science and Philosophy* (New York: Philosophical Library, 1948), pp. 9–21.
[2] B. Russell, "Alfred North Whitehead," *Harper's Magazine*, Vol. 205, No. 1231 (December, 1952), pp. 50–52; P. Weiss, "Alfred North Whitehead: 1861–1947," *The Atlantic Monthly*, Vol. 181, No. 5 (May, 1948), pp. 105–07; W. E. Hocking, "Whitehead as I Knew Him," *The Journal of Philosophy*, Vol. 58, No. 19 (September 14, 1961), pp. 505–16.
[3] See especially V. Lowe, *Understanding Whitehead* (Baltimore: Johns Hopkins Press, 1962); I. Leclerc, *Whitehead's Metaphysics* (New York: Macmillan, 1958).

exact. His birthplace was Ramsgate, on the Isle of Thanet, Kent, in England. His father was an ordained Anglican clergyman. Following the course of studies of those who prepare for a university, Whitehead was sent, at the age of fourteen, to school at Sherborne in Dorsetshire. He received a classical education, with courses in Latin and Greek, and tells us that, in general, the level of teaching was high. He was excused from some of the work in Latin so that he might have more time for mathematics. The scientific world owes a debt of gratitude to the un-named pedagogue who had the foresight to make this decision. In his free time, which seems to have been ample enough, Whitehead was able to do private reading. His great interest in history and in the po-etry of Wordsworth and Shelley is reflected in the writing of his philo-sophical period.

In 1880 Whitehead entered Trinity College, Cambridge. To those who believe that the education given at that renowned university is limited to the study of the Greek and Latin classics, it will come as a surprise that, in his undergraduate days, Whitehead took all his lec-tures in pure and applied mathematics: "I never went inside another lecture room." [4] But formal studies were only part of the educational process; students and staff members engaged in discussions that con-tinued late into the night or early morning. "We discussed everything —politics, religion, philosophy, literature—with a bias toward litera-ture," [5] and all this led to a good deal of extra reading. The value of these aspects of life at Cambridge was not lost on Whitehead, and in his later years he expresses his gratitude for it.

In 1885 Whitehead acquired a fellowship and teaching position at Cambridge. His association with the university continued until 1910, when he resigned as Senior Lecturer, a breach of manners his alma mater has never quite forgotten. His resignation was followed by three years (1911–14) at University College, London. The years roughly from 1891 until 1913 can be called his mathematical period.[6] During this time he wrote A *Treatise on Universal Algebra* (1898), the monu-mental *Principia Mathematica* in three volumes (1910–13) with Bertrand Russell, and numerous articles on algebra, geometry, and logic. From 1914 until 1924, Whitehead taught at the Imperial Col-

[4] Whitehead, *op. cit.*, p. 13.
[5] *Ibid.*, p. 13.
[6] In grouping Whitehead's intellectual development into three periods and in dating each period, I follow the chronology of Lowe, *op. cit.*, Part II, though he admits uncertainty (p. 121).

lege of Science and Technology in Kensington. During these years his attention turned to the philosophy of natural science, with special application to physics.

Whitehead's final period began in 1924 when, at the age of sixty-three, he was invited to teach in the Philosophy Department at Harvard University. William Ernest Hocking, who was teaching there when Whitehead arrived, gives an account of the latter's career. Though Whitehead was only two years away from retirement, President Lowell wisely engaged him for five years in order to give him time to develop his ideas. Actually, he taught for thirteen years and remained as Professor Emeritus for ten more, until his death in 1947.[7]

Why did Whitehead come to America? It was truly a momentous decision for a man of advanced years to leave his native land and begin a whole new career. It would be impossible to give any one reason or even to single out a dominant one; the motivation was probably quite complex. First of all, in a letter to Charles Hartshorne, Whitehead said that he had always wanted to teach philosophy in order to develop ideas that had been going through his mind for some time. So his interest in philosophy did not begin in America; otherwise, it would be scarcely credible that, in the short space of four or five years, without previous long reflection, he could have developed such books as *Science and the Modern World, Religion in the Making,* and *Process and Reality*—to name but three, and each of these a classic. The invitation to teach at Harvard gave him the hoped-for opportunity to work out his ideas. So well did he succeed that, as Bertrand Russell notes, he became known as a philosopher in America, whereas in England he was looked upon only as a mathematician.[8] According to Paul Weiss, Whitehead said that he felt at Harvard a new-found freedom to express himself and to begin a whole new life. However, Professor Weiss shows more than a slight prejudice for Harvard and America when he says of Whitehead "that he began to make evident to the world the breadth of his interests, the brilliance of his mind, and the freshness, profundity, and boldness of his thought."[9] Whitehead had manifested all but the first of these traits in his own country. But then again, it was the one exception, the "breadth of his interests," that made all the difference and that gave a new dimension to his thought.

[7] Hocking, *op. cit.,* pp. 505–07.
[8] Russell, *op. cit.,* p. 50.
[9] Weiss, *op. cit.,* pp. 105–06.

Whitehead gives witness to another reason for the change to America. In England, with the passing of years, he began to feel cramped by a narrowness of outlook characteristic of English education. Hocking writes that he simply could not believe it when he heard that Whitehead had attended only lectures in mathematics while an undergraduate at Cambridge. Apparently a student in other circumstances was just as apt to specialize in classics to the exclusion of all else. We have seen how the students, in informal discussions, overcame the narrowness of specialization. Hocking sees in the typical British university a conflict between traditional humanism and the new science and maintains that no such problem existed at Harvard, where "science and the 'genteel tradition' were finding a common ground." [10] In Hocking's view, this was an important influence on Whitehead's decision.

But British education was apparently narrow in other ways as well. Whitehead, of course, appreciated the university training characteristic of the late nineteenth century in that it prepared career men for the England of those days. Nonetheless, he did not hesitate to say that it was far too limited for the new world that was emerging. At Sherborne the students knew little or nothing about the ruthless competition of modern industrial life or about the problems that arise in such a society.[11] Cambridge, and Oxford, too, showed a contempt born of ignorance for "the seething mass of artisans seeking intellectual enlightenment, of young people from every social grade craving for adequate knowledge, [and] the variety of problems thus introduced." [12] Whitehead became aware of all this only after he had gone to the University of London, and he felt that this university was attempting to face the problems of contemporary society. It is not too much to conclude that he saw American universities as trying to meet the same problems and that he was attracted by their vision and boldness. This seemed exceedingly important to him, and he thought that the future of civilization depended on the university's ability to adapt to changing conditions.

Whitehead spoke glowingly of America's prospects for future greatness. He saw in America "a zeal for knowledge which is reminiscent of the great periods of Greece and the Renaissance." [13] He thought the future of the world's intellectual civilization rested in the hands of America's great eastern universities. America, he felt, has an opportu-

[10] Hocking, op. cit., p. 507.
[11] Whitehead, op. cit., pp. 42, 46.
[12] Ibid., p. 18.
[13] Ibid., p. 21.

nity for greatness comparable to that of ancient Greece and the medieval European countries,[14] and Harvard itself he called "the greatest of existing cultural institutions." [15] Even when we allow for exaggeration, this is high praise and makes manifest the respect he had for America. All this was said after he had lived in America for some time, but he surely had formed an opinion of this kind even prior to his coming to this country.

An interesting question remains: how much was Whitehead's philosophy influenced by American thought? Hartshorne says that it is anybody's guess.[16] I suppose we could say that America's broader outlook toward the purpose of education gave him the freedom to widen his perspective. How much individual American philosophers influenced him is also difficult to evaluate, except to say that he admired men like James, Dewey, and Peirce. Can we then classify him as British or American? Hocking says he always remained British in affection and in politics.[17] Regarding his philosophy, I myself have never considered him as anything but an American. He shares with our tradition an openness to the changing conditions of contemporary life, an appreciation for the value of modern science, and an awareness of the need for human interaction with nature. It seems to me that it is not really important to settle the question of how much America influenced him or of whether he is American or not; the point is that he has something to say to us and that he belongs to our tradition. Whether England or America should be given the credit is relatively unimportant, but, as Victor Lowe points out, this much is clear: Whitehead's metaphysics has been given a far greater hearing by the philosophic world of America than by that of England.[18]

Search for Meaning

By the time Whitehead came to his metaphysical period, he had brought to focus a current of thought that had been forming for some years. His outlook had gradually been broadened, allowing him to

[14] *Ibid.*, p. 219.
[15] *Ibid.*, p. 235.
[16] C. Hartshorne, "Whitehead, the Anglo-American Philosopher-Scientist," *Proceedings of the American Catholic Philosophical Association*, Vol. 35 (1961), p. 163.
[17] Hocking, *op. cit.*, p. 506.
[18] Lowe, *op. cit.*, p. 13.

stand back and take a wider view of the universe. His previous years had been devoted to specialized problems, first in mathematics and then in the philosophy of natural science. His research in these fields had certainly helped him to answer many questions regarding the world in which he lived, and he found great intellectual stimulation in his work. But his searching mind was not quite satisfied with the solution of limited problems; his perspective widened until he began to ask questions of more inclusive import.

If we were to characterize the orientation of his thought at this time, we would say that he was looking for the ultimate meaning behind the whole of reality. When we read the works of his metaphysical period in the order in which they were written, we observe a groping toward such a meaning. It is as though by some intuitive sense he came to know that all he had done thus far had not completely satisfied his quest for the meaning of the universe. He himself said that he was searching for "something that matters." [19]

It would be going too far to suggest from this that he had grown disillusioned with everything he had done before. There is no indication in his writings that he had second thoughts about the value of the interests he had pursued for so many years and through so much labor. Bertrand Russell has suggested that Whitehead turned to philosophy largely as result of the grief he felt when his eighteen-year-old son was killed in World War I. There is no doubt that this was a tragic blow for Whitehead and that thereafter he continued his work only with great difficulty, but Russell seems to exaggerate when he says that the loss caused Whitehead "to seek ways of escaping from belief in a merely mechanistic universe." [20] This remark seems to be an expression of pique on the part of Russell because his former colleague turned to theism. Victor Lowe admits that the national and personal tragedy of the war had some influence in broadening his thought, but sees no evidence that his metaphysics would have been much different without this event.[21] I think we can find in Whitehead's own autobiography both the reason for his turn to metaphysics and the indication that this interest arose very early, even though he did not begin expressing it until quite late. In speaking of his wife he says: "Her vivid life has taught me that beauty, moral and aesthetic, is the aim of

[19] A. N. Whitehead, *Modes of Thought* (New York: Macmillan, 1938), p. 159.
[20] Russell, *op. cit.*, p. 50.
[21] Lowe, *op. cit.*, pp. 220–21.

existence; and that kindness, and love, and artistic satisfaction are among its modes of attainment." [22] But whatever its origins, the quest for a deeper meaning behind reality became his main interest, and it was for this reason that he developed his metaphysics.

Whitehead's search for meaning can be seen, first of all, on the level of civilization and culture. There is in the universe an "aim at social perfection" or an "aim at fineness." [23] The universe is always in the process of achieving value to the extent possible to it at a definite period of time.[24] Each epoch of mankind comes out of a definite past and drives forward to surpass itself in the achievement of things that men prize most because they fulfill the human urge for satisfaction.[25] This is the drive to what Whitehead called "peace," by which he meant, with obvious reference to Plato, a "harmony of harmonies" that tames the discordant forces in nature and brings civilization to the highest point of development possible to it at a given moment.[26] In his view, each age has a definite degree of excellence possible for it to achieve, given the past from which the age has emerged and the potentialities at its disposal. Deficiencies and limitations are inevitable, for no age is perfect, but the forward thrust of the world will enable it to develop according to its potential.[27]

The Advance of Civilization

What are the conditions for the advance of civilization? First of all, we should not set up a fixed ideal regarding the past. During Whitehead's school days at Sherborne, the civilization of Greece in its finest period was taken as the standard of what civilization ought to be. Athens was held up as the model of an ideal city.[28] But such an ideal is too static; it does not take into consideration the fact that growth in knowledge and technology gives a new shape to the growth of civilization itself. The attempt to apply rigidly the model of ancient cultures to a chang-

[22] *Science and Philosophy*, p. 15.
[23] A. N. Whitehead, *Adventures of Ideas* (New York: Macmillan, 1933), p. 363.
[24] *Modes of Thought*, p. 16.
[25] *Adventures of Ideas*, pp. 7–10.
[26] *Ibid.*, p. 367.
[27] *Ibid.*, p. 375.
[28] *Science and Philosophy*, p. 42.

ing world closes the door to new opportunities. "The result is static, repressive, and promotes a decadent habit of mind." [29]

The only alternatives open to an age are advance or decadence; to hold a fixed position is to go counter to the whole direction of the universe. This is precisely what the pure conservative tries to do, and the attempt can only lead to failure.[30] What is needed then is *adventure*, which for Whitehead is "the search for new perfections." [31] This is the theme of his important book, *Adventures of Ideas*. In the main, the book consistently makes the point that civilization has within itself a drive for the continued development of its potentialities. In the light of this position, Whitehead maintained that an age cannot rest in the jealous preservation of past achievements and that the attempt to ape the past is doomed to failure; worse than that, it will lead to full decay.[32]

With all his emphasis on novelty, it must not be supposed that Whitehead had a disdain for the past. Writing as an octogenarian, he recalls with appreciation and affection the historic places that studded the countryside of his childhood and school days.[33] Near his home was the magnificent Canterbury Cathedral, and often, in imagination, he reconstructed the violent death of the Archbishop, Thomas à Becket, in 1170. The relics of Romans, Saxons, and Normans were familiar scenes and set his young mind dreaming of England's historic past. The school at Sherborne dated back to the eighth century and boasted of King Alfred as one of its pupils, while the school song rang with the legend of King Arthur and his royal court. The bells of the Abbey Church attached to the school stirred memories of Henry VIII, who brought the bells from Tournai and gave them to the Abbey. Thus Whitehead's roots were deeply set in tradition, and he never lost his respect for it. He charged contemporary civilization with the solemn duties of assimilating what is best in the past and of striving to imitate it, for it can serve as a guideline in projecting possibilities for the future.

But Whitehead still sees that the real problem is to balance a respect for what is best in ancient cultures with a discernment of their limitations. Changing conditions will render many elements of the past

[29] *Adventures of Ideas*, pp. 352–53.
[30] *Ibid.*, pp. 353–54.
[31] *Ibid.*, p. 332.
[32] *Ibid.*, p. 360.
[33] *Science and Philosophy*, pp. 10–11.

irrelevant, and we must be able to judge what should be retained and what should be discarded.[34] A similar discernment is needed in evaluating novelty; experience has shown that the new is not necessarily good. For some time now we have been schooled to render fairly accurate decisions regarding the past, and this has come about through hard experience. "But in regard to novelty our critical apparatus is only half developed. Each generation runs into childish extremes. Today we adore, to-morrow we will flog the images of our saints or at least desert their shrines." [35] This task is made all the more difficult in view of the fact that with each generation the time span of change is being accelerated. We have reached the stage where it is impossible to prepare ourselves fully for the future, simply because the past is largely no longer relevant and change is happening too rapidly for us to delay over long and careful preparation. This would indeed seem to be a discouraging outlook except for the facts that Whitehead has confidence in the dynamic, purposeful striving of the whole universe toward greater perfection and that he believes that by the power of foresight we shall be able to meet the challenges of a changing present and an unknown future.[36]

One of the greatest obstacles, as well as one of the greatest aids, to the progress of modern civilization is our technological society. It can give rise to the decline of religion, the abuse of material power, the increase of poverty, and the decay of creativity in art.[37] All these evils have undoubtedly followed upon the wake of a technological and industrial society. But, at such times, it will not do to wax eloquent about the glories of the past, to moan over the failures of the present, or to grow pessimistic regarding the prospects for the future. Each age has its weakness: "Decay, Transition, Loss, Displacement belong to the essence of the Creative Advance." [38] But it has been the glory of the past that it has been able to rise above weakness and move on to greater strength. Material progress in itself is neutral regarding the growth of civilization; it can be used for either good or evil. In the long run, Whitehead maintains, our present age has the potentiality, unequaled in history, for social progress and for the development of great

[34] *Ibid.*, pp. 212, 217.
[35] *Ibid.*, pp. 212–13.
[36] *Adventures of Ideas*, p. 118.
[37] A. N. Whitehead, *Science and the Modern World* (New York: Macmillan, 1925), p. 286.
[38] *Adventures of Ideas*, pp. 368–69.

men endowed with creative genius.[39] He has confidence that in each age there will arise men who will meet the challenges of that age and enable mankind to continue its advance.

The Fulfillment of the Individual

The cultural striving for meaning is based on the individual and the type of development he is able to realize. The individual, too, has a destiny toward harmony and peace. This consists in excluding the restless preoccupation with the self.[40] Value, for the individual, is found when the importance of the self is fused with the importance of others. What matters is what gives personal satisfaction and enjoyment, which cannot be achieved unless they include the enjoyment experienced by others.[41] The harmony that one finds in oneself and that is the basis for the harmony found in civilization consists in the ideal aims of going beyond personal satisfaction and of surpassing personality. It is at this point that the ego enjoys an importance that transcends preoccupation with self-interest.[42] In moments such as these the individual experiences a sense of harmony, which for Whitehead means "peace," in the realization that one has done something worthwhile because his interests have broken through the narrow bounds of selfishness and have centered themselves on the welfare of others.[43]

It is not difficult to see where Whitehead is leading: he is not embarrassed to say that peace and harmony can be achieved only through love for all mankind.[44] In its finest hour, love so transforms personal desire that it centers upon the one loved. The lover then no longer thinks of self, for at that moment he has passed beyond himself so that his only preoccupation is the good of the beloved. Such love gives meaning and importance to the whole of life and to the individual activities of that life. The present moment has value because one's interest and activity have gone out to another. At the same time direction is given to future interests and activities because the individual, on

---

[39] *Science and the Modern World*, p. 287.
[40] *Adventures of Ideas*, p. 367.
[41] *Modes of Thought*, pp. 160–61.
[42] *Modes of Thought*, p. 165; *Adventures of Ideas*, pp. 367, 371.
[43] *Adventures of Ideas*, pp. 372–73.
[44] *Ibid.*, p. 368.

the basis of his love for others, is anxious to build a world that will further the welfare of those who are loved.[45]

It can be seen how the harmony achieved in the individual contributes to the harmony of the whole of civilization: the vigor and vitality of a civilization are in direct proportion to the diffusion of the feeling that selfless and transcending interests are worthwhile.[46] If people of a given age share this sense of the value of selfless love and self-sacrifice for others, such an age will reach a maximum of harmony and peace. Examples of love—parents for children, spouses for one another, members of a community for their fellow citizens—are but particular instances of the dynamic aim in the universe, which is ever striving for a higher degree of peace according to its inner capacity.[47]

Views of the Universe

In the description above of Whitehead's search for meaning, we have centered attention on the larger issues of culture and civilization. These issues were the subject matter of such books as *Adventures of Ideas* and *Essays in Philosophy* and, to some extent, *Science and the Modern World*. His analysis of man's cultural history arose from what he called "moral intuitions." [48] But when Whitehead reviewed the picture of the world given by science, he seemed to discern a serious discrepancy. Until the recent past, the scientific picture has been characterized by a "materialistic mechanism" that conflicts with moral intuition because it fails to give meaning and importance to the objects and events studied by the physical sciences. To heal this gap between "the materialistic mechanism of science and the moral intuitions, which are presupposed in the concrete affairs of life," Whitehead launched into a critique of the scientific picture of the universe.

The classical view, which is expressed in the Newtonian physics, is characterized principally by the category of "simple location." According to this view, the universe is made up of a succession of particles existing at a durationless instant of time. It as though a high-speed camera were to take a picture and "freeze" material bodies in a fixed

[45] *Modes of Thought*, pp. 160–61.
[46] *Adventures of Ideas*, p. 371.
[47] *Ibid.*, p. 373.
[48] *Science and the Modern World*, p. 112.

position. No particle is viewed in movement or in a state of change; each bit of matter occupies a particular position in space at a durationless instant of time.[49] The only relationships that particles of matter have are spatial. Thus particle A is related to particle B only because A and B are situated in a certain position in space in reference to each other. Change consists merely in a change of position and, consequently, in spatial relationships.[50] As a consequence, "Nature is thus described as made up of vacuous bits of matter with no internal values, and merely hurrying through space." [51] This is the familiar "billiard ball theory" of matter, which was prevalent in the period of mechanistic determinism during the latter part of the nineteenth century.

What bothers Whitehead regarding this picture is that "scientific materialism," as he calls it, renders matter "senseless, valueless, purposeless." [52] The Newtonian physics failed to give meaning or value to nature. It is true that it explained the movement of bodies by the laws of gravitation and motion, but a further question remained unanswered: why should material bodies be related at all? Newtonian physics, of course, made enormous contributions by the determination of the particular laws of motion of material bodies, but the larger question as to why such laws should exist was left unanswered.[53] This is a question that science, as such, does not even raise. But our larger experience seeks deeper understanding of the universe. It is this mode of understanding, which Whitehead calls "intuitive," that is omitted.

Such an intuitive understanding is not satisfied with a "dead" universe pushed around by external laws. A universe of this sort has no reason, no aim, no intrinsic value, and it is these that our deeper intuitions are seeking.[54] Modern physics thus becomes a "mystic chant over an unintelligible Universe." [55] Whitehead by no means intends to deride science; after a long career of interest in mathematics and science he is well aware of the contribution these have made to the progress of civilization. But what he criticizes is science's narrow view, which remains satisfied with "an ultimate irrationality" characteristic of positivistic philosophy. This he calls "muddle-headed," because it

[49] Modes of Thought, p. 199.
[50] Ibid., p. 179.
[51] Ibid., p. 217.
[52] Science and the Modern World, p. 24.
[53] Modes of Thought, p. 183.
[54] Ibid., p. 184.
[55] Ibid., p. 185.

maintains that the processes of nature can be completely described by the formulae of physics and chemistry. We are left with isolated and unrelated facts that do not penetrate into the deeper meaning of the world and its activities and that omit the richer dimensions of importance, value, and enjoyment.[56]

Hopefully, there are signs within science itself that indicate a widening of the narrow view characteristic of classical physics. The whole universe is seen as a field of force and of continued activity; it is no longer viewed as bits of matter statically located in a particular place and moved about by external forces. Matter is energy or incessant activity, or, better still, interconnected activity.[57] Instead of the concept of "simple location," we have the fundamental categories of activity and process. According to this view, "Nature is a theatre for the interrelations of activities." [58] Process itself becomes a name to sum up the various activities going on in the universe, with relations that are internal and essential to the various elements.[59]

This change of viewpoint has but slowly seeped into human consciousness, taking the better part of four centuries, and even yet has not gained complete possession of our thinking. In spite of its increased sophistication, science continues to give only "rules of succession" and thus takes into account only part of the data given to us by human experience.[60] The part that is left out is actually the most important, and this omission is what Whitehead considers the great failure of science, for it has given rise to the "discord between the aesthetic intuitions of mankind and the mechanism of science." [61] The human mind is not content with formulae that describe how things will act physically when put into contact with one another; it seeks for a deeper meaning underlying these mechanical activities.

Process and Teleology

From what has been said so far, it is clear that in Whitehead's opinion the universe is engaged in a truly creative advance—an advance leading to higher forms of value, importance, and richness. It is essen-

[56] Ibid., pp. 203–04, 211, 223.
[57] Ibid., pp. 182, 186, 188, 191.
[58] Ibid., p. 191.
[59] Ibid., p. 198.
[60] Ibid., p. 211.
[61] Science and the Modern World, p. 122.

tial to the universe that it comes from a definite past and moves ahead, sometimes after failures and regressions, to higher achievements.[62] The whole world is dynamic and has a thrust for higher values.

On the cultural level, mankind is ever striving for the realization of some ideal, proper to each age, to be achieved within a certain period of time. The ideal is never realized in its perfection, but it is under the attraction of the ideal that men, as individuals and as members of a society, have the incentive to move ahead to the best of their ability.[63] If there were no drive toward the fulfillment of some ideal, there would be "no meaning for purpose, hope, fear, energy." [64] Science, too, gives evidence of a progressive evolution at work that shows that nature, as we know it today, has passed through higher and higher stages—from inorganic matter to man.

Looking at the universe from these perspectives, Whitehead concludes that the fundamental fact of our experience is process. But this does not mean sheer activity operating at random; a question that continues to bother him is: "Why should there be process?" [65] Why should the world, on the broad cultural level and on the narrower scientific level, be continually striving for higher achievement? The laws of science merely tell us how things will act under certain conditions. Whitehead feels that more basic questions remain to be answered: why should things act at all? Why should they act in precisely this way? And why should we witness in ourselves and in things at large the constant thrust toward higher forms of realization? It is questions such as these that Whitehead feels science has left unanswered and that demand a deeper insight into the "metaphysical nature of things." [66] He developed his philosophy in the hope that he might illuminate "the ultimate aim infused into the process of nature." [67]

Theism

In 1925 Whitehead's *Science and the Modern World* appeared. Paul Weiss has said, "We have not yet entirely recovered from the shock of

[62] *Modes of Thought*, pp. 16, 73, 206–08.
[63] *Ibid.*, pp. 164–65.
[64] *Ibid.*, p. 139.
[65] *Ibid.*, p. 73.
[66] *Ibid.*, p. 217.
[67] *Ibid.*, p. 16.

its appearance." [68] Professor Weiss is referring in general to the wealth of original ideas found in the book, but his statement could also apply to the theistic position Whitehead develops here for the first time. It came as a surprise to those who were familiar with his works during his mathematical and philosophy-of-science periods, for they were not prepared by anything he had written up to that time for the theistic turn he gave to his thought. Following this first appearance in his writing, the subject of theism became a significant part of his work.

Whitehead's theism was not something that had to be imposed upon his system in order to make room for a belief in God; it is not as though he believed in God first and then tried to force this belief into his system. He followed the lead of experience, his "moral intuition," as it viewed the universe in which he lived. The more he probed into the meaning of reality, the more he felt that the picture of the universe as he saw it required a God, and a God of a particular nature. As early as his *Science and the Modern World*, where, incidentally, his theism is but hurriedly developed, he was led from a statement of *what* things are to an explanation of *why* things are. In other words, he felt that nature is not self-explanatory and that an analysis of reality would lead to depths whose meaning we can dimly discern but cannot fully comprehend.[69] In *Process and Reality* he proposed to examine "dispassionately" what the metaphysical analysis of reality required.[70] In Part V of that work he tries to show that the metaphysical principles developed throughout the book require a God. A beginning is made with our "higher intuitions," which seek for meaning in the things and events of everyday life and lead to religious experience. Yet, even in its purest form, such intuition can lead to erroneous, superstitious, and even brutal practices. Hence it must be purified by speculative philosophy, which seeks for ultimate meanings that rise above the immediate situation and give ultimate value to all reality.[71]

Principle of Limitation

The key notion leading to Whitehead's theism is his concept of the "creative advance." We have seen how he develops this in relation both to the broad cultural currents of history and to individual enti-

[68] Weiss, *op. cit.*, p. 106.
[69] *Science and the Modern World*, p. 130.
[70] A. N. Whitehead, *Process and Reality* (New York: Macmillan, 1929), p. 521.
[71] *Adventures of Ideas*, p. 30.

ties. He sees he whole universe and all nature involved in an advance that is creative, inasmuch as it is not merely repeating the cycle of the past but breaking out into new forms and new fulfillments. If we take our stand at any moment of history and look to the future, we note that the creative advance is confronted with a "boundless wealth of alternatives." [72] There are many forms the universe can take in its drive for higher values. In a sense, it can be said that the universe has infinite freedom to develop itself by actualizing any number of potentialities facing it. But, in the last analysis, this creativity and these infinite possibilities are powerless to move the universe forward unless something is given to resolve the indeterminacy that lies at the heart of reality.[73] Why should the universe move this way and not that? Why should it develop along these lines and not those? Why should such and such potentialities be realized and not others? These are the questions to which Whitehead's metaphysical principles have led. He phrases the difficulty and begins his solution of the problem:

> The boundless wealth of possibility in the realm of abstract form would leave each creative phase still indeterminate, unable to synthesize under determinate conditions the creatures from which it springs. The definite determination which imposes ordered balance on the world requires an actual entity imposing its own unchanged consistency of character on every phase.[74]

Whitehead's theism, then, comes as the ultimate term of his metaphysics. His metaphysical principles "require" that the universe, "riddled with ambiguity," have the incentive to arrive at a definite outcome.[75] For this reason Whitehead calls God "the actual but nontemporal entity whereby the indetermination of mere creativity is transmuted into a determinate freedom." [76] Whitehead also calls God the "ultimate limitation" that brings down the indetermination of infinite potentiality to the limited range of particular realizations. In a strange-sounding phrase he characterizes God as the "ultimate irrationality." [77] By this he does not mean that God is completely incomprehensible, though, as we have already noted, he will admit that we

[72] *Modes of Thought*, p. 208.
[73] A. N. Whitehead, *Religion in the Making* (New York: Macmillan, 1926), pp. 119–20.
[74] *Ibid.*, p. 94.
[75] *Process and Reality*, p. 523.
[76] *Religion in the Making*, p. 90.
[77] *Science and the Modern World*, p. 249.

cannot fully understand His nature. What he means is that, though there is a "metaphysical need" for a principle of determination, there is no final explanation of the principle itself: "No reason can be given for the nature of God, because that nature is the ground of rationality." [78]

In order to make Whitehead's position a bit clearer, perhaps we can approach it from the standpoint of process and evolution. For him, evolution is the gradual development of things that are important and of value and that go beyond what has been achieved before.[79] This is observed in the inorganic and organic worlds of nature. The process of evolution exhibits a steady progress from less well-adapted to better-adapted forms. We can apply the same analysis to historic process: history shows a gradual improvement in civilization and culture, whereby each age surpasses its predecessor in the achievement of value and richness of experience. History reveals a dynamism toward the achievement of ideals that transcend the dead facts of science.[80] In other words, we are confronted once again with the fact of creativity, here seen as a movement toward the emergence of higher values or of "things that matter."

Whitehead draws the same conclusion from his analysis of the emergence of value as he did from his examination of the indeterminacy of reality: he maintains that there must be value beyond the present moment; otherwise there would be no incentive in things to improve by going beyond themselves. Without this incentive, each actuality would be just a "barren detail" existing by itself. The creative advance continues because each actuality, in a sense, measures itself in accordance with what it is not and could be. "A solipsist experience cannot succeed or fail, for it would be all that exists." [81] There would be no standard of comparison proposed and hence no incentive to advance. Whitehead, of course, is applying this analysis mainly to human experience, but it is quite clear that he also means that it applies to the whole of reality.

In the light of Whitehead's position on value, we can appreciate several other terms he uses in reference to God. He calls Him "the lure for feeling," "the eternal urge of desire," and, finally, "the initial ob-

[78] *Ibid.*, p. 249.
[79] *Ibid.*, p. 132.
[80] *Modes of Thought*, p. 142.
[81] *Ibid.*, p. 141.

ject of desire." [82] In a sense, these express best of all how God enters into Whitehead's metaphysical thinking. God is seen, then, to be the explanation of process and evolution, for He draws all things to develop and to seek higher values; He is the reason for the initiative and dynamism in the universe—the purpose, aim, and goal of all striving. Evolution toward higher values finds its term and explanation in God. It is God, too, who gives determination to the infinite potentiality in nature, for He is the ideal toward the realization of which all things strive. God is the ultimate value which grounds all value in the universe by presenting Himself as the ideal value that serves as model for all other things. If we may be permitted the example, all evolution can be looked upon as a gigantic wave that rises, swells, and moves forward, ever breaking and ever gathering new force, drawn by some mysterious attraction that gives it direction. In these terms, evolution and process have a meaning and purpose, which is in some limited way to fulfill themselves according to the value, importance, and model of God, who, like a huge magnet, draws all things to develop and realize themselves according to His pattern.

In this way Whitehead hoped to answer the questions his metaphysics ultimately posed. Things did not just move at random, without aim or purpose. In fact, without such aim, Whitehead thought that there could not be any movement or process at all. It was not sufficient to say that things moved in such and such ways; the fundamental question as to why things should act at all was left untouched. It is God who sets the whole world in process as He draws all things to fulfill themselves according to His ideal. He is, then, truly the lure, the urge, the object of all desire and of all striving. Without Him the process of the universe would halt, and things would remain just themselves in isolation, without any incentive for movement or development.

God's Nature

When Whitehead came to delineate the features of God's nature, he likewise asked what was required to satisfy his metaphysical principles.[83] First of all, he would not be satisfied with a static God whose

---

[82] *Process and Reality*, p. 522.
[83] Whitehead distinguishes between God as primordial and God as consequent. A thorough discussion of this distinction would take us too far afield. Briefly,

nature is complete and finished. The basis of this conclusion was undoubtedly his view that reality essentially involves the creative advance into novelty, which he looked upon as the ultimate metaphysical ground of all reality.[84] From our own experience, we see that to be is to develop, to express the self in new ways. Whether he looked at the broad cultural level of history or at the individual actualities in existence, he thought that development was at the heart of reality and that for a being not to push forward toward novelty is to stagnate and decay. This helps us to understand Whitehead's basic principle regarding God, which he places as the cornerstone of his discussion about the Deity. "In the first place, God is not to be treated as an exception to all metaphysical principles, invoked to save their collapse. He is their chief exemplification." [85] For him, development was a perfection and the adoption of a static position was a defect. Worse than that, it meant the very end of the actuality itself. This follows from the first of his fundamental categories that explain reality: "that the actual world is a process, and that the process is the becoming of actual entities." [86] To be is to be in process; this, to Whitehead, was fundamental, and to say that God stands outside his principle was to deny His existence. This is what he means when he says, "Neither God, nor the World, reaches static completion. Both are in the grip of the ultimate metaphysical ground, the creative advance into novelty." [87]

Another reason Whitehead puts God into process is that, for God to be related to the world and to be meaningful for it, He must in some way interact with it. As we have seen, God is the reason for the whole movement of process and evolution of the world. So important is He to the universe that without Him the universe becomes meaningless. In other words, God is *relevant* to the world, so much so that without Him the world lacks meaning. Now, what about the converse? Can we assume that the world means nothing to God, that He is completely unaffected by the development of nature, a development He Himself has initiated and encouraged? Does it mean that God stands

God as primordial is the lure for feeling, the eternal urge of desire, the ideal aimed at by all potentialities. As such, He is complete, eternal, and unchanged. God as consequent is in interaction with the world and involved in the creative advance. Hence He is incomplete and in process. This does not mean that there are two Gods but two ways of viewing his nature.

[84] *Process and Reality*, p. 529.
[85] *Ibid.*, p. 521.
[86] *Ibid.*, p. 33.
[87] *Ibid.*, p. 529.

off in splendid isolation, completely indifferent to and unmoved by all the fruitful development of which He is the initiator, final cause, and term? Whitehead did not think so. It would seem to be a strange state of affairs that the very lure and object of desire for improvement, drawing all things to higher perfection, should be completely unaffected by what He had initiated.

For these reasons, Whitehead concluded that God and the world are mutually affected by the "creative advance into novelty." There is an interaction that is creative for both: one becomes the incentive for the other to express itself in new ways. "Either of them, God and the World, is the instrument of novelty for the other." [88] Both God and the universe are seen to be coming to completion together. God is concerned for the growth of the world—for the development of entities on the inorganic and organic levels; for the growth of civilization and culture; for social, industrial, economic progress; for whatever makes for value and contributes to the multiplication of things that matter.

Since God is the reason why new perfections come into existence and why the whole world brings forth new values, He is deeply concerned over the world's joys, sorrows, triumphs, and failures. His aim is that, in some way, what is good in the world be preserved and what is evil be redeemed and turned to good. Hence Whitehead says that God's nature is best thought of as "a tender care that nothing be lost." [89] Since God, like a parent, has brought things into existence by drawing them to fulfill themselves, He cannot forget them once they have been born. Whitehead expresses this even better when he says that God has a love for the world, for by a particular providence He has brought forth particular beings. Here we see that Whitehead's metaphysical conclusions are perfectly in accord with his whole orientation to God. He is extremely critical of an approach to God that looks upon Him as the God of fear and not the God of love.[90] He takes issue with the saying of Proverbs (i.7) that "The fear of the Lord is the beginning of knowledge," for he considers this to be quite strange in view of the fact that "God is love." It should not surprise us that Whitehead is much attracted to John the Evangelist, who conceived of God in terms of love and whose writings are saturated with the insight into that love.

In Whitehead's admiration for John he allows himself to take a

[88] *Ibid.*, p. 529.
[89] *Ibid.*, p. 525.
[90] *Religion in the Making*, p. 75.

position that is slightly harsh toward Paul. He quotes the text of Second Thessalonians, i.8–9, where Paul calls down fire and everlasting destruction on those who do not acknowledge the Gospel of Jesus Christ. This criticism would surely seem to be unfair, for there are many texts in Paul that give expression to the love of God for mankind. But if we grant the bias of Whitehead for John as against Paul, we can appreciate his statement that "If the modern world is to find God, it must find him through love and not through fear, with the help of John and not of Paul." [91] In Whitehead's view, we must go back to the "Galilean origin of Christianity" in its purity, with its emphasis on the slow and quiet operation of God's love over the world.[92]

If God loves the world, He will also be concerned with the suffering found in it. As the lure for feeling and the ideal of all developing value, He intends that all things develop toward higher values. He cannot be indifferent, therefore, when things do not progress toward a happy completion. God has a concern for suffering humanity and, in this sense, He is "the great companion—the fellow-sufferer who understands." [93] In His concern for suffering, God will make sure that what is good is preserved and what is evil will be overcome in His own nature.[94] In Him, human evil and woe will be turned to good and joy, and sorrow and pain will be transformed into triumph: "This is the notion of redemption through suffering, which haunts the world." [95] Because of this viewpoint, Whitehead prefers to look upon God as redeemer rather than as creator: "He does not create the world, he saves it; or, more accurately, he is the poet of the world, with tender patience leading it by his vision of truth, beauty, and goodness." [96] To Whitehead, a creator God is an impersonal God who is above and beyond the world and who has no concern for the work of His hands.[97] But a God who interacts with the world and hovers over it in His anxiety to move it forward to greater perfection is a God who is involved with the destiny of the universe. It is through Him that the universe develops, for "the world lives by its incarnation of God in itself." [98]

[91] *Ibid.*, p. 76.
[92] *Process and Reality*, p. 520.
[93] *Ibid.*, p. 532.
[94] *Religion in the Making*, p. 155.
[95] *Process and Reality*, p. 531.
[96] *Ibid.*, p. 526.
[97] *Religion in the Making*, pp. 71, 86–87.
[98] *Ibid.*, p. 156.

Reconciliation of Extremes

By his doctrine concerning the nature of God, Whitehead hoped to reconcile the extremes he thought have been plaguing religion and theology for centuries. In several places he expresses these extremes as he understood them:

> . . . the doctrine of God as the impersonal order of the universe, and the doctrine of God as the one person creating the universe.[99]

> . . . the extreme monotheistic doctrine of God, as essentially transcendent and only accidentally immanent, and on the other hand the pantheistic doctrine of God, as essentially immanent and in no way transcendent.[100]

> . . . God as eminently real, and the World as derivatively real. God as necessary to the World, but the World as not necessary to God.[101]

Whitehead tries to resolve the first contradiction by proposing a personal God who introduces order into the universe and who loves, suffers with, and shows concern for the progress of finite reality, yet does not create the world and, therefore, does not completely transcend finite reality or lose contact with it. The second set of extremes is resolved by a God who is essentially transcendent because He contains the infinite possibilities for the perfection of all actualities and yet is essentially immanent because He is the eternal urge of desire, drawing all things to future development because He interacts with the world, has concern for the world, and develops with it and ultimately redeems all things in Himself. Lastly, regarding the third extreme, God is eminently real and necessary to the world, for, again, He contains in Himself all possibilities and is the eternal urge leading the world to develop according to these possibilities; further, though the world is derivatively real by reason of its dependence on God, it is also necessary to God because, through His interaction with finite reality, He is engaged with it in the creative advance toward greater perfection.

In reconciling these extremes, Whitehead felt assured that he had also confronted another problem that has consistently bothered philosophers and theologians: the problem of evil. Any theistic position is confronted with this problem as soon as it proposes a God who is

[99] *Ibid.*, p. 150.
[100] *Adventures of Ideas*, p. 154.
[101] *Ibid.*, p. 217.

either a creator or infinite, or both. If He is a creator, then the objection can arise that He is also the cause of evil; and if He is infinite, it would seem to follow that He includes evil in His nature. This dilemma is nicely avoided if God is neither a creator nor infinite. This is precisely the position Whitehead proposes; and though he would maintain that a finite, noncreator God follows from his metaphysical analysis of reality, one cannot help but get the feeling that a dominant influence leading him to this position was the difficulty arising from the problem of evil. Whitehead himself, I am sure, would be the first to admit that his own position is beset with difficulties. In *Science and the Modern World*, where his theistic position was first proposed, he admitted that, in attempting to find an ultimate explanation of reality, we could not hope for a full understanding.[102] His more systematic treatment, as found in *Process and Reality*, makes even more explicit this admission, for here he confesses that we shall be confronted with certain inadequacies and that, guided by the metaphysical principles of reality, we shall have to be content with little more than suggestions concerning the nature of God.[103] In spite of this, he was satisfied that it was of the utmost importance to propose a God who is relevant to the universe and, therefore, more meaningful for man, even though this proposition might leave unresolved more theoretical problems regarding God's nature.

Religion

Was Whitehead a religious man? The answer to the question will depend on what one is looking for. We do not find in his works a personal involvement in such matters as God's relation to specific human problems, or the relation of dogma to modern life, or the meaning of liturgical worship. This follows from the whole orientation of his metaphysical period, during which he was trying to work out a system of general ideas in order to interpret our experience.[104] He wanted metaphysics to be as independent as possible of shifting events, so that even change could be integrated into a general scheme. This does not mean that his system has no bearing on the contemporary scene. He

---

[102] *Science and the Modern World*, p. 130.
[103] *Process and Reality*, p. 521.
[104] *Process and Reality*, pp. 4, 177–79; *Religion in the Making*, pp. 88–89.

meant his general ideas to be applicable and applied, but, for the most part, he himself did not work out the details. Something similar can be said of his theory of religion. In redoing metaphysics, he tried to go back beyond the various expressions of religion to general ideas unaffected by previous structures, so as to form a basis of a purified religion.

His treatment of religion is not exclusively abstract. In his school days he had read the Old and New Testaments with more than a casual interest. Biblical themes appear in his pages—the psalmist's hymn of God's glory,[105] the agonizing soul-searching of Job,[106] the loneliness of the prophets, the wisdom of the sapiential works,[107] and the love of our Lord, of John, and of the early Christians. Though Whitehead's aim was not to produce a book of pastoral theology, he gave some valuable indications of how such a book could be written.

Perhaps this happened because, during his boyhood, he saw in his clergyman-father the model of what a pastor should be to his flock. Whitehead remembers him best as reading the Bible over a dying Baptist minister, greeting the parishioners who jammed his church, walking through town and countryside and stopping to talk with young and old, sharing their concerns both important and trivial, giving kind and sympathetic advice.[108] This was the type of pastor Whitehead felt was passing out of existence. These impressions must have lasted for some time, for we are told that during his undergraduate days he often spoke of religion and expressed an interest in foreign missions.[109] Russell relates that Whitehead was almost converted to Roman Catholicism through the impact that Cardinal Newman (1801–90) had upon him.[110]

Early in his married life, for about eight years, he read many books on theology.[111] Since he married in 1890, this period would have extended from his early to late thirties. Then, for some mysterious reason, he lost interest and sold the books. It would be helpful to know what volumes he read: if they were dry, technical treatises, his loss of interest would not necessarily argue a loss of religion. More significant

[105] *Religion in the Making*, pp. 54–55.
[106] *Ibid.*, pp. 48–49, 55.
[107] *Ibid.*, pp. 52–53.
[108] *Science and Philosophy*, p. 10.
[109] Lowe, *op. cit.*, p. 231.
[110] Russell, *op. cit.*, p. 96.
[111] L. Price, ed., *Dialogues of Alfred North Whitehead* (London: William Clowes and Sons, 1954), pp. 147–48.

is the report that, for a time, Whitehead became a militant agnostic.[112] How long this lasted we do not know, nor are we sure of the dates. It is curious, though, that concern for a deity is practically nonexistent in his work until *Science and the Modern World* in 1925. It would seem that his agnosticism lasted for some time, even if we grant that his interest in philosophy went back some years before 1925. But this is a question we shall have to leave for our hoped-for biographer.

Whitehead maintained that there was no such thing as a separate religious sense.[113] Religion emerged quite naturally from his whole analysis of reality. Whitehead, we remember, was continually bothered by nagging questions as to the meaning of reality, where it was leading, its importance. The questions affected the whole of reality, whether we consider the development of culture and civilization or the process of the organic and inorganic elements of the universe. What was behind process and evolution that makes them important to the human person? The answer to this question is precisely what Whitehead meant by religion. In *Science and the Modern World* he had already arrived at this position. This is surprising in view of the fact that he had not yet had time to think through his theory of theism and religion. From the description already given, we can appreciate his prophetic sense, manifested in the following statement:

> Religion is the vision of something which stands beyond, behind, and within, the passing flux of immediate things; something which is real, and yet waiting to be realised; something which is a remote possibility, and yet the greatest of present facts; something that gives meaning to all that passes, and yet eludes apprehension; something whose possession is the final good, and yet is beyond all reach; something which is the ultimate ideal, and the hopeless quest.[114]

It is amazing how the text above anticipates in a general way the direction his subsequent thought took in analyzing the meaning of the universe in terms of metaphysical principles. Later on, he expressed the same thing in briefer fashion when he said that religion "provides a meaning, in terms of value, for our own existence, a meaning which flows from the nature of things." [115]

Since God emerges as the term of metaphysics, He is also the basis

---

[112] Lowe received this information from Bertrand Russell in a letter dated September 26, 1959. See Lowe, *op cit.*, p. 232.
[113] *Religion in the Making*, pp. 123–24.
[114] *Science and the Modern World*, pp. 267–68.
[115] *Religion in the Making*, p. 124.

of religion. In this sense metaphysics and religion are synonymous. Man—in viewing or, more exactly, in *experiencing* the universe—is led to seek its meaning in God. He is, as we have seen, both the origin and term of all process. Once the reality of the Deity seizes man's consciousness, religion becomes the manner in which he reacts to Him.[116] For a human being who allows the awareness of God's love for him to permeate the inner recesses of his personality, the only response can be a return of love. This response was characteristic of the message of John and motivated the lives of the early Christians. On the strength of this love, man will desire to be united with God, and thereby will find the eternal harmony and peace the whole universe desires and toward which it is striving through its evolving process and under the attracting influence of "the lure for feeling." [117]

Effect on the Individual

When Whitehead develops further his notion of religion and its effect on man, he seems to depart radically from one of his fundamental positions. There is nothing he had stressed more than the interconnection between entities—whether these be material bodies or human beings, tiny particles or larger masses. Yet, when he discusses religion, he stresses the response of the individual. The reason for this seeming conflict in his thought is not hard to find: he feels that, in its more primitive forms, religion had overemphasized membership in a tribe or community, where the individual was submerged in the group. People were led like sheep without an awareness of the nature of their commitment. This resulted in mere routine or in the uncritical acceptance of superstitious and even brutal practices. Man has since arrived at a higher level of maturity, which makes him capable of purifying his approach to religion by giving a more individual response to a belief in God. The accent now should be on individual responsibility through personal commitment.

This helps to explain some rather vague expressions Whitehead uses to describe religion. For example, he states that "Religion is what the individual does with his own solitariness." [118] Stripped of the emotionalism generated by "herd-psychology," we can arrive at "the awful fact, which is the human being, consciously alone with itself, for its

[116] *Science and the Modern World*, p. 266.
[117] *Ibid.*, p. 268.
[118] *Religion in the Making*, p. 16.

own sake." [119] When the human person stands before God with no one else to lean upon, he cannot be lost in the crowd, accepting beliefs whose validity he has never really evaluated or going through rituals whose meaning he does not understand. Fully conscious of what God means to himself and to the whole universe, each man is able to accept Him on the basis of personal conviction and to respond to Him on the basis of personal love.

So insistent is Whitehead on the response of love that he is critical of many things associated with religion:

> Collective enthusiasms, revivals, institutions, churches, rituals, bibles, codes of behaviour, are the trappings of religion, its passing forms. They may be useful or harmful; they may be authoritatively ordained, or merely temporary expedients. But the end of religion is beyond all this.[120]

What is "beyond all this," of course, is the love of the individual person for God. Everything else should serve to foster that love. Rituals, modes of thought, doctrine in the form of systems of general truths—all should have as their purpose to transform the person, to shake him to the very core of his being, to turn his mind to God as the very basis of finite existence, and to inspire him to unifying love. If ritual and doctrine do not accomplish this purpose, they can be useless and even harmful.[121]

Whitehead knew well the advantages and disadvantages of symbolism. Sometimes symbols have been examples of "the follies of humanity" because through them men have descended to sheer barbarism. It has been one of the glories of civilized men to have eliminated such aberrations. There is always danger that such follies will crop up again like weeds, and there is constant need to guard against them. Humanity must also examine its symbolic expressions so that they may be adapted to the needs of the present social structure. But because man is human, he will always express himself in symbols, for through these the importance of the things he prizes is enhanced.[122] So it is not symbol or ritual in themselves that Whitehead criticizes, but a use of them that would obscure the loving response of the person to God.

[119] *Ibid.*, p. 16.
[120] *Ibid.*, p. 17.
[121] *Religion in the Making*, pp. 15–18; *Science and the Modern World*, pp. 268–69.
[122] A. N. Whitehead, *Symbolism: Its Meaning and Effect* (New York: Macmillan, 1927), pp. 60–63.

The same can be said of dogma. Whitehead does not deprecate the value of dogmatic expression; he feels that it gives rise to a coherent doctrine that sheds light upon the world and gives guidance for thought and action.[123] But dogmas become a hindrance when they lose contact with the changing order of things because they have become too abstract or because men have failed to rethink them and to find more fruitful ways of applying them to areas of contemporary life.[124] Religion, on its doctrinal side, also stands in the way of loving response when it insists on rules of conduct and stifles the freedom of the human spirit. This stage marks "the ebb of religious fervor" because it snuffs out the intuitive response of the individual and substitutes a code of behavior without the dynamic spirit that should animate our lives.[125]

Relation to the Contemporary World

In the first paragraph of his *Religion in the Making,* Whitehead shows himself aware that each generation must examine its own attitude toward religion.[126] He could not have thought otherwise, since so much of his writing was devoted to the task of showing how civilization and culture are ever changing. Man's changing outlook toward himself and the universe in which he lives must have some effect on the response he gives to God in religion. For this reason, Whitehead turned his attention to the relation between religion and the contemporary world.

A primary function that religion must fulfill, in Whitehead's view, is to make the world meaningful for contemporary man. He maintains that, during the Middle Ages and for some time thereafter, the thinking of religious men was dominated by the Platonic-Christian tradition. The tendency has been to minimize the importance of this world. Some have gone so far as to write it off as a lost cause and to abandon it to the Power of Darkness. The best that man can do is to endure the precarious existence that is this life and to wait for the final day, when all evils will be dispelled in the joys of heaven.

Whitehead did not share that view. He believed that there is an inherent goodness to be found in this world and that it is the duty of

[123] *Religion in the Making,* p. 144.
[124] *Ibid.,* pp. 142–43.
[125] *Science and the Modern World,* p. 267; *Religion in the Making,* p. 144.
[126] *Religion in the Making,* p. 13.

religion to discover it. In looking ahead to the future of religion in a modern age, he made the following significant statement:

> I hazard the prophecy that that religion will conquer which can render clear to popular understanding some eternal greatness incarnate in the passage of temporal fact.[127]

His own reflections on religion were always guided by this conviction, and he tried to fashion the outlines of a religion that would discover in present experience a meaning and a purpose that were relevant to the present world but that still went beyond it.[128] By this he meant that the human spirit can find no value or meaning in present existence unless it finds them in the concrete contact with the present world. This is what he meant when he said that "religion is world-loyalty," for he believed that man cannot find the meaning of his own existence, a meaning that is essentially religious, unless he sees himself as essentially related to the present world.[129]

The implications of this insight are important. What does he mean by "world"? It is not merely the material universe of rocks, trees, mountains, rivers, and organic life on all levels. He includes the civilizations that have been built up through the intelligence of human beings; he includes the development of art, science, societies, and nations, with their political, social, and economic institutions. This is the world for Whitehead, a world that is undergoing the process of evolution every bit as much as living species. It is in relation to this world that the human person is to develop as a religious man.

Whitehead has said that God develops through contact with the changing world. Again, by "world" he means all that we have said above. It may be true that the notion of a developing God will be unacceptable to many religious people, and there are good reasons for such opposition. But what is incontestable is the emphasis Whitehead places upon the contemporary world. It has developed by reason of the attraction God works upon the processes found in nature. In some mysterious way, God Himself develops through contact with this world. Moreover, God is not indifferent to the world, for at each moment that it comes into a new stage of development, God looks upon it with love and concern.

Perhaps most significant of all for the development of a religion in a

[127] *Adventures of Ideas,* p. 41.
[128] *Process and Reality,* p. 520.
[129] *Religion in the Making,* p. 60.

modern age is Whitehead's statement that God does not create the world, but saves it. Whitehead has not drawn out a fully developed eschatology, and a statement like this is both irritating in its incompleteness and breathtaking in its implications. In some way or other, nothing that has come into existence is lost. The world will be purged of the evil in it, and the goodness found in nature will be preserved by finding objective immortality in God's nature. God has concern that "nothing be lost," and whatever good that man does in the present life will find completion and continued existence in God. No doubt Whitehead's treatment of the afterlife is in many respects unsatisfying, and yet there can be no doubt that he did not look for the final destruction of the world as we know it but for the "new heavens and a new earth" prophesied so mysteriously by Peter in his Second Epistle. Whitehead was so deeply concerned in his writing with criticizing past culture and projecting guidelines for its future development because he saw all this as necessary for the religious growth of man and because he believed that all that the processes of the world had developed would somehow find a final consummation in God. If all this is true, then man's engagement in the world is truly sacred in a way that far surpasses the concept of John Dewey. Man becomes God's cooperator in a meaningful way because he assists in the birth of new forms in nature and thereby enables the evolution of the world, of man, and of God to continue in more fruitful ways. This concept is daring and, some will say, misguided, but we must admire Whitehead's attempt to see the "eternal greatness incarnate in the passage of temporal fact."

Any consideration of contemporary society must take into account the role of science. It is understandable that Whitehead, with a long and brilliant background in science, was appreciative of the great contributions it had made to the growth of civilization. Through his metaphysical analysis of reality he came to see the role of religion, and he lamented the fact that, when we think of science and religion, it is usually in terms of conflict. The importance of both is, for the most part, obscured in their oppositions. Hence he says:

> It seems as though, during the last half-century, the results of science and the beliefs of religion had come into a position of frank disagreement, from which there can be no escape, except by abandoning either the clear teaching of science, or the clear teaching of religion.[130]

[130] *Science and the Modern World*, p. 252.

What were the reasons for this conflict? The main deficiency Whitehead saw in science was that, in spite of its positive contributions, it assumed a role that it could not possibly fulfill—namely, that of giving ultimate meaning to the universe. All we can expect from science is the statement of facts and of the interrelatedness of facts. He felt that science could not give the reasons for these facts and for their connections and that, when it pretends to do so, it comes into irreconcilable conflict with religion.

Whitehead was ready to accord to religion the supreme role of going beyond facts and of showing what it is that gives them importance. But he was highly critical of its tendency in the past to harden itself against new discoveries in science. He believed that, too often in its intransigent opposition to change and novelty, religion had adopted an exaggerated position it was later forced to abandon or modify. This led to the repetition of an "undignified retreat," which was detrimental to the status of religion in the eyes of the scientific community and of society in general.

Whitehead called for a new way of thinking on the part of those engaged in the task of explaining and propagating religious belief: religious men must not be afraid of change but should welcome it as a challenge to the powers of their belief to express itself in new ways. Religion is like life itself, which is ever growing, expanding, and developing: "But you cannot permanently enclose the same life in the same mould." [131] Sooner or later the mould becomes too narrow for the life that is expanding within it. While granting that the principles of religion may be eternal, Whitehead emphasized that the form in which these principles are expressed called for continuous development.[132] He was not afraid to say that religion will recover its power and influence only when it learns to face change in much the same spirit that science faces it. The very survival of the churches depends on it: "The Church will perish unless it opens its windows and lets out the dove to search for an olive branch." [133] To Whitehead, extinction of the church would be a tragedy, just as it would be tragic were religion to close its mind to the contributions science can make to the progress of mankind. He expressed his own feelings as to the importance of both science and religion when he wrote:

[131] *Science and the Modern World*, p. 262.
[132] *Ibid.*, p. 188; *Religion in the Making*, p. 140.
[133] *Religion in the Making*, p. 146.

When we consider what religion is for mankind, and what science is, it is no exaggeration to say that the future course of history depends upon the decision of this generation as to the relations between them. We have here the two strongest general forces (apart from the mere impulse of the various senses) which influence men, and they seem to be set one against the other.[184]

This is why he considered it to be of the utmost importance that the conflict between the two be resolved as soon as possible.

Conclusion

There is little doubt that, of the philosophers we have considered so far, Whitehead is the most difficult to understand. Not the least among the reasons is that, in the works we have considered, he is a metaphysician. I know that this term is not in good favor in many circles today, but it should not frighten us. As often as philosophers and scientists try to bury it, we see it popping up again and again in articles and discussions. It becomes not only a harmless word but even quite respectable if we define it as *a study of the generic traits of nature in all its aspects.* John Dewey found no difficulty with this meaning, and no one was more critical of metaphysics than he. Whitehead called metaphysics "the science which seeks to discover the general ideas which are indispensably relevant to the analysis of everything that happens." [135]

If we understand metaphysics in this sense, we can also understand why Whitehead can be looked upon as having accomplished the task of unification of experience even more successfully than James, Peirce, or Dewey. Remember what these men were trying to do: each was attempting to show how religion could be viable in a scientific age. Each set about the task in his own way, with varied results.

James came out of a scientific background, but he did not develop along strictly scientific lines even in his own specialty, psychology; yet the scientist in him had difficulty in coming to terms with religion. His solution was to appeal to ordinary experience for his theism and for his outlook on religion. He resisted the attempt of science to rule out the evidence of such experience on anything, and particularly on theism and religion. For James, one's scientific and religious aspirations could

---

[184] *Science and the Modern World,* pp. 252–53.
[135] *Religion in the Making,* p. 84, n.

be reconciled, and all conflicts could be resolved. Science and religion could clasp hands and live together in peace.

For all that, James did not accomplish the complete unification of scientific and religious experience. To say that science and religion are not incompatible is not the same as saying that they are one. I am sure James would admit that man can be religious even while pursuing science, but this is not made explicit in his work. A dualism of a radical kind has indeed been overcome, but a complete unification has not yet been achieved.

Something of the same can be said of Peirce. He was far more the scientist than James by temperament, training, and practice, but his theism does not come precisely out of his science. When he considers the question of God and religion, he talks very much like James. We see the same refusal to allow science to block the road of ordinary experience and the same appeal to such experience as verification for the hypothesis of theism. But the successful integration of science and religion is still to be made.

In Dewey, the integration is complete. Though not a scientist in the strict sense, he is open to science's implications. Moreover, in calling religious all experience that is consummatory, he has effected a unification of experience and has shown that all types of it, even the most ordinary, can be called religious. He has attempted to explore the meaning of man's entire life as well as of the individual experiences that go to make up that life. The cost of this enterprise was, of course, disastrous for God and religion in any traditional meaning of these terms. Dewey simply did not see how God and religion could be relevant to modern man, and so he rejected them because he feared that any other choice would cut off the hope of future development for humanity.

Whitehead is more authentically a scientific man than James or Dewey. His orientation goes beyond that of his contemporaries, for he draws up a theory of reality that is applicable to ordinary experience and to all reality, right down to the very roots of the material universe. He thereby tries to heal the breach between "the materialistic mechanism of science and the moral intuitions, which are presupposed in the concrete affairs of life." The same general principles applied both to the scientific development of the universe and to the cultural growth of mankind. From an analysis of both of these and from the same general principles, God emerges quite naturally as the source and term of all process. In this respect, Whitehead develops not parallel experiences in the manner of James or Peirce, but a unity of experience after the fashion of Dewey, but without sacrificing theism and religion. He is thus more conscious of the place of scientific thinking in his theism, and vice versa. His work is not so much a departure from the thought of James and Peirce as an extension, precisely along scientific lines, through which he breaks down the distinction between scientific, religious, and ordinary experience. In this he agrees with Dewey, though he does not sacrifice God and religion.

As science becomes more dominant, it is interesting to speculate whether the future approach to God will be more like that of Whitehead than that of James, Peirce, or Dewey. I personally do not believe that there will ever be a complete separation from the appeal to direct experience, as seen in these last three men. It is abundantly evident that for Whitehead, scientific, religious, and ordinary experience are one. His is a better example of a modern scientist's approach to God, because he comes from a strictly scientific background and effects a unification of this background with his theism and religion. For the same reasons, he should appeal to the large and increasing number of scientists and scientifically minded men of our generation.

As a final question we may ask: is Whitehead a naturalist? Roy Wood Sellars is quite emphatic in stating that Whitehead was opposed to everything that naturalism stands for. Among other reasons, he gives the following: ". . . he is a theist; he flirts with the idea of immortality; he believes in religious and moral intuitions as significant guides in ultimate matters." [136] If naturalism calls for the contrary, then certainly Whitehead was not a naturalist. However, as I have tried to show in the opening chapter, one can question whether the exclusion of God and religion is essential to naturalism. It depends on how one wishes to frame his definition: James and Peirce were theists, and Dewey was not, yet they agreed in their fundamental approach to reality.

Whitehead is in agreement, too, regarding this approach. He himself used a term that best sums up the basic characteristic of a naturalist: "world-loyalty." The word appears in his book on religion, and, in fact, as pointed out above, he defines religion itself as world-loyalty.[137]

[136] R. W. Sellars, "Philosophy of Organism and Physical Realism," in P. A. Schilpp, ed., *The Philosophy of Alfred North Whitehead*, 2nd ed. (New York: Tudor Publishing, 1951), p. 409.
[137] *Religion in the Making*, p. 60.

As we have seen, for Whitehead religion is the response man makes to the meaning of reality, and meaning cannot be found until the individual has merged his own interest with that of the universe.[138] Concretely, this means that growth of the human person and of the religious man depends on the extent to which he engages himself in scientific, technological, social, political, and economic interests, and especially on the extent to which each one gives himself in love and sacrifice for his fellow man. These characteristics are essential to Whitehead's philosophy. For this reason, I do not hesitate to call him a naturalist, just as I would classify James, Peirce, and Dewey as naturalists. But for all that, I do not think we should allow ourselves to quarrel over terms. Whatever label we use for him, Whitehead's emphasis on the relation of man to the universe puts him in the ranks of those whose philosophy deserves a hearing because it has a message for contemporary man.

[138] *Ibid.*, p. 60.

VI

JOSIAH ROYCE

AND SALVATION
PHILOSOPHY

There would seem to be no more convenient place at which to end discussion of American religious philosophy than at Whitehead. We have explored the religious thinking of our four most influential philosophers, and that would seem to be sufficient for a book of limited purpose and length. In reality, it was my original intention to end it all right there, but a haunting refrain that sounds something like "and then there is Josiah Royce" keeps going through my head. Royce— the forgotten man among American philosophers.

It wasn't always so. Josiah Royce was the foremost representative of

American idealism at a time when idealism itself was the reigning philosophy. But then Royce and his idealism fell upon hard times. They came under fire from science and from philosophy as influenced by science. Roycean idealism was criticized because, it was alleged, it went beyond the empiricism so dearly loved by the scientifically minded; because it proposed an Absolute; because it was closed to science, progress, and chance; and because its theory of ideals separated man from nature. For the same reasons, it was branded as alien to the whole American temperament in its novel approach to a changing universe. So strong and persistent was the attack that idealism soon lost its hold upon the philosophic world. As a result, the picture we are given in the histories of American philosophy is that of an outmoded idealism being swept away by triumphant pragmatism and naturalism. And with the demise of idealism we also see the almost total eclipse of Josiah Royce. Good reason, then, for calling him a forgotten man!

But just how reliable is this picture? It is true that on the philosophical level pragmatism and naturalism won the day. Their influence was felt in religion, education, science, social and political theory, and law. There would seem to be no doubt that the picture is accurate. But what happens if we reverse the ordinary sequence? I mean, suppose that we treat idealism *after* pragmatism and naturalism? Does our perspective also change? I think it does. For one thing, we notice that Royce actually outlived two of the five classical philosophers, James and Peirce. Further, Royce was well aware of the movement of pragmatism, for he was a contemporary of Peirce's and a colleague of James's at Harvard. For years he carried on with James a long series of discussions on the merits of idealism and pragmatism. So he was not an idealist through ignorance of the pragmatic movement.

If Royce is treated before the others, as is usually done, it gives plausibility to the commonly voiced beliefs that idealism was surpassed and that it should be treated as a museum piece, historically interesting but currently irrelevant. But once reverse the order, and idealism seems to be not only contemporary with pragmatism and early naturalism but a definite challenge to them. Reading Royce can be a stimulating experience and, for those who tend to become complacent with pragmatism and naturalism, a disturbing one. For Royce probes, needles, knocks you off balance. A study of him brings to the forefront once more questions that the pragmatist and naturalist often like to think of as answered, but that have really never been settled.

An examination of Royce today will not necessarily reverse the trend of the times and bring us back beyond pragmatism to the days when idealism ruled the philosophical world in America. Pragmatism and naturalism were too much manifestations of America's growth in self-awareness to be removed from the scene as though they never existed, and there are many aspects that are too valuable to be wholly discarded. Moreover, not all of Royce's philosophic ideas can be judged acceptable to contemporary man. Royce himself was open to that possibility; he was not so naive as to think that his philosophy, any more than the philosophy of the men of the past, could or should be transmitted, whole and unchanged, to subsequent generations. He saw that philosophy was, in the last analysis, but one man's attempt to express his critical reflections on the more serious questions faced in daily life.[1] To his way of thinking, the role of the philosopher throughout history has been to describe the thoughts and feelings of the people of his own age.[2] If a philosophy is a faithful expression of its time, it will not wholly pass away. A future age will be able to draw upon it as it, too, attempts to give expression to the new thoughts and feelings that are emerging. The philosopher may not always know ahead of time what the future will find valuable in his thought, but if he is a great philosopher he will have "builded better than he knew." [3]

Royce also voiced the opinion that a new generation of thinkers will always find it easy to refute old doctrines. But he expressed the view that new doctrines may merely seem to oppose the old, when in reality they complete them,[4] and that the truth is neither in the old nor the new but in a synthesis of both.[5] After all, evolution itself is not a complete creation out of nothing, but a gradual development of an old stock. This is true of language, institutions, beliefs, and ideas.[6]

In actuality, Royce has suffered the very fate he claimed should be avoided in viewing the philosophy of the past. Both his contemporaries and his successors raised strong objections to several elements of his thought. Royce attempted to answer them, but he failed to satisfy his critics. And because his idealism was rejected on partial grounds, the

[1] J. Royce, *The Spirit of Modern Philosophy* (New York: Houghton Mifflin, 1892), p. 1.
[2] *Ibid.*, pp. 8–9.
[3] *Ibid.*, p. 10.
[4] *Ibid.*, p. 13.
[5] *Ibid.*, p. 15.
[6] *Ibid.*, p. 283.

result was a wholesale rejection of his thought. This was the fate of Aristotle, Descartes, Kant, and Hegel, to name a few. But in each of these cases, to a greater or lesser degree, subsequent ages have learned, with William James, that "nothing is nothing but" and that exclusive positions are usually dangerous.

With this in mind, I would like to look again at the philosophy of Josiah Royce. To some it will appear that I am stacking the cards in his favor when I present him after a discussion of pragmatism and naturalism, as though to give him the final say. But I adopt this order with no intention of retracting what has been said in previous chapters of this book.

No, my only purpose in treating Royce last is to bring out those questions that still remain to be faced by American philosophy. The treatment of Royce as a whipping boy by later philosophers has, I am afraid, made it seem that these questions have been answered or that they are no longer relevant. A failure to face them squarely has been in part the reason why, since World War II, American pragmatism and naturalism have themselves been overshadowed by the logical and analytic schools of philosophy. A rereading of Royce could help to prevent the complete decline of pragmatism and naturalism and with it the loss of their valuable insights.

Biography

Josiah Royce was born in Grass Valley, a mining town in California, in 1855.[7] Six years earlier, his parents and older sister had been among the forty-niners who went West in search of gold. Josiah himself was born near the abandoned and crumbling mines. Schooling, like everything else, was primitive, and he received his first lessons at home with

[7] The best sources for the details of Royce's life are J. Royce, "Words of Professor Royce at the Walton Hotel in Philadelphia, December 29, 1915," *The Philosophical Review*, Vol. 25, No. 3 (May, 1916), pp. 507–14; G. H. Palmer, "In Dedication: Josiah Royce," in C. Barrett, ed., *Contemporary Idealism in America* (New York: Russell and Russell, 1964), pp. 1–9; G. H. Howison, "Josiah Royce: The Significance of His Work in Philosophy," *The Philosophical Review*, Vol. 25, No. 3 (May, 1916), pp. 231–44; R. B. Perry, *In the Spirit of William James* (Indiana University Press, 1958), chap. 1, "Two American Philosophers: William James and Josiah Royce"; J. H. Randall, Jr., "Josiah Royce and American Idealism," *The Journal of Philosophy*, Vol. 63, No. 3 (February 3, 1966), pp. 57–83.

his mother as teacher. One of his sisters taught him to read. He even attributes to his mother and three sisters his first lessons in philosophy, and he had to be punished occasionally when his arguments with his sister nearest in age became too philosophical! [8]

Royce himself admits, and his friends agree, that he was homely in appearance. George H. Howison says that, when he first met Royce in 1884, he was struck by his middle-aged (Royce was then twenty-nine) "British head" and countenance set on a small, youthful body.[9] His liberally freckled face was topped by a shock of red hair. When the family moved to San Francisco in 1866, his unusual appearance and countrified ways made him the butt of many a schoolboy prank. All this may account for a shyness that was always to characterize him, though his sincerity, generosity, and open-mindedness won him many close friends among his fellow pupils and later among his students and colleagues.

Royce attended the University of California and received the bachelor's degree in 1875. Some businessmen were so impressed by his senior thesis, "The Theology of Aeschylus's *Prometheus Bound*," that they gave him the financial means for a year of study in Germany. There he was a student of the great German philosopher Rudolph Hermann Lotze (1817–81), at Göttingen, and he was influenced by the writings of Arthur Schopenhauer (1788–1860) and Immanuel Kant (1724–1804). The strong influence of Hegel did not come until after 1890.[10]

On his return from Germany Royce was awarded a fellowship at Johns Hopkins University; he received the doctorate in 1878. Immediately he was offered a position at the University of California as an instructor in rhetoric and logic. He was sufficiently successful in his work to publish a small book on logic.[11] But Royce was not content in California: his first love was philosophy, and, in a letter to William James in January, 1879, he wrote with a touch of despair that "There is no philosophy in California." And so, in spite of feeling at home among good friends and freedom to arrange his own courses—adding a little philosophy—he longed for an atmosphere more in accord with his philosophical interests.[12]

[8] Royce, "Words of Professor Royce," pp. 507–08.
[9] Howison, *op. cit.*, pp. 234–35.
[10] Royce, "Words of Professor Royce," p. 510.
[11] J. Royce, *Primer of Logical Analysis for the Use of Composition Students* (San Francisco: Bancroft, 1881).
[12] R. B. Perry, *The Thought and Character of William James* (Boston: Little, Brown, 1936), I, 781.

Howison, however, gives a slightly different explanation for Royce's discontent in California: he claims that many of Royce's colleagues and some of the Regents voted that he stick to English and not become too involved in logic. In any event, James sympathized with the lot of this "solitary philosopher," as he called Royce, and began the movement to bring him to Harvard. Royce had met James in 1877 during graduate days at Johns Hopkins and visited James in Cambridge. Many years later he acknowledged his great affection for his colleague and his gratitude that James had encouraged him to take up a career in philosophy.[13]

In 1881 Royce's first application for a position at Harvard was turned down, since there were no openings, but in the spring of 1882 he was invited to fill in while James was on leave during the academic year 1882–83. The appointment was only for a year, with no guarantee of a renewal of contract. It meant that Royce would have to leave his position in California and travel clear across the country with no security beyond one year. The salary was to be $1,250.[14] A family man himself, James sent to Royce an estimate of expenses: $360 rent for "a good little furnished house" and $30 a week for "first-class board" for himself and his wife.[15] Royce reflected the pioneering spirit of his forebears by taking the risk and accepting the position. In the summer of 1882, he made the trip East with his wife and their baby. The risk was well worthwhile: Royce was to remain at Harvard until his death in 1916—thirty-four years later!

Royce's career at Harvard was a busy and productive one. According to Palmer, he taught more hours of class than anyone else in the department.[16] His schedule was augmented by the many requests he received for outside lectures: he gave the Gifford Lectures at the University of Aberdeen, Scotland, and the Hibbert Lectures at Manchester College, Oxford. A bibliography of his works, composed shortly before his death, shows twenty-three books and ninety-four articles.[17] His work played an important role in making idealism so influential in academic philosophical circles and placed him among the ranking American philosophers.

[13] *Ibid.*, p. 779–80.
[14] *Ibid.*, p. 795. Palmer says it was $1,000. He also claims some part in bringing Royce to Harvard. See *Contemporary Idealism in America*, p. 6.
[15] *Ibid.*, p. 795.
[16] Palmer, *op. cit.*, p. 7.
[17] B. Rand, "A Bibliography of the Writings of Josiah Royce," *The Philosophical Review*, Vol. 25, No. 3 (May, 1916), pp. 515–21.

What of his religious background? We do know that his mother, Sarah Royce, had a strong Puritan faith. Josiah later recalls that he enjoyed hearing the Bible stories she read to him in his early years, though he likewise states that he had a stubborn dislike for Sunday observance. This he attributes to the fact that he was a "born nonconformist." [18] He attended the church of his parents until he entered college, but thereafter he never committed himself to any organized religion.[19] Palmer states that this was due partly to his independent spirit and partly to a reaction against "certain rigidities of his boyhood," though what these rigidities were Palmer does not say. He adds that Royce admitted to him that his aversion for organized religion was a bit childish.[20]

It has been remarked more than once that there is a curious contrast between James and Royce.[21] James was born and raised in the highly cultured atmosphere of New England and Europe and yet developed a philosophy that seems more characteristic of the pioneer spirit of the American frontiersman. A "slouchy philosopher," he called himself, with a definite dislike for tidy systems, like packages whose ends are neatly tucked in and whose ribbons are carefully tied. Life, he claimed, just wasn't that way, and a philosophy that tried to make it so was artificial and unrealistic. Royce, however, who came out of the raw West, where informality was the order of the day and improvisation was the only means of dealing with real-life situations, developed a philosophy that was carefully structured and highly systematic, where everything was made to fit into a harmonious pattern.

This is a convenient way of summing up the two men, and it makes the task of analyzing them easy. There is only one difficulty: it doesn't fit the facts, at least not as far as Royce is concerned. I would be more willing to grant the summation regarding James. He was, indeed, a "slouchy philosopher," and his philosophy is a perfect mirror of the man. It would be difficult to name any of his works that is carefully and systematically worked out, with all inconsistencies reconciled. This, as we have seen, has been the despair of more than one man who has tried to understand his thought.

But to oppose Royce as a perfect contrast is to take only half the man. Surely, if we concentrate only on a part of his work, the contrast

[18] Royce, "Words of Professor Royce," pp. 507–08.
[19] Perry, *In the Spirit*, p. 14.
[20] Palmer, *op. cit.*, p. 8.
[21] See Perry, "Two American Philosophers," *In the Spirit*, pp. 1–43.

will stand. Book II of *The Religious Aspect of Philosophy*, the two ponderous volumes of *The World and the Individual*, and *The Conception of God* show Royce to be the most systematic of all our American philosophers. These works merit the criticism of George Santayana, who maintained that in his most important works Royce tried to show that all reality was part of the one divine life in which all problems found their solution and all evils their explanation.[22] This was the period of his writing during which Royce pursued relentlessly the task of arguing to the existence of the divine behind finite reality and of showing how the divine gives reality its ultimate reason and explanation. For those who like logical reasoning, Royce's writing is a masterpiece: no problem is left untouched, no possible difficulty left open. Step by step he worked his way through his task. We could say that Royce played "impeccable logician" to James's "slouchy philosopher."

It would not take long to find in Royce's background good reason for his love of system and logic. We would have only to recall that he spent a year of study in Germany and that he was a pupil of the master logician, Lotze, who more than once was the object of James's good-natured but pointed witticisms. Lotze, Kant, Schopenhauer, Hegel—these were the men from whom Royce drew his early inspiration. The German school's great love for system was in his blood, and he never fully divested himself of its influence. Moreover, one could argue that his frontier experience was the very thing that drove him to seek guidance from foreign sources. In many respects, of course, the taming of a wilderness forced the American to devise new methods of handling novel situations; Americans wanted to stand on their own feet and work out their own problems. But here was a young man of twenty, with little background in philosophy and at a time when America did not even have a philosophy it could call its own, given the opportunity to study in Germany, where Americans by the hundreds were going for graduate work, especially in the new psychology. Like many another, Royce was awed by the prestige of German scholarship, and he was eager to absorb as much of it as he could in the short space of one year. Two more years of graduate study gave him further opportunity to broaden and deepen his knowledge of the German tradition.

Consider the man as he began his teaching career at Harvard: a definite orientation had already shaped his thinking, and the ideas

[22] G. Santayana, *Character and Opinion in the United States* (New York: Scribner's, 1920), p. 100.

bubbling within him naturally took the direction given to them by his German training. It could also be granted that, in the process, he may have missed aspects of these ideas that were more native to his own country. Both George Santayana and George Herbert Mead (1863–1931) criticized him for failing to be wholly American in his thinking. But should anyone be surprised that he did not fully adjust to the American experience in his philosophy? It would be more remarkable if he did. We find, then, that the problems he faced, at least in his earlier writings, were cast in the mold of a dialectic that was elaborated into a grand system with every item accounted for. Pragmatists like James found this method quite alien to their thinking and so waged relentless warfare against it. The philosophy that was to win the day was more in accord with the American mentality of facing situations as they arose, of meeting them with the best adjustment possible, and of leaving it to the future to decide whether the adjustment should stand.

The reaction in the early part of the century against systematic philosophy will also explain why it took so long for Peirce and Whitehead to be recognized in our own country: the philosophy of both of them, especially Whitehead, is highly systematic. For sheer massiveness of content and care in logical development, Whitehead's *Process and Reality* will rival anything that Royce ever wrote. But there are important differences: both Peirce and Whitehead were representatives of the new logic that has since gained prominence in America, and they also had a strong background in science, which formed an important part of their work. Though the American intellectual world was simply not ready for Peirce in the early 1900's, he has come into his own in the last two decades. Whitehead fared much better, since he lived until the middle of our century, but he, too, had to be "discovered."

What particularly bothered the rising pragmatists was Royce's attempt to handle traditional problems in a systematic way. Difficulties had been raised concerning German and British forms of idealism before: their proponents were pressed to explain how all minds could be part of one mind and how evil could be reconciled with universal, overall good. But these difficulties were particularly irksome to the American temperament, and Royce had to bear the full force of the attack. His answers were no better or worse than those of his predecessors; it was just that his listeners were less willing to accept them.

If this were all that could be said for Royce's philosophy, it would be just as well to leave him as the forgotten man. America is no more ready now for his systematic form of idealism than it was fifty years ago, and perhaps far less so. But there is another side to Royce that shows him much more American than his critics have acknowledged. How could he have lived in America and still be untouched by its influence? Even if it were theoretically possible, it just didn't happen that way. This is clear from the early part of his first major work, *The Religious Aspect of Philosophy*, and from all his works after the second volume of *The World and the Individual* (1901). These include *The Philosophy of Loyalty* (1908), *The Sources of Religious Insight* (1912), and the two-volume *The Problem of Christianity* (1913). These works are Jamesian in their whole approach, which means that actual experience is the starting point of Royce's philosophy and that in the working out of problems that arise he resolutely tries to stay in contact with experience. His conscious aim is to state only what he can verify by experience. To read *The Philosophy of Loyalty* after *The World and the Individual* is like entering a whole new world. I really think that, if one did not know that Royce wrote both, one would suppose that they were the work of two different authors.

Royce, then, does not so much stand at the end of an old era as at the beginning of a new one: he is the link between a fading idealism and a nascent pragmatism. For a long time, he was to be the last of our home-grown American philosophers who came out of a European tradition. Some would say that it was precisely this tradition that hindered him from becoming truly American. In the course of this chapter, I shall try to show that there is a dimension of Royce's thought that came out of his American experience and that poses important problems and suggests valuable insights for the future of American religious philosophy. This can be seen only if we become aware of the fact that Royce was more than a systematic philosopher bent on reconciling all reality with a divine spirit through a dialectic of idealism. He certainly attempted this, but he did something else besides. It is this something else that shall engage our attention.

Religious Philosophy: Man's Need of Salvation

The year before he died, Royce related to a group of his friends his earliest recollections of the scenes that surrounded his boyhood. He remembered vividly that not far from the house there yawned the gaping mouth of an abandoned mine. Close by, there stood the lonely grave of some miner who had come West with bright hopes of striking it rich but whose body was broken in a few short years by the cruelty of the elements or the ravages of disease. These symbols, like the hulks of ruined ships washed up on the shore, were melancholy reminders that here human beings like himself had been buoyed up by high hopes and had died without ever seeing them realized. It would be pure conjecture to say that such memories, going back to boyhood, shaped the whole direction of his thought. But whatever set him thinking, there is no doubt that at its source was the feeling that there is in every human being a cry welling up from the depths of his personality for a destiny greater than himself. It is a dynamism that sets man thinking and acting, reaching out for a goal beyond himself. Royce also believed that this goal could not be attained by human effort alone and that man must be saved. It was by no logic that he came to this conviction; he drew it from his own inner experience. Man feels an existential need for salvation, and this cannot be reached by his own powers.

This was by no means a new insight, nor did Royce pretend that it was. It is a familiar theme met on every page of Scripture, from the story of man's fall in the Garden of Eden to the promise of paradise made to the good thief on the cross. It is embodied in Christian eschatology, both Roman and Protestant, different though the forms of presenting it may be. The theme was not new, though it was conceived by Royce in novel terms, as we shall see. As the title of this chapter indicates, I have come to view Royce's thought under the heading of "salvation philosophy." Actually, the notion of salvation becomes explicit only in the later part of his philosophy, but, as I shall try to show, it had taken root and it grew as his ideas developed. It is the course of this development that will be traced in the following pages.

In his first major book, *The Religious Aspect of Philosophy*, Royce gives us two bits of information that are valuable for the understanding of his thought: first, he states that religious problems drove him to philosophy.[23] Then, in trying to explain what he means by religious problems, he tells us what he means by religious philosophy. The terms involved here are "religon," "philosophy," and "religious philosophy," or philosophy with a religious aspect.

[23] J. Royce, *The Religious Aspect of Philosophy* (New York: Houghton Mifflin, 1885), p. ix.

Religion includes three elements: First, it teaches a moral code of action—that is, it teaches what should be done and what should be avoided. Further, it inspires the individual to act according to the moral law—with devotion, reverence, and love. The faithful are then able to commit themselves fully to a way of life with gladness and, if necessary, to suffer pain and even loss of life in that commitment. Such dedication is brought about by those things usually considered to be an essential part of religion—parable, myth, ceremony, and song. Lastly, in order to teach a commitment to a code of action, religion must develop a theory of reality—that is, it must propose a body of beliefs.

Philosophy, meaning here purely theoretical philosophy, is concerned merely about finding out all it can regarding the real world. It has a passion for truth and does not pay attention to the consequences. Philosophy with a religious aspect, or religious philosophy, is also concerned with the truth, but beyond that it seeks *value*. It asks what in reality is worthy of worship as the good, what is capable of inspiring us and moving us to a wholehearted commitment, what, if anything, is of infinite worth.

By way of clarifying these headings, we may make the following summary: *religion* brings the individual to action and belief and, in addition, tries to inspire him to an enthusiastic commitment through parables, myths, ceremonies, and song. *Philosophy* includes belief but does not concern itself with enthusiastic commitment. Philosophy with a religious aspect, or *religious philosophy*, in seeking things of value and objects of infinite worth that lead to a personal commitment, is the same as religion, except that it does not include myths, parables, ceremonies, and song.

We see, then, that the "religious problems" that drove Royce to philosophy are those that concern the serious questions facing man in his daily life. Royce was concerned with neither cold and detached truth nor organized religion. The first did not enter into the real problems confronting human experience and the latter contained dogmas imposed from above and attempted to interpret them through symbol and ritual. We shall see later the reasons for Royce's difficulties regarding organized religion, but for the moment it is enough to say that he was trying to give an interpretation of the meaning of human life without having recourse to revealed dogma.

To Royce, man's most constant quest is to find some unifying principle in his life, some one ideal that will integrate the varied sequence of his thoughts and actions. Throughout his life the individual finds himself drawn to many different objects he hopes will satisfy the inquietude that constantly besets him. At one moment he is drawn to pleasure, at another to power over others, at another to material success, or again to self-sacrifice. Not only are these goals different, but they are often contradictory. Royce calls this predicament a "spray of aims," a "confused and blinding cloud of purposes" that causes the individual to experience a sense of confusion and disunity at the very center of his personality.[24]

In his quest for an ideal that will effect the needed unification in man, Royce tries to show that it cannot be achieved by the individual.[25] Individualism develops into a selfish guarding of one's own prerogatives against the real or imagined encroachments of others, leading to the ceaseless conflict of one man against another and to the destruction of any hope of unity and peace. Or it causes one to isolate himself in the belief that he is self-sufficient, bringing him to utter disappointment and disillusionment. Finally, individualism and the separation of man from man can only result in a sense of aloneness that makes unity of life impossible.

Having rejected individualism as incapable of unifying and satisfying man, Royce concludes that inner personal harmony can be reached only in union with others. No matter what the highest human good may be, man can reach it only by achieving a unity of thought and purpose with other men. Royce was willing to conclude that without such unity there could be no satisfactory life for man. The only way of achieving human satisfaction is by a sense of community, which means a unity of aims and the ability to work with others. So important is this that he considered it to be the first need of mankind.[26] Once this need is realized, men should strive to make sure that others, too, come to this realization. It is man's first duty and first commandment.[27]

Royce tries to suggest ways in which this duty may be implemented. He is not content to leave it in the theoretical order but wishes that it find expression in some practical way. He asks what activities will enable the individual to lose himself in interest for the welfare of others

[24] *Ibid.*, p. 143.
[25] *Ibid.*, pp. 201–11.
[26] *Ibid.*, p. 175.
[27] *Ibid.*, pp. 175–76.

and suggests three areas.[28] The first is art, wherein each man can contribute to beauty and esthetic enjoyment in life. The second is the area of scientific knowledge. (It is interesting to note here that, though Royce does not exhibit any first-hand or profound acquaintance with science and its development, he is aware enough of its importance to realize that the pursuit of scientific knowledge can well become a means of unifying men's interests and activities.) The third area is that of political life, for the development of the ideal state demands that men submerge their selfish interests to work for the common welfare of all those united in the political community.

Such are the three areas suggested by Royce for communal thought and action: Beauty, Knowledge, and the State—the esthetic, theoretical, and social. For those familiar with the notion of community as developed by Dewey—with his long discussion of esthetic, scientific, and political theory—the treatment of Royce seems quite rudimentary; he hardly did more than draw the broad outlines of community life in its practical aspects and discuss it in merely general terms. But for all that, the whole orientation of his theory of community is strikingly in accord with that of Dewey and of anyone else who was writing on the subject. He states clearly and emphatically that, whatever may be the final ideal that unifies man's aspirations, his vocation in this life must be to make his contribution to human happiness by uniting in heart and action with others.

Such is the development of Royce's thought as found in the first part of The Religious Aspect of Philosophy. He has worked out his ideas through an analysis of man's experience in much the same way as they were worked out by men like James and Dewey: his starting point is man and his quest for personal fulfillment, and, by an appeal to experience, he seeks for what will enable man to gain his end. There is a minimum of appeal to logical proof. The main reason, no doubt, is that he did not feel the need of such proof. He was calling upon the common experience of all men, and he was led to much the same conclusions that had been reached by others. In this regard, he shows himself very much an American in his thinking and quite in line with the tradition of James and Peirce, Dewey and Whitehead.

So much can be said of the early part of The Religious Aspect of Philosophy. After that, Royce tried to work out a proof that the search for inner harmony and the development of community-mindedness

[28] Ibid., pp. 212–18.

finds its ultimate completion in the divine. Quite suddenly his mood changes: before, he had relied almost entirely on human experience and what it could tell us about man. In trying to link this up with the divine, he uses a method quite different; it is as if he felt that a justification of the existence of the divine had to be established by rigorous argument. He suddenly abandons the lead of human experience in order to prove God's existence through logic. In other words, his whole approach changes from an examination of human experience to a method of logical analysis. He uses a ponderous and technical argument to the effect that error and truth demand an all-knower who encompasses all reality by knowledge and gives meaning to all reality by his own being. This theory follows the main lines of idealism as it has been developed in the history of philosophy. Royce's unique contribution consists in the argument from error to an all-knower. The argument begins in the second half of *The Religious Aspect of Philosophy* and continues through *The Conception of God* (1897) and the two thick volumes of *The World and the Individual* (1899 and 1901). These works, especially the last mentioned, bore the brunt of the attacks by the rising school of pragmatism.

It is not my intention to work my way through an exposition of these volumes. What I would like to do instead is give an interpretation of that aspect of Royce's thought that has become obscured in all the criticism of his idealism. My purpose is to show that an estimate of Royce need not depend on his idealism, but may rest on those elements that are very much in the stream of American philosophy. I shall also go out on a limb by trying to show that his approach on some points is not far from the pragmatism of William James, in spite of their long and sharp criticism of each other!

The Philosophy of Loyalty

It was a good many years before Royce returned to the themes discussed in the early part of *The Religious Aspect of Philosophy*—twenty-three to be exact. Having worked out the metaphysics of his idealism to his satisfaction, he returned, in a book called *The Philosophy of Loyalty* (1908), to the problems he had dropped so abruptly in the second part of his earlier work. His starting point again is human experience, which raises questions that plague the mind and heart of every human being: "For what do I live? Why am I here? For what am I good? Why am I needed." [29] These are questions each man finds either explicitly or implicitly pressing for an answer. They are not ones that can be easily dismissed, and sooner or later each man tries to find a solution. Each wants some unifying purpose to give meaning to his life; but when the individual looks within himself, he finds "vague cravings for happiness, a chaos of desires, a medley of conflicting instincts." [30] Left to himself, man feels pulled every which way in the attempt to give meaning to his life. What each man seeks is a unified cause and some plan of action that will give him personal fulfillment.[31]

Royce finds that the personality can be expressed and enriched only by a commitment to some outside cause.[32] He gives the example of patriotism in time of war: the individual commits himself to a cause, forgets himself and his own interests, pursues the cause with enthusiasm, overcomes difficulties that stand in the way, and, if need be, gives up his life for his cause. The example of patriotism brings out clearly what Royce is trying to say, though he by no means limits himself to it. On the contrary, a commitment should be made to causes that engender peace and harmony, not discord. It can take many forms: it can concern the home, religious belief, or business and professional life.[33] Royce calls this kind of commitment *loyalty* and defines it as "the willing and practical and thoroughgoing devotion of a person to a cause." [34] It is willing when it is freely assented to by the individual; it is practical when it leads to positive action; it is thoroughgoing when the individual is ready to bear hardship and even death in his dedication to it.

The most essential thing about the cause to which loyalty attaches itself consists in the fact that the individual dedicates himself through love to the service of other human beings. Man is social by instinct, and he finds his fulfillment in dedicating himself to others. He engages in social activities because they focus all his instincts on a single aim, unify his passions and impulses, and bring order into the chaos of his desires.[35] Royce thus stresses the need of the individual to engage in community life, just as he had done in his earlier work.

[29] J. Royce, *The Philosophy of Loyalty* (New York: Macmillan, 1916), p. 57.
[30] *Ibid.*, p. 57.
[31] *Ibid.*, p. 42.
[32] *Ibid.*, p. 42.
[33] *Ibid.*, p. 43.
[34] *Ibid.*, pp. 16–17.
[35] *Ibid.*, p. 32.

Royce is quite definite in the stress he places on loyalty as the only means by which a man can fulfill and enrich his personality. Without it, one can find no unity or peace in his life.[36] This has been shown by the fact that, in the course of history, men of all times and places have grouped together and have dedicated themselves to some cause. The cause may not always have been the best one, or even a good one, but it has always been something that takes individuals out of themselves and focuses their interest and energies on the welfare of others. And yet, as great as is the importance Royce attaches to loyalty as we have described it, he nonetheless maintains that it is not enough. Drawing on his own experience and that of others, he states that any human cause to which a person attaches himself will indeed satisfy him, but not completely; there is always something lacking. Any unity that is attained through loyalty is only partial and fragmentary, leaving the person ultimately incomplete.[37] We feel a deep need for a cause "which we cannot successfully express in any set of human experiences of transient joys and of crumbling successes." [38] What successes we do experience give us a hint of complete success and point in its direction. The dynamism of the human personality pushes on toward a higher unity. The individual finds within himself a desire for what wholly fulfills his personality.

Having brought the discussion to this point, Royce is well aware that many following the same line of thought have concluded that the human mind can go no further. Ultimate incompletion is of the nature of things, and man himself must face the fact that he can never realize all his aspirations. It is simply something that man must learn to expect and live with, and this he can do by settling for an effort to make the best of the situation. But Royce was not ready to settle for this: "I am discontented with mere discontent." [39] He did not believe that the dynamic striving of the human person for complete fulfillment was to be in vain. He admitted that every cause is in some sense a "lost cause." [40] The pursuit of it can gain some measure of completion, but it can never be wholly successful. And yet he believed that every lost cause will be redeemed: "The *loyal*, and they alone, know the one great good of suffering, of ignorance, of finitude, of loss, of defeat," namely, the knowledge that ultimately they will be saved by finding their com-

[36] *Ibid.*, p. 46.   [39] *Ibid.*, p. 11.
[37] *Ibid.*, p. 43.   [40] *Ibid.*, pp. 284–86.
[38] *Ibid.*, p. 387.

pletion with the divine in an eternal life.[41] The ultimate destiny of man, then, is not discouragement, defeat, and loss, but hope, victory, and redemption.

Where did Royce derive the justification for this conclusion? Not from a carefully worded argument of the type found in his previous books. As we have seen, he has taken up the approach begun in his first philosophical work and put aside for over twenty years: the appeal to human experience and to the dynamism of the human personality. He is willing to admit that, in recognizing a need for unity of life, he does have a pragmatism. In fact, if we compare his discussion of loyalty with James's approach, we can see that they are quite similar.

Royce follows human experience to the point where it indicates that man has a drive for completion; he then expresses his unwillingness to believe that such a drive can be frustrated. He claims to borrow merely a phrase from James when he gives his revised definition of loyalty as "the Will to Believe in something eternal, and to express that belief in the practical life of a human being." [42] He has in fact borrowed more than a phrase; he has developed the same line of approach. He is even willing to admit that the conclusion drawn does not follow with compelling clarity; it has no final authority in its own right. He is simply trying to express "in a reasonable way" man's position in the universe.[43] He can force no one to accept his view; he simply invites "thoughtful people" to consider what ordinary experience tells us. More than that he cannot do.

It is strange that neither James nor Royce realized how close they were on the matter under discussion. The only explanation I can offer is that, in centering attention on points of obvious disagreement, they did not see their equally obvious areas of agreement. This is a common and understandable failing of those who are defending positions. As a result, James hammered away at Royce's Absolute, "the all-experiencer," which he roundly derided; he was repelled by this attempt to argue carefully and exhaustively through a sharp and well-honed logic; he complained that, in the process, the concrete events of daily life were passed over or only casually treated. Meanwhile, he missed Royce's openness to human experience and his close touch with human feelings and suffering, as expressed in his later works. Royce

[41] *Ibid.*, p. 393.
[42] *Ibid.*, p. 357.
[43] *Ibid.*, p. 360.

likewise allowed himself to concentrate too much on the looseness of terminology that is characteristic of James's style. He was rightly bothered by terms like "cash-value," "expediency," "consequences," and "useful," [44] but this caused him to misconstrue James's whole notion of truth. And he certainly was in error when he said that James merely collected examples of religious experience without ever trying to explain what the term of these experiences was.[45] To take this viewpoint is to center attention on *The Varieties of Religious Experience* and ignore his other works. He also misrepresents James when he says that, for him, religious convictions have their origin in the subconscious.[46] Meanwhile, both men failed to realize that they were in agreement in their justification of God's existence through human experience. But no matter; it is not important to try to show that Royce was Jamesian or vice versa. The important point is that, following a course a great many people are likely to find congenial to their own way of thinking, they both found a place for God.

The Notion of Salvation

Though the notion of salvation is implicit in the philosophy of loyalty, it consciously comes to the fore in *The Sources of Religious Insight* (1912). Royce continues the fundamental idea that there is something in human nature that needs redeeming and that man by himself is incapable of accomplishing it. The language is a bit more theological, and he takes his ideas from religion in the technical sense, but he stays within the realm of religious philosophy.[47] According to Royce, history gives witness to the fact that there is in man a cry for salvation that is not confined to any age or to any religious faith. Man is prey to "some vast and universal burden, of imperfection, of unreasonableness, of evil, of misery, of fate, of unworthiness, or of sin," [48] and he feels the need of being free from these. There are two basic ideas here. The first is that human life is destined for some great purpose that comprises man's highest good and in comparison with which

[44] *Ibid.*, pp. 322–23, 346–48.
[45] J. Royce, *The Sources of Religious Insight* (New York: Scribner's 1912), p. 30.
[46] *Ibid.*, p. 82.
[47] *Ibid.*, pp. 9–10.
[48] *Ibid.*, p. 8.

all other purposes are unimportant. The other idea is that man is always under the threat of failing to achieve this good and hence needs help beyond himself.[49] The highest good, the supreme goal of life for which man is destined, is victory over the conflict that is part of man's lot; and it is a goal that will unify all his desires, focus all his actions, and bring him a sense of fulfillment.[50] It is a good that is to be obtained by membership in a social group whose members are drawn together by love and motivated to action for the benefit of all.

We notice immediately from these brief remarks that there is a great similarity between *The Philosophy of Loyalty* and *The Sources of Religious Insight*. The basic notions are repeated, and even the mode of development in one book bears strong resemblances to that in the other. But in the latter we find the notion of salvation made much more explicit and religion given greater emphasis. As a matter of fact, in developing his philosophy of loyalty, Royce speaks of it in terms of religion; he even calls it "the religion of loyalty." [51] If we go all the way back to the opening pages of *The Religious Aspect of Philosophy*, we will realize that he is really speaking about a philosophy of religion, for he does not mean that his philosophy of loyalty involves dogmas, creeds, rite, or ritual, which are connected with religion in the traditional sense. His concern is to find out what he can about reality, and in the pursuit of it he is led to a belief in a superhuman and eternal world without which finite existence cannot be fully explained. This is the meaning he intends when he calls his philosophy of loyalty a religion.[52]

Salvation and Christianity

In his last great work, *The Problem of Christianity* (1913), in two volumes, Royce turns his attention more explicitly to salvation and religion. The work is an examination of Christianity to find out what it means in its essentials.[53] He is especially interested in determining what message Christianity has for the modern world and whether this

[49] *Ibid.*, pp. 12, 171–72.
[50] *Ibid.*, pp. 44–45.
[51] *Ibid.*, chap. V, "The Religion of Loyalty."
[52] *The Philosophy of Loyalty*, pp. 377, 381–84; *The Sources of Religious Insight*, pp. 181, 206–07; J. Royce, *The Problem of Christianity* (New York: Macmillan, 1914), I, p. 360.
[53] *The Problem of Christianity*, pp. 20–21.

message will still be viable in a changing universe.[54] In order to do this, he feels that he cannot depend on creeds or dogmas proper to any particular sect within Christianity, for these have given rise to controversy and disagreement. Instead, he will try to interpret Christianity through human experience and in empirical terms. He hopes that the result will be a core of doctrine that can still speak to modern man.[55] In making this interpretation, he will at the same time be writing a philosophy of the Christian religion.

At the very beginning of *The Problem of Christianity*, Royce maintains that his "philosophy of loyalty" had been taking shape in his mind since 1908. As the idea deepened, he moved toward a "religion of loyalty," and this in turn led him to express his views on the essence of Christianity.[56] He gradually came to the conviction that Christianity, in its essence, is precisely a religion of loyalty, and the most highly developed kind that has as yet emerged. He also believed that, however Christianity may develop in its institutions and traditions, it is essential for the salvation of man that the religion of loyalty continue in existence and direct both religion and mankind.[57] In other words, when stripped of its deposit of controversial dogma and examined purely in empirical terms and from the point of view of human experience, Christianity appears as the most perfect example of loyalty. It is important to keep in mind that Royce is not writing a theory of natural religion. He does not necessarily deny the supernatural aspects of Christianity nor the belief in direct revelation of God to man; he tries to prescind from these. He maintains that, in the course of history, disputes have arisen regarding individual points of dogma, and that these have served no purpose save to obscure what is viable and applicable to a modern world. In order to recover the value of Christianity and its basic message, he tries to study it as a "religion of loyalty," which can be evaluated in purely human terms.

Three Christian Ideas

Let us come more directly to Royce's interpretation of Christianity in terms of his religion of loyalty. There are three Christian ideas that

[54] *Ibid.*, p. 420.
[55] *Ibid.*, pp. ix, xxxviii.
[56] *Ibid.*, pp. viii–ix.
[57] *Ibid.*, pp. xviii–xix.

form the focal point of his discussion: Community, Lost Individual, and Atonement. These ideas are very closely intertwined, but, in spite of some overlapping, they can be discussed separately.

Community If we examine what Christianity teaches about community, we find that it is the same as that taught by the philosophy of loyalty.[58] Thus, in the Sermon on the Mount of the Gospels, salvation is spoken of as membership in a community, or more precisely, in the Kingdom of Heaven. In order to be saved, the individual has to join that community and remain in it until he reaches the place prepared for him by the Father in heaven. Beyond certain general prescriptions, the Master did not specify the form the Christian community was to take in future ages. The early Christians who continued the community tradition and formed small communities or churches tried to spell out in greater detail what had been merely suggested in parable form. The Kingdom of Heaven had to be realized in a fellowship of the faithful who made up the Church, while the continuing presence of the divine Spirit was to guide it as it carried out its saving function.

Though Royce is in basic agreement with the notion of the community and its mission of salvation as presented by Christianity, he is afraid that, in the course of history, dogmatic controversy has caused that ideal to become confused. This is unfortunate, since this ideal is important for contemporary man. Hence Royce tries to show that the basic elements of the Christian notion of community are preserved in his philosophy of loyalty.[59] It is a development with which we are already familiar. The individual feels both within and without a sense of disunity caused by conflicting desires and ambitions; these are a constant source of frustration in his personal life. The only way in which the individual can be saved—that is, can find fulfillment—is by becoming a member of the universal community of the loyal, "a community which, despite all warfare and jealousy, and despite all varieties of gods and of laws, is supreme in its value." [60] This is the ideal to which all humanity should strive—namely, to become members of the universal community and to achieve what Christianity calls salvation.[61]

[58] *Ibid.*, pp. 39–73.
[59] *Ibid.*, pp. 61–73.
[60] *Ibid.*, p. 72.
[61] *Ibid.*, p. 73.

The description above has been purposely brief, since it can be presupposed from our discussion of *The Philosophy of Loyalty*. We may note in passing that it should be apparent now, and will become even more so as we move on, how important the aforementioned book is to the understanding of Royce's thought: it looks back to his previous works and lays the groundwork for those that came later. Be that as it may, we shall assume that the notion of community as developed in Royce's philosophy of loyalty is familiar and concentrate on his understanding of the contrast between the doctrines of Christ and Paul.[62]

According to his interpretation, Christ left certain practical problems of community untouched. He described the Kingdom in its most rudimentary form, usually in parables, and did not give precise instructions for the future. He did this purposely so as to give the future Church free scope to develop according to the changing times. The spirit of love that was to prevail among all men was stressed, but, like the mustard seed, it must in the course of time take root and grow.

Paul made a new contribution to the notion of community although he believed that he received it from the Master's Spirit, which was moving in the Church. Paul introduced the notion of a new corporate being, which he called the body of Christ, whose head was the divine Master, now gloriously risen and reigning in heaven. Here we see a whole transformation of the meaning of neighbor as presented by the Gospels in the parable of the Samaritan. This parable describes only in general terms the notion that everyone is my neighbor and worthy of my love. But now my neighbor is seen to be more than the one whom I meet by the wayside and whom I momentarily stop to help in time of need. He is a fellow member of a community, a person whom I not only love but with whom I work for the common good and salvation of all mankind. Royce then concludes that Paul has also transformed the notion of Christian love, which before was seen to be extended only to separate individuals but which now goes out to all men as part of the one Christian community. Christian love, as taught by Paul, is nothing but the religion of loyalty Royce has described in his other works.

Royce maintains that his religion of loyalty is all the more important in view of the fact that Paul and the early Christians had supposed the end of the world to be near. They could not have envisioned the Christian community as enduring for vast ages of time. But, as a matter of fact, the small apostolic churches gradually gave way to the

[62] *Ibid.*, pp. 75–106.

organized religion of Christianity, the simple belief of the faithful in the basic notions of love and salvation in the Church grew into complicated dogmas, and the idea of the Christian community became largely lost. Royce thought that loyalty could do a service by recovering the universal community.

The Lost Individual   The second of the three Christian ideas discussed by Royce is the Lost Individual.[63] It is an idea that is foreign to the modern mind, for it teaches that man is weighed down by a burden of sin and that he is doomed to destruction if he does not receive divine intervention. Royce realizes that modern man balks at such a notion but insists that it is by no means something that has been dreamed up by the theologians. It is not peculiar to Christianity, but it can be discovered by anyone who takes the trouble to examine the experience of man as we know him empirically.

What Royce is really doing is describing the conflicts man experiences in himself and in his relation with the environment. The individual is the subject of deep-seated drives and inclinations. Some of these cannot be satisfied because of obstacles in the way; others meet with opposition from the moral principles according to which the individual guides his life. But most important of all is the social environment in which one lives. The individual sees himself in constant conflict with others. In primitive times, these oppositions arose because individuals asserted their private interests against others without any control from existing social laws. But the growth of civilization has increased rather than lessened such strife: the social group tries to settle conflicts by setting up structures to govern the behavior of the individuals within the community. But this only increases the burden because it brings the rights of the individual into conflict with the collectivity.

The problem, simply stated, is this: in civilized society, members of the community are taught independence, initiative, and self-reliance. They are encouraged to make their own decisions and to take up their own course of action. At the same time, as civilization becomes more complicated, further restrictions are placed upon the individual. The claims of the individual—the "ye shall be as gods" of Scripture—grow stronger and more unruly, and the restrictions on independent thought and action grow tighter. Royce sees in this the exemplification in natural terms of Paul's statement that he did not recognize the evil tenden-

[63] *Ibid.*, pp. 109–59.

cies within him until he came to a knowledge of the law that told him, "Thou shalt not covet." [64] Something similar happens to a member of the community: the necessary restrictions of community life become occasions for irritation within the individual. As a result, he becomes a "divided self" who, with Paul, finds himself omitting the good that he wants to do and doing the evil of which he disapproves.[65] Paul's answer was a community that was divinely instituted and guided by the abiding Spirit of God. But Royce again feels that, in order for this concept to be effective, it must be translated into natural terms. And so Paul's doctrine of the "mystery" that is the body of Christ, the Christian community through which the faithful are saved, becomes for Royce the community of those bound together in the religion of loyalty.

Sin and Atonement   The third Christian idea is atonement for sin. In discussing it, Royce's procedure is the same as with the other Christian ideas: he explains how it has been conceived by Christianity and then reinterprets it in terms of loyalty.[66] The Christian position on this subject is familiar enough, since it is contained in those passages of the Gospel that are most frequently quoted, and it is generally considered to form an essential part of the message the founder of Christianity came to proclaim. Briefly, it teaches that the faithful are members of the Kingdom through wholehearted love of God and neighbor. The individual commits himself to that Kingdom and to the good of all its members. Sin means that a member wilfully performs some act that is disruptive of love in his relations either with God or neighbor, and he thereby separates himself from God and the Kingdom. This separation can only be healed when the individual repents of his sin, recommits himself by love, and, in addition, becomes the object of God's forgiveness, without which repentance would be futile. Without such repentance and forgiveness, the sinner receives the stern judgment of eternal punishment.

Royce notes that in his day the doctrine of sin and atonement met with widespread opposition on the part of men. It is perhaps even more widely opposed today: "The modern man is one who does not believe in hell, and who is too busy to think about his own sins." [67] As

[64] Romans vii.7–13.
[65] Romans vii.18–25.
[66] *The Problem of Christianity*, pp. 227–67.
[67] *Ibid.*, p. 236.

before, Royce regrets the passing of notions he believes to be extremely important for the fulfillment of man in the world, and he attempts to reconsider the Christian idea of sin and atonement. He asks if there is any core of doctrine that can be retained and that can be meaningful to modern man. He again prescinds from theology and dogma in order to get at what we can find to be essential from human experience.

Since so many object to the terms "sin" and "sinner," Royce uses the word "traitor." A traitorous act involves two things: first, the traitor is one who has set for himself an ideal of finding his fulfillment through selfless dedication to a community. The good of the community has become his highest goal in life and the focal point of all his thoughts and activities. At the same time, this commitment is a voluntary one. The individual is free either to persevere in it by continuing his love for the members and his efforts on their behalf or to put an end to all this. The traitor is one who freely chooses to take back his love and break faith with those who have given him their love. He has betrayed love and has separated himself from the community.

What will atonement mean in the case of the traitor? Royce leaves aside the question of a penalty imposed upon the traitor by the community. He does not necessarily think that it is valueless but he considers the inner recognition on the part of the traitor—that he has violated love—to be much more important. Simply because he has put aside theological dogma and is considering only what he can learn from human experience, Royce is still less concerned with some sanction imposed by a deity. He presupposes that the traitor will inwardly repent of his wrongdoing, reaffirm his love for the members of the community, and rededicate himself to the task the community has set before itself. On their part, the members will accept in good faith the sincere manifestation of repentance and renewed love on the part of the traitor. It would seem that everything has been done to fulfill the meaning of atonement in any ordinary sense of the word. In fact, one would say that the ideal presented is a rather lofty one and worthy of admiration and imitation.

But Royce's position on atonement presents a higher ideal still. It goes beyond the case of those people who, through the traitorous act of a member of the community, have received some crushing blow and yet, in spite of it, have risen above their sorrow and engaged in activities of a demanding kind so that others might prosper. Royce is thinking of a person who has been the victim of a traitor's act. He has known what it means to be hated by men and rejected from their company: he has been ridiculed, humiliated, injured, and yet, through it all, he has remained loyal to the community. Let us suppose that this man comes forward to represent the community in order to atone for the traitorous act of another. He brings to his task competence, skill, and good judgment. In addition, he performs a task that could not have been done except for the fact that the traitor had performed his own malicious act; moreover, the act of atonement is of such value that the world is improved in a way that would not have been possible had the evil act never taken place. When all this has been done, we have an example of an act Royce considers to be an act of atonement as he understands it.

Many observations undoubtedly come to mind regarding Royce's position on atonement. One cannot help reflecting, for example, that even in the cases he has passed by in order to develop the example he finally accepts, he has presented a high ideal. In a world grown cynical about human goodness through overexposure to the inhumanity of man against man, it is refreshing to hear someone speak about repentance and amendment on the part of a traitor, forgiveness on the part of those who receive the traitor with love, the selfless act of one who has been crushed by a traitor's act and still devotes himself to the welfare of others. Royce claims to know such people in his own experience, and he is sure that others will recall examples of their own.

There are also some aspects of his final example that are a bit puzzling. For instance, the metaphysics of his idealism is apparent in his attempt to explain how the final act of atonement improves the world in a way that would not have been possible had a traitorous act not been committed. It is difficult not to suspect that this aspect of atonement was influenced by the idealist's position that evil actually contributes to universal good. This seems confirmed by the fact that atonement means that the "unscarred love" of the community can be restored only by the act of the humiliated person and not by the traitor himself, no matter how strong and sincere his repentance may be. This, too, seems under the influence of the tendency within idealism to insure that good is triumphant over evil and that the lost state of goodness is restored.

But there is another influence at work. The characteristics of the humiliated member who assumes the work of atonement are those Royce understands to be attributed to Christ by the Christian tradition. Christ's presence in the world and the work He performed are of such worth that "The world as a whole was a nobler and richer and worthier creation than it would have been if Adam had not sinned." [68] Royce claims that he drew his idea from real-life examples, but it is difficult not to see a direct influence of his own understanding of the Christian concept upon his own ideal. It is also difficult to believe that he would have presented his own position in quite the same terms but for this influence.

The Realm of Grace

There is one more aspect of Christianity that Royce discusses. It does not constitute a completely different idea from the three he develops, but it affects all of them. It is the question of divine grace.[69] In Pauline theology, grace is the supernatural means by which the convert becomes a member of the Christian community, enters into loving union with God and neighbor, and receives forgiveness from his sins, all of which are beyond his own natural strength to accomplish. Royce tries to interpret the Pauline notion of grace through his religion of loyalty. He maintains that entrance into the companionship of the loyal is likewise the work of grace, for in order that one may enter into that community, he must find it lovable and thus capable of overcoming his own spirit of independence. But this presupposes that those who are already members became so because they found the community lovable. And if we try to trace it back to its origins, the same problem is met: people will not join the community until they find it lovable, and it cannot be lovable until it is made up of dedicated members. We move in a vicious circle. The community of the loyal, then, needs some "grace" analogous to the grace of Christianity.

The last is a good example of the subtle mode of argument Royce is capable of using. It is not found often in the books we have been discussing, though it forms the methodology of a work like *The World and the Individual*. Without passing judgment on that work or on others in which the same methodology is employed, it is safe to say that the argument above is far from convincing. Moreover, Royce is not at all clear as to what he means by grace when it applies to loyalty. In *The Philosophy of Loyalty* and *The Sources of Religious Insight*,

[68] *Ibid.*, p. 319.
[69] *Ibid.*, pp. 163–213.

Royce had already proposed the thesis that the community of the loyal is superhuman and eternal. As we have seen, in these works he maintains that the whole dynamism of the human person for fulfillment can be satisfied only in a community that, in turn, finds its completion in God. This is a key point in the development of his philosophy of loyalty. Why does it become obscured in *The Problem of Christianity?* One reason I could suggest is that Royce becomes more concerned with giving point by point explanations in natural terms of what is contained in Christianity. Since the latter includes the notion of grace, he must find a place for it in his religion of loyalty, even though it cannot be directly translated. Or, very possibly, he thought that in his previous works on loyalty he had sufficiently shown that the union of the loyal reaches out to the divine. The superhuman character of loyalty had already been proposed by Royce, and his position on it had been made clear.

Conclusion

One of the objectives in the study of Josiah Royce's philosophy has been to show that he is in the mainstream of American thought. In spite of objections to the effect that he relied too heavily on the abstract methodology of the German tradition, he is clearly open to the lead of human experience. This is especially evident in his examination of Christianity and in his attempt to explain it in purely human terms. At the close of his study, he maintains that "Religion is, historically speaking, a product of certain human needs; and its endurance depends upon its power to meet those needs. A religion which ceases to strengthen hearts and to fulfill the just demands of the human spirit for guidance through the wilderness of this world, is doomed." [70] Though he is quite emphatic in his belief that religion goes beyond this material world, he is equally emphatic in his conviction that the message religion has to give can reach man only through his human experience —that is, through his needs, desires, longings, and satisfactions. Any religion that fails to do this will not survive.[71]

The critics of Roycean idealism have continually complained that he did not give enough consideration to man's existence in this world. If

[70] *Ibid.*, p. 385.
[71] *Ibid.*, p. 387.

this means that he did not treat explicitly and at length the specific problems facing his generation, the criticism is justified. But, in a general way, he did oppose any religion that would counsel a flight from the world, an indifference to modern civilization, or a disdain for the significance of time, change, and an open future. The Church, the beloved community, does not come into being fully formed; it must be created throughout the course of history.[72] In this work of creation, and in the quest for salvation, the loyal must become active in human affairs and must work strenuously to solve the social problems that arise in an industrial society.[73]

In his own time, Royce was accused of being too pessimistic. He wrote about sorrow, loss and defeat, about moral weakness and depravity, and about the impossibility of achieving salvation without superhuman help.[74] He was writing at a time when the current was turning away from a stress on man's helplessness before the elements and toward the emphasis on his ability to control the environment by scientific means. The great catchword was man's responsibility to create a new world by guiding the future progress of matter and of humanity. For the times in which he lived, Royce was sounding a familiar theme, but unfortunately it was a bit too familiar. The philosophy and theology then needed had to emphasize human responsibility.

Royce may well provide the ground for reconciliation of the extremes of American optimism and of European existential pessimism. He has said that man by himself is inadequate; he has never even intimated that man is completely helpless. In his recognition of the dim side of reality, he is well within the existentialist tradition, and that is why the French philosopher Gabriel Marcel, who knows that tradition well, has not hesitated to say that Royce marks the transition between absolute idealism and existentialist thought.[75] If this is so, he deserves to be heard again.

[72] *Ibid.*, pp. 355–59.
[73] *Ibid.*, pp. 398–402.
[74] *The Sources of Religious Insight*, pp. 224–26.
[75] G. Marcel, *Royce's Metaphysics*, trans. by V. and G. Ringer (Chicago: Henry Regnery, 1956), p. xii.

VII

EXPERIENCE AND
RELIGIOUS PHILOSOPHY

In the course of this book, particular emphasis has been placed on the philosophical orientation of William James. In a number of instances I tried to show similarities between his position and those of the other philosophers we have considered. Quite possibly, I have given the impression that I consider him to be the last word in American philosophy; this was certainly not my intention. If similarities have been highlighted, it is because they are there and because they are important.

What, to me, is especially significant in the thought of a man like

James is the emphasis he has placed on experience in its full meaning. As we have seen, he opposed every attempt to screen out aspects of experience that could in any way give us knowledge about ourselves or external reality. To him this was a dogmatism that could not be tolerated. This is why he was so much opposed to idealism: he saw in it a rationalism that tries to work out its ideas without sufficient reference to daily life. This procedure isolates specialized aspects of reality, makes them the whole of it, and leaves out what touches the human heart most deeply. We have seen James's critique of the attempt to defend the eternal goodness of things while ignoring human suffering. He also opposed the dogmatism of science, when it excludes every type of evidence save the empirical. In this he was one with Peirce, who pleaded with science not to block the road to inquiry. To both of these men, ordinary human experience is a source of information that must be respected if man hopes to learn more about himself and the universe in which he lives.

James's approach lays the groundwork for a sound psychology of the self. It involves an alertness to the possibilities that the promptings of the human spirit are data to be consulted in the search for a rational order of things and that, if properly handled, these data can give us knowledge of reality. But for all that, his position never received a hearing from the philosophical or scientific world, which became preoccupied with his term "passional nature." This term appears in the relatively early work, "The Will to Believe," and was taken to mean an emotionalism that is open to all kinds of illusion. By the time James came to write his *Pragmatism*, the phrase was considered to be clearly objectionable, and the concept that actually stood behind it was never seen in the context of his whole pragmatic theory. His contemporaries and his successors have embraced his theory of truth and empirical verification and have rejected the rest.

If James's personalism ever had any chance of being heard, the door was firmly closed on that chance by the rise of behaviorism under John B. Watson (1878–1958). In 1908, Watson went to Johns Hopkins University, where behaviorism was born. He reacted strongly against all forms of introspection in psychology. He also acknowledged the greatness of Wilhelm Wundt (1832–1920), the founder of experimental psychology in Leipzig, Germany, and conceded that Wundt favored a scientific psychology. But, he maintained, Wundt's psychology was only a compromise between philosophy, with its mind-body problem, and science. It discarded soul but retained conscious states as its field of study. This was true also of American schools of psychology set up by those who had gone to Leipzig to study under Wundt.

Psychologists studied consciousness by a method of introspection, which means looking in on what takes place within us. The only valid scientific method, it was held, was to treat consciousness as we would any other object in science—that is, through the objective method of laboratory technique.[1] For these reasons, Watson launched a campaign to make psychology as objective and as scientific as physics or chemistry. His campaign was so successful that in the 1920's American psychology went behaviorist. Though behaviorism subsequently went through a series of modifications, it has had a lasting influence on the development of American psychology. Its positive result was that psychology gained respectability as a science, opening the way for experimentation and research of a high order. Characteristically, the behavioral approach attempts to make psychology a strict positive science: it limits itself to externally observed behavior, it emphasizes statistical aids in the treatment of data, it gives wide scope to investigation of physiological functions, and it has made experimentation on animals an important tool for the study of human behavior.

The stress on the purely objective method has led to a strong bias against all forms of introspection or reflection, and psychology has become to a great extent a study of stimulus and response. Analysis of the self and its conscious operations has become suspect and is even branded as subjectivism. For these reasons psychology in America has failed to develop a theory concerning self-hood or problems affecting the self. One might even say that the self has completely vanished. The main source of the difficulty would seem to be the supposition that the self can be handled like any other object of scientific procedure: science must face objects as problems confronting the observer, and they must be dealt with in a completely objective manner. But, in many situations, the self stubbornly refuses to be treated as an object. It enters intimately into the data, so much so that it is both the observer and the observed.

[1] J. B. Watson, *Psychology from the Standpoint of a Behaviorist*, 3rd ed. rev. (Philadelphia: Lippincott, 1929), pp. 2–4; J. B. Watson, *Behaviorism*, rev. ed. (New York: Norton, 1930), pp. 3–5.

The French philosopher Gabriel Marcel grasped the point at issue when he made his famous distinction between "problem" and "mystery." He wrote:

> A problem is something which I meet, which I find complete before me, but which I can therefore lay siege to and reduce. But a mystery is something in which I am myself involved, and it can therefore only be thought of as *a sphere where the distinction between what is in me and what is before me loses its meaning and its initial validity.* A genuine problem is subject to an appropriate technique by the exercise of which it is defined: whereas a mystery, by definition, transcends every conceivable technique. It is, no doubt, always possible (logically and psychologically) to degrade a mystery so as to turn it into a problem. But this is a fundamentally vicious proceeding, whose springs might perhaps be discovered in a kind of corruption of the intelligence.[2]

We see that a problem concerns what is "out there," what confronts me, what I can handle empirically and scientifically. Mystery, however, is something that deeply involves the self and that can be grasped only by a process of reflection. In the one, I am a detached observer; in the other, I am deeply involved. In the one, the focal point of my attention is something external to me, and I introduce the self only at the peril of departing from a genuinely scientific approach; in the other, the self is excluded only at the risk of losing what is essential to the whole situation.

Marcel singles out love and evil as examples of mystery. We need not emphasize how much these touch the inner dimensions of the person. How can we ever handle them as problems? They can be adequately explained only insofar as they involve the self. Thus, evil merely stated or observed is no longer evil, because there is no longer one who suffers. The same is true of love: it is never something that merely comes to me, that merely "happens" to me, as though I were a passive bystander witnessing an event. In love the person is the unique source of the event—even as he is surrounded by it and penetrated through and through by it.[3] It would be incredible that, in an experience so intimate, the self could be excluded or one could fail to learn something about himself that he could not possibly observe by objective analysis.

[2] G. Marcel, *Being and Having: An Existentialist Diary* (New York: Harper & Row, 1965), p. 117.
[3] G. Marcel, *The Philosophy of Existentialism*, trans. by M. Harari (New York: Citadel Press, 1963), pp. 19–20.

This line of thought reveals Marcel's fundamental attitude toward philosophy: it is not a complete system, but a journey, a quest, an inquiry. It can even be looked upon as a wondering, almost like letting the mind range at will over whatever comes to it. It follows a line of thought for a while, then comes upon a point that needs further reflection. This new point becomes a digression from the main theme. Often the inquiry consists more in raising difficulties than in solving them.

In 1949 and 1950, Marcel was invited to give two series of Gifford Lectures. He states that he approached the task with some trepidation: surely now he would be expected to formulate into a system what had always been a quest.[4] But he declared this to be impossible. He preferred to be a Socrates rather than an Aristotle, and so he continued his usual form of inquiry.

He is never in a hurry; no quick, cryptic statement sums up what he has said. Marcel writes as he thinks, leisurely pursuing a line of thought, often without coming to any definite conclusion. For him philosophy is a phenomenological analysis that places man's fundamental situation squarely in the center of things. He aims to explore this situation as thoroughly as possible without hoping to achieve the exhaustive knowledge that is proper to science. In this way, he tries to avoid the anonymity that is proper to science. Though this is the only way in which the scientific man should proceed, its exclusive use leads to the "functional man" that is so much a part of our technological society. Man is no longer considered in terms of his inherent worth, but in terms of functions that can be tabulated on a card: his taxable earnings, his social security number, his draft status, his previous business experience, his skills, and so on. There is hardly an aspect of his life that has not been so recorded.

Marcel is frequently critical of modern technological society.[5] He claims that it undermines human freedom and creativity by reducing the individual to a "mass man"; it depersonalizes human relationships and turns them into functions; it is in danger of losing the higher values of affection, love, and friendship. Many Americans will never excuse him for what they would call his pessimistic view toward science and technology, in spite of his expressions of esteem for their impor-

[4] G. Marcel, *Mystery of Being*, trans. by G. S. Fraser (Chicago: Henry Regnery, 1960), I, p. 2.
[5] See G. Marcel, *Man Against Mass Society*, trans. by G. S. Fraser (Chicago: Henry Regnery, 1962).

tance. But if he has shown any bias against modern technology, it can be explained by his firm conviction that the self is of primary importance and by his anxiety that this truth be not lost from view.

Until recently this type of thinking had little effect on American psychology, but there are signs that the climate may be slowly changing. In a remarkable little book called *Existential Psychology*, several psychologists and psychotherapists have stated that psychology is seriously in need of an existential outlook.[6] They warn against an exclusively laboratory approach to the human person. Psychology must not limit itself to a study of conditioning, drives, or mechanisms, as important as these may be. It must consider man in the concrete situation of suffering, struggling, and experiencing conflicts; it must deal with the person as a unique source of freedom and responsibility and not merely as a battleground of drives and psychological problems; it must include among its data the ability of the individual to be conscious of himself and of his situation, an ability that marks man as distinctively human. The authors of *Existential Psychology* are implicitly maintaining that, for a full view of the person, we must take into consideration *all* the data of experience and not limit ourselves to what can be handled by laboratory techniques. If necessary, science must be revised in order to take into account the uniqueness of the individual.[7]

Within American philosophy, naturalists of the Deweyan type have succeeded in avoiding an extreme objectivism that would consider the human person as just one object among others or separated from everything else. The leading principle is that one cannot know the self —indeed cannot even be a self—except in interaction with the environment. Everything is seen in relation to the self: the self develops only in relation to and in interaction with things. A view of this kind changes radically one's whole attitude toward external reality, and its positive contributions can be seen especially in the work of Dewey. His analysis of interaction between self and environment merits a place among the "I-Thou" theories of the person that have become familiar in philosophical and theological literature.

[6] R. May, ed., *Existential Psychology* (New York: Random House, 1961). This book contains articles by Rollo May, Abraham Maslow, Herman Feifel, Carl Rogers, Gordon Allport, and Joseph Lyons. See also R. May, E. Angel, H. F. Ellenberger, eds., *Existence: A New Dimension in Psychiatry and Psychology* (New York: Basic Books, 1958).
[7] A. H. Maslow, "Existential Psychology—What's in It for Us?" *Existential Psychology*, pp. 57–59.

But there is a serious limitation to Dewey's approach. Beginning as an attempt to "de-objectify" things and people by bringing them into relationship with each other, the approach has changed quite subtly, the interaction itself becoming objectified and considered to be "out there." There is still a reluctance to get inside the self, even for a moment, for fear that one will become subjective. Dewey and those who follow his theory of interaction continue to stand outside the self, coming close to it but never entering the door. There is a failure to appreciate the fact that, though man is like every other being in his close relationship with the whole of the universe, he is unique in that he can reflect upon himself and see that the self is not completely absorbed in the environment.

Some philosophers have taken tentative steps lately toward a reflective psychology, the substance of which can be illustrated by considering the relation of the person to his own material body.[8] He may distinguish three levels of things. The first comprises objects that I have. For example, I have a book, a pen, a suit of clothes. These I recognize as belonging to me, as things that I "have," but in no real sense can I say that they are the real ego. No matter how important they may be for the expression of my personality, I realize that they do not constitute the self.

Then there is my body. It is certainly closer to me than the objects that I own; it is not completely external to me. For example, I do not say that my hand lifts the book but that I lift the book—unless, of course, I wish to specify the part of the body that is functioning. In this sense, I do not "have" my body, but I "am" my body.

By a further process of reflection, however, I can see that there is a dimension of the self that is in no sense "had" or "possessed" but that "has" everything else, even my body. This is seen most of all in personal decisions. At times the body is the ally of the self when its inclinations favor a choice that has been made. At other times the body is an obstacle opposing personal choice—as anyone will know who has made a decision to rise early in the morning.

Summing up this analysis, we may say that there are things that I have but that in no real sense I am; these are external objects that I

[8] For the development of this idea, I am indebted to the treatment of my colleague, J. Donceel, S.J., in his book *Philosophical Psychology*, 2nd ed. rev. (New York: Sheed & Ward, 1961), pp. 445–50. See also S. Strasser, *The Soul in Metaphysical and Empirical Psychology* (Pittsburgh: Duquesne University Press, 1957).

own. Then, there is an object that I both am and have, and that is my body. Lastly, there is that which I am but in no sense have, and this is the inner core of the self. It is this last dimension that, so far, American philosophers have not analyzed: they are afraid to enter into this area because they are sensitive to the dangers of an excessive introspectionism. As a result, very subtly the self remains objectified, no matter how much one may talk about interaction between the self and the environment. More significantly, an avenue of approach to more fruitful knowledge of self and reality is forever barred to the inquirer.

One serious difficulty is raised against any attempt to penetrate into the deeper dimensions of the self: it is argued that this penetration will lead only to probability and will sacrifice the demand for certainty that is so dear to the scientific mind. Science has shown how exacting and demanding is the evidence of the scientific laboratory and what precise results it can obtain. Impressed by this, American philosophers in the last few decades have embarked upon a movement that has caused Professor Lewis S. Feuer to say that American philosophy is "dead." [9] By contemporary standards, that should be enough to guarantee its immortality! Professor Feuer complains that academic philosophy has attempted to imitate the certainty of mathematics and the physical sciences; it has gone over to mathematical logic and linguistic analysis. This approach has taken over our philosophy journals, our annual conventions, and whole departments at many of our leading universities. It is posing as the authentic voice of philosophy in contemporary America.

What is the result of this trend? In Professor Feurer's view, American philosophy has screened out the problems of men and has taken for its subject matter only what can be handled by numbers, symbols, or dictionary terms. Because of this exclusive orientation, our philosophers have made little or no impact on the intellectual history of contemporary America. Young students come to philosophy with an enthusiasm generated by some religious problem or by a search for a way of life, but their enthusiasm is soon stifled by endless quibbling over questions that have no reference to real life.

Now, no one can find fault with a sincere desire to achieve certainty; the difficulty comes when we try to determine what we mean by "certainty." The difficulty goes back at least to Hume, who made the rigid

[9] Lewis S. Feuer, "American Philosophy is Dead," *New York Times*, April 24, 1966, Sec. VI, pp. 30–31, 122–24.

distinction between certainty and probability. Certainty, which for Hume meant knowledge, includes propositions of quantity and number, and they are the result of demonstration. Probability, or belief, includes matters of fact, such as the existence of the self and the external world. According to this division, certainty, or knowledge in the genuine sense, is confined to a narrow range of truths, principally mathematical propositions. All else, and this includes practically every other statement we can make, is relegated to the domain of probability.[10]

We can sympathize with Hume for attempting to tighten up the meaning of certainty by modeling it along scientific—and by this he meant mathematical—lines. The excitement caused by the growth of science had profoundly affected men's approach to traditional philosophical problems. René Descartes (1596–1650) had a vision of one science, built according to the model of mathematics, done by one man. He tells us that he considered his proofs for the existence of the self, God, and the external world to surpass in certainty and evidence the demonstrations of geometry.[11]

Baruch Spinoza (1632–77) developed an "ethics demonstrated according to the geometrical order," so we should not be surprised that Hume thought along similar lines. Enamored of the certainty of mathematics and aware of errors regarding matters of fact, Hume drew a sharp line between mathematics and facts. Once he had done this, he filled page after page in trying to establish his own existence and that of the external world. He could not prove these philosophically, since philosophy for him had come to mean what we know with certainty. Yet he had to admit that we do acknowledge the existence of self and the external world from "ordinary experience." Hume almost painted himself into a corner by the stringency of the requirements that he insisted be met if something were to be designated knowledge. But he was honest enough to admit that what he doubted as a philosopher he believed as an ordinary man.[12]

By far, the greater number of things men accept as true do not have the clear-cut certainty of mathematics and logic. Peirce was eminently aware of this fact when he made a distinction between theoretical

[10] D. Hume, A Treatise of Human Nature, Book I, Part III (Garden City, N.Y.: Doubleday, 1961), pp. 63–164.
[11] R. Descartes, "Dedication," Meditations on First Philosophy, trans. by E. S. Holdune and G. R. T. Ross (New York: Dover, 1955), I, pp. 133–37.
[12] Hume, op. cit., Part IV, Sec. II.

science—which includes mathematics (with its subdivision of mathematical logic), philosophy (with its subdivision of logic), and the physical sciences—and practical science—which include vitally important matters. Regarding theoretical science, he called for a precision in method and results befitting the nature of the subject. His great interest in this branch of knowledge is evident from the amount of space he devoted to it in his written works and from the original contributions he made to it, especially in the areas of logic and mathematical logic. But his great insistence on exactitude should not make us think that he was obsessed with the desire for absolute certainty or that he thought he could achieve it: he was ready to concede that error was possible even in mathematics and the positive sciences.[13] Moreover, though he extolled the precision of theoretical science, we should not forget that he had a high regard for evidence in practical affairs. We have shown how Peirce accepted evidence drawn from the dynamism of man's personality toward growth and fulfillment. He was careful to point out, too, that, in spite of his scientific background and the high standards he had set for exactness, the evidence he proposed was "eminently sane and wholesome" [14] and that he was ready to shape his life according to it. The acceptance of such evidence he called belief, which he defined more fully as the adoption of a "principle upon which we are willing to act." [15] This is exactly what James was saying, and both would agree to the following proposition: I can accept as true and make the guiding principle of my life whatever it is reasonable to accept, that being whatever contributes to the growth of the human person.

John Dewey, too, for all his insistence on the scientific method, accepted something less than empirical or scientific accuracy. Take, for example, the ideal he proposed as the goal of human existence—that is, self-realization. Man achieves this ideal when he casts off selfishness and labors for the good of mankind now and in the future. For Dewey, this idea was the motive for human thinking, striving, and cooperative activity, and it was also the fulfillment of man's hopes and aspirations. And where does he ever justify empirically the validity of that goal? Nowhere. Dewey felt sure that men would see the value of it without

[13] 1. 55, 131, 248; 2. 75. A. Burks, C. Hartshorne, and P. Weiss, eds., *Collected Papers of Charles Sanders Peirce* (Cambridge, Mass.: Harvard University Press, 1931–58), 8 vols. References are by volume and paragraph.
[14] 1. 662.
[15] 1. 636.

having to have it proven. In this respect, the goal of self-realization is closely connected with his esthetic theory. He did not think that you could prove to an individual that a work of art is esthetic. You can point the way to an esthetic experience, you can prepare a man for it, but, in the end, he either appreciates the work of art in an esthetic way or he does not; no amount of scientific or mathematical manipulation can convince another of an object's esthetic value. The same is true of the goal of self-realization: either one sees the value of working for the good of humanity or one does not. All that can be done is to prepare the way so that the value of such an ideal will be appreciated by the individual.[16]

Whitehead is another who has drawn deeply from personal experience. It was not through any disillusionment with mathematics or the philosophy of science that he turned to metaphysics and theism. He simply lifted his vision beyond limited problems to some ultimate meaning behind all reality. He looked for the "harmony of harmonies" that would fulfill the human urge for satisfaction both on the individual and cultural levels. His vision widened until it embraced all of reality, for he saw the drive for higher perfection as characteristic of all beings in the universe. Finally, Royce, in seeking something that would unify all aspects of human existence, placed full confidence in the dictates of human experience, despite the dry abstractionism of his idealistic philosophy. His search brought him to see that only in community could man find fulfillment, and his discontent with discontent led him to the conclusion that true loyalty must find its completion in God.

These men were one, then, in their trust in human experience and in their conviction that its dictates gave ample grounds for a reasonable judgment. The conclusions reached were sufficient to elicit a commitment of their whole lives without fear that they would be disappointed.

It is evident from the study of James, Peirce, Dewey, Whitehead, and Royce that the orientation of American philosophy in its classical period was experiential. But it was also mathematical and logical, as is clear from the work of Peirce and Whitehead, who combined what is best in both orientations.

[16] Elsewhere I have tried to show that, in his ethical theory, Dewey does not adhere strictly to the empirical method in grounding the notion of the good and the "ought." See my article "Naturalistic Ethics: Problem of Method," *The New Scholasticism*, Vol. 40, No. 3 (July, 1966), pp. 285–311.

We have dwelt so long on the place of personal experience in the thought of our five philosophers because it is important for an understanding of their religious philosophy. Four of them not only made personal experience a central part of their thought, but followed its lead until it brought them to a deity; Dewey alone stopped short of that goal.

The men who came to a deity did not do so by a casual examination of their inner experiences, but by a carefully thought-out argument after much soul-searching. The controlling thought was that, without God, the inner drive of the human personality for completion would be denied. The denial these men were talking about is total. They did not mean that this or that desire would have to go unfulfilled, but that the whole personality would be deprived of that without which everything else is meaningless. And so they simply asked themselves if they were willing to accept such a view of human existence. Each in his own way decided that this would be irrational; they felt justified in believing that there is something behind finite reality that gives it an ultimate meaning and that makes life worthwhile.

We know, of course, that Dewey rejected such belief. He did it neither arrogantly nor triumphantly. One can easily point out factors that influenced his decision: more so than the other four, he saw the importance of involvement in the world for human growth and he felt that theism and religion essentially alienated man from the world and, hence, from the possibility of development. He committed himself to a naturalistic view and placed on mutual cooperation the hopes of mankind for present and future progress. He saw the goal he proposed as sufficient to sustain man and nourish his inner drive for fulfillment. For all his opposition to theism and religion, Dewey deserves a place in this book: he has given guidelines for any future attempt to work out a theory of God and religion in contemporary society.

This is, indeed, the value one can derive from the study of all five philosophers selected for discussion: they can help us toward a viable religion today. They have emphasized the value of human experience; they have cautioned against the hardening of doctrine, rite, and ritual, which would cause a loss of contact with contemporary needs; and they have lamented the scandalous divisions that have opened between the churches. It is rather startling to read some statement by a modern theologian which is hailed as revolutionary only to find it almost verbatim in the works of our own American philosophers.

Conclusion

Just as it is difficult to assess how religious America really is, so is it difficult to predict whether it will be more religious or more secular in the future. At the moment, the mystic chant of "God is dead" seems like a rising wind drowning out all other voices. Whether it will whip up into a storm or blow itself out to the sea of oblivion cannot now be foretold.

To some, it is a puzzling and even a disturbing fact that the four philosophers who accepted God did not belong to any particular religious group. One explanation is that they were highly individualistic and, hence, could never conform to particular beliefs or to a particular way of life. This may have some surface plausibility, especially in the case of Peirce, who found it difficult to get along with people, but we are not dealing here with men who, after the fashion of Thoreau, took themselves off to a Walden Pond to live in isolation from all human companionship. We have to take these men at their word. In their view, religious rites and expressions of creed were no longer applicable to a contemporary world; they missed the Gospel spirit of charity; they were scandalized by the divisions between the churches; they were dismayed that religion lost its appeal for men as soon as they became better educated. For them these issues were crucial enough to give up traditional religion and to go their own way in following the God in whom they believed.

For all that, the philosophers we have considered present insights, modes of approach, and outlooks that can be fruitful for religion in a modern age. If I have insisted on anything, it is that American philosophers have shown that the way of personal experience is a starting point that can lead to theism. With William James, I can say only that this way to God is not one that I am forced to take, but one that I *may* take, that I have a *right* to take, and still remain a reasonable man.

SELECTED
BIBLIOGRAPHY

SELECTED
BIBLIOGRAPHY

Chapter I

BERTOCCI, PETER ANTHONY. *Introduction to the Philosophy of Religion*. Englewood Cliffs, N. J.: Prentice-Hall, 1951.

BLAU, JOSEPH L. *Men and Movements in American Philosophy*. Englewood Cliffs, N. J.: Prentice-Hall, 1952.

BRIGHTMAN, EDGAR SHEFFIELD. *A Philosophy of Religion*. Englewood Cliffs, N. J.: Prentice-Hall, 1940.

CALLAHAN, DANIEL, ed. *The Secular City Debate*. New York: Macmillan, 1966.

COX, HARVEY. *The Secular City*. New York: Macmillan, 1965.

EDWARDS, DAVID L., ed. *The Honest to God Debate*. Philadelphia: Westminster Press, 1963.

HERBERG, WILL. *Protestant, Caholic, Jew: An Essay in American Religious Sociology*. 2nd ed. rev. Garden City, N. Y.: Doubleday, 1960.

HOFSTADTER, RICHARD. *Social Darwinism in American Thought*. Philadelphia: University of Pennsylvania Press, 1945.

"HUMANIST MANIFESTO." *The New Humanist*, Vol. 6 (May–June, 1933), pp. 58–61.

KRIKORIAN, YERVANT H., ed. *Naturalism and the Human Spirit*. New York: Columbia University Press, 1944.

NIEBUHR, REINHOLD. *An Interpretation of Christian Ethics*. New York: Harper & Brothers, 1935.

NIEBUHR, REINHOLD. *Moral Man and Immoral Society.* New York: Scribner's, 1932.

RANDALL, JOHN HERMAN, JR. Review of Robert J. Roth's *John Dewey and Self-Realization. Thought,* Vol. 39, No. 155 (Winter, 1964), pp. 629–31.

ROBINSON, JOHN A. T. *Honest to God.* Philadelphia: Westminster Press, 1963.

ROTH, ROBERT J. "The Challenge of American Naturalism." *Thought,* Vol. 39, No. 155 (Winter, 1964), pp. 559–84.

SCHNEIDER, HERBERT W. *A History of American Philosophy.* New York: Columbia University Press, 1946.

SMITH, H. SHELTON, ROBERT T. HANDY, and LEFFERTS A. LOETSCHER, eds. *American Christianity: An Historical Interpretation with Representative Documents.* New York: Scribner's, 1963. 2 vols.

SMITH, JOHN E. *The Spirit of American Philosophy.* New York: Oxford University Press, 1963.

TAYLOR, GEORGE ROGERS, ed. *The Turner Thesis: Concerning the Role of the Frontier in American History.* 2nd ed. rev. Boston: Heath, 1956.

Chapter II

PRIMARY SOURCES

JAMES, WILLIAM. *Essays in Radical Empiricism.* New York: Longmans, Green, 1912.

———. *The Meaning of Truth.* New York: Longmans, Green, 1909.

———. *A Pluralistic Universe.* New York: Longmans, Green, 1909.

———. *Pragmatism.* New York: Longmans, Green, 1908.

———. *The Varieties of Religious Experience.* New York: Longmans, Green, 1902.

———. *The Will to Believe and Other Essays in Popular Philosophy.* New York: Longmans, Green, 1897.

COMMENTARIES

BARRETT, WILLIAM. *Irrational Man.* Garden City, N. Y.: Doubleday, 1958.

KENNEDY, GAIL, ed. *Pragmatism and American Culture.* Boston: Heath, 1950.

LOVEJOY, ARTHUR O. *The Thirteen Pragmatisms and Other Essays.*
Baltimore, Md.: Johns Hopkins Press, 1963.
LUBAC, HENRI DE. *La pensée religieuse du Père Teilhard de Chardin.*
Paris: Aubier, 1962.
MAY, ROLLO, ed. *Existential Psychology.* New York: Random House,
1961.
PERRY, RALPH BARTON. *In the Spirit of William James.* New Haven,
Conn.: Yale University Press, 1938.
———. *The Thought and Character of William James.* Boston:
Little, Brown, 1936. 2 vols.
PERSONS, STOW, ed. *Evolutionary Thought in America.* New Haven,
Conn.: Yale University Press, 1950.
ROTH, ROBERT J. "American Pragmatic-Naturalist Thought." In
Jesse A. Mann and Gerald F. Kreyche, eds. *Perspectives on Reality.*
New York: Harcourt, Brace & World, 1966, pp. 290–309.
———. "The Religious Philosophy of William James." *Thought,*
Vol. 61, No. 161 (Summer, 1966), pp. 249–81.
WIENER, PHILIP P. *Evolution and the Founders of Pragmatism.*
Cambridge, Mass.: Harvard University Press, 1949.

Chapter III

PRIMARY SOURCES

BUCHLER, JUSTUS, ed. *Philosophical Writings of Peirce.* New York:
Dover Publications, 1955.
BURKS, ARTHUR, CHARLES HARTSHORNE, and PAUL WEISS, eds. *Collected Papers of Charles Sanders Peirce.* Cambridge, Mass.: Harvard
University Press, 1931–58. 8 vols.
COHEN, MORRIS R. *Chance, Love and Logic: Philosophical Essays
by C. S. Peirce.* New York: Braziller, 1956.
TOMAS, VINCENT, ed. *Charles S. Peirce: Essays in the Philosophy of
Science.* New York: Liberal Arts Press, 1957.
WIENER, PHILIP P., ed. *Charles S. Peirce: Selected Writings.* New
York: Dover Publications, 1966.

COMMENTARIES

BUCHLER, JUSTUS. *Charles Peirce's Empiricism.* New York: Harcourt,
Brace & World, 1939.
FEIBLEMAN, J. K. *An Introduction to Peirce's Philosophy.* New
York: Harper & Brothers, 1946.

GALLIE, W. B. *Peirce and Pragmatism.* Baltimore, Md.: Penguin, 1952.

GOUDGE, T. A. *The Thought of C. S. Peirce.* Toronto: University of Toronto Press, 1950.

MURPHEY, MURRAY G. *The Development of Peirce's Philosophy.* Cambridge, Mass.: Harvard University Press, 1961.

ROTH, ROBERT J. "Charles Sanders Peirce: 1839–1914." *America,* Vol. 111, No. 5 (August 1, 1964), pp. 108–10.

————. "Is Peirce's Pragmatism Anti-Jamesian?" *International Philosophical Quarterly,* Vol. 5, No. 4 (December, 1965), pp. 541–63.

Chapter IV

PRIMARY SOURCES

DEWEY, JOHN. "Antinaturalism in Extremis." In Yervant H. Krikorian, ed. *Naturalism and the Human Spirit.* New York: Columbia University Press, 1944, pp. 1–16.

————. *Art as Experience.* New York: Minton, Balch, 1934.

————. *The Child and the Curriculum and the School and Society.* Chicago: University of Chicago Press, 1956.

————. *A Common Faith.* New Haven, Conn.: Yale University Press, 1934.

————. *Democracy and Education.* New York: Macmillan, 1916.

————. *Experience and Education.* New York: Macmillan, 1939.

————. *Experience and Nature.* New York: Norton, 1929.

————. "From Absolutism to Experimentalism." In George P. Adams and William Pepperell Montague, eds. *Contemporary American Philosophy,* Vol. 2. New York: Macmillan, 1930, pp. 13–27.

————. *Individualism Old and New.* New York: Minton, Balch, 1930.

————. *The Influence of Darwin on Philosophy.* New York: Holt, 1910.

————. *Liberalism and Social Action.* New York: Putnam's, 1935.

————. *Philosophy and Civilization.* New York: Minton, Balch, 1931.

————. *The Public and Its Problems.* New York: Holt, 1927.

————. *Reconstruction in Philosophy.* 2nd ed. rev. Boston: Beacon Press, 1948.

————. "Religion and Our Schools." In Joseph Ratner, ed. *Characters and Events,* Vol. 2. New York: Holt, 1929, pp. 504–16.

————. *Theory of the Moral Life.* New York: Holt, 1960.

COMMENTARIES

BLEWETT, JOHN, ed. *John Dewey: His Thought and Influence*. New York: Fordham University Press, 1960.

CREMIN, LAWRENCE A. "The Progressive Movement in American Education." *Harvard Educational Review*, Vol. 27, No. 4 (Fall, 1957), pp. 251–70.

————. *The Transformation of the School: Progressivism in American Education, 1876–1957*. New York: Knopf, 1961.

DENNES, WILLIAM R. *Some Dilemmas of Naturalism*. New York: Columbia University Press, 1960.

DYKHUIZEN, GEORGE. "An Early Chapter in the Life of John Dewey." *Journal of the History of Ideas*, Vol. 13, No. 4 (October, 1952), pp. 563–72.

FELDMAN, W. T. *The Philosophy of John Dewey: A Critical Analysis*. Baltimore, Md.: Johns Hopkins Press, 1934.

GEIGER, GEORGE R. *John Dewey in Perspective*. New York: Oxford University Press, 1958.

HANDLIN, OSCAR. *John Dewey's Challenge to Education*. New York: Harper & Brothers, 1959.

HOOK, SIDNEY. *John Dewey: An Intellectual Portrait*. New York: John Day, 1939.

————, ed. *John Dewey: Philosopher of Science and Freedom*. New York: Dial Press, 1950.

————. *The Quest for Being*. New York: St. Martin's Press, 1961.

————. "Some Memories of John Dewey." *Commentary*. Vol. 14, No. 9 (September, 1952), pp. 244–53.

KRIKORIAN, YERVANT H., ed. *Naturalism and the Human Spirit*. New York: Columbia University Press, 1944.

LAMONT, CORLISS, ed. *Dialogue on John Dewey*. New York: Hanzon Press, 1959.

————. "New Light on Dewey's *Common Faith*." *The Journal of Philosophy*, Vol. 58, No. 1 (January 5, 1961), pp. 21–28.

LAMPRECHT, STERLING P. "Naturalism and Religion." In Yervant H. Krikorian, ed. *Naturalism and the Human Spirit*. New York: Columbia University Press, 1944, pp. 17–39.

LARRABEE, HAROLD A. "Naturalism in America." In Yervant H. Krikorian, ed. *Naturalism and the Human Spirit*. New York: Columbia University Press, 1944, pp. 319–53.

OLAFSEN, F. A. Review of S. Hook's *The Quest for Being*. *The Journal of Philosophy*, Vol. 59, No. 13 (June 21, 1962), pp. 355–59.

PRAT, J. B. *Naturalism*. New Haven, Conn.: Yale University Press, 1939.

RANDALL, JOHN HERMAN, JR. "The Nature of Naturalism." In Yervant H. Krikorian, ed. *Naturalism and the Human Spirit*. New York: Columbia University Press, 1944, pp. 354–82.

ROMANELL, PATRICK. *Toward a Critical Naturalism*. New York: Macmillan, 1958.

ROODKOWSKY, NIKITA D. "Marxism's Appeal for American Intellectuals." *The Catholic World*, Vol. 192, No. 1147 (October, 1959), pp. 35–39.

ROTH, ROBERT J. "American Pragmatic-Naturalist Thought." In Jesse A. Mann and Gerald F. Kreyche, eds. *Perspectives on Reality*. New York: Harcourt, Brace & World, 1966, pp. 290–309.

———. "The Challenge of American Naturalism." *Thought*, Vol. 39, No. 155 (Winter, 1964), pp. 559–84.

———. "The Importance of Matter." *America*, Vol. 109, No. 25 (December 21, 1963), pp. 792–94.

———. *John Dewey and Self-Realization*. Englewood Cliffs, N. J.: Prentice-Hall, 1963.

———. "Naturalistic Ethics: Problem of Method." *The New Scholasticism*, Vol. 40, No. 3 (July, 1966), pp. 285–311.

SCHILPP, PAUL ARTHUR, ed. *The Philosophy of John Dewey*. 2nd ed. rev. New York: Tudor Publishing, 1951.

SHELDON, W. H. "Critique of Naturalism." *The Journal of Philosophy*, Vol. 42, No. 10 (May 10, 1945), pp. 253–70.

THOMAS, MILTON H. *John Dewey: A Centennial Bibliography*. Chicago: University of Chicago Press, 1962.

WHITE, MORTON G. *The Origin of Dewey's Instrumentalism*. New York: Columbia University Press, 1943.

Chapter V

PRIMARY SOURCES

WHITEHEAD, ALFRED NORTH. *Adventures of Ideas*. New York: Macmillan, 1933.

———. *Essays in Science and Philosophy*. New York: Philosophical Library, 1947.

———. *Modes of Thought*. New York: Macmillan, 1938.

———. *Process and Reality*. New York: Macmillan, 1929.

———. *Religion in the Making*. New York: Macmillan, 1929.

———. *Symbolism: Its Meaning and Effect*. New York: Macmillan, 1927.

BIXLER, JULIUS. "Whitehead's Theory of Religion." In Paul Arthur Schilpp, ed. *The Philosophy of Alfred North Whitehead*. 2nd ed. New York: Tudor Publishing, 1951, pp. 487–512.

CHRISTIAN, WILLIAM. *An Interpretation of Whitehead's Metaphysics*. New Haven, Conn.: Yale University Press, 1959.

ELY, STEPHEN. *Religious Availability of Whitehead's God*. Madison, Wis.: University of Wisconsin Press, 1942.

HARTSHORNE, C. "Whitehead, the Anglo-American Philosopher-Scientist." *Proceedings of the American Catholic Philosophical Association*, Vol. 35, (1961), pp. 163–71.

————. "Whitehead's Idea of God." In Paul Arthur Schilpp, ed. *The Philosophy of Alfred North Whitehead*. 2nd ed. New York: Tudor Publishing, 1951, pp. 513–60.

HOCKING, WILLIAM ERNEST. "Whitehead as I Knew Him." *The Journal of Philosophy*, Vol. 58, No. 19 (September 14, 1961), pp. 505–16.

LAWRENCE, NATHANIEL. *Whitehead's Philosophical Development*. Berkeley, Calif.: University of California Press, 1956.

LECLERC, IVOR. *Whitehead's Metaphysics*. New York: Macmillan, 1958.

LOWE, VICTOR. *Understanding Whitehead*. Baltimore, Md.: Johns Hopkins Press, 1962.

MAYS, WOLFE. *The Philosophy of Whitehead*. New York: Macmillan, 1959.

PRICE, LUCIEN. *Dialogues of Alfred North Whitehead*. Boston: Little, Brown, 1954.

RUSSELL, BERTRAND. "Alfred North Whitehead." *Harper's Magazine*, Vol. 205, No. 1231 (December, 1952), pp. 50–52.

SCHILPP, PAUL ARTHUR, ed. *The Philosophy of Alfred North Whitehead*, 2nd ed. New York: Tudor Publishing, 1951.

SELLARS, ROY WOOD. "Philosophy of Organism and Physical Realism." In Paul Arthur Schilpp, ed. *The Philosophy of Alfred North Whitehead*, 2nd ed. New York: Tudor Publishing, 1951, pp. 405–34.

STOKES, WALTER. "A Select and Annotated Bibliography of Alfred North Whitehead." *The Modern Schoolman*, Vol. 39, No. 1 (January, 1962), pp. 135–51.

WEISS, PAUL. "Alfred North Whitehead: 1861–1947." *The Atlantic Monthly*, Vol. 181, No. 5 (May, 1948), pp. 105–07.

Chapter VI

PRIMARY SOURCES

ROYCE, JOSIAH. *The Conception of God.* New York: Macmillan, 1897.

———. *The Philosophy of Loyalty.* New York: Macmillan, 1908.

———. *Primer of Logical Analysis for the Use of Composition Students.* San Francisco, Calif.: Bancroft, 1881.

———. *The Problem of Christianity.* New York: Macmillan, 1913. 2 vols.

———. *The Religious Aspect of Philosophy.* Boston: Houghton Mifflin, 1885.

———. *The Sources of Religious Insight.* New York: Scribner's, 1912.

———. *The Spirit of Modern Philosophy.* Boston: Houghton Mifflin, 1892.

———. "Words of Professor Royce at the Walton Hotel in Philadelphia." *The Philosophical Review,* Vol. 25, No. 3 (May, 1916), pp. 507–14.

———. *The World and the Individual.* New York: Macmillan, 1900–01. 2 vols.

COMMENTARIES

BURANELLI, VINCENT. *Josiah Royce.* New York: Twayne Publishers, 1964.

FUSS, P. L. *The Moral Philosophy of Josiah Royce.* Cambridge, Mass.: Harvard University Press, 1965.

HOWISON, G. H. "Josiah Royce: The Significance of His Work in Philosophy." *The Philosophical Review,* Vol. 25, No. 3 (May, 1916), pp. 231–44.

MARCEL, GABRIEL. *Royce's Metaphysics.* Trans. by Virginia and Gordon Ringer. Chicago: Regnery, 1956.

PALMER, GEORGE HERBERT. "In Dedication: Josiah Royce." In Clifford Barrett, ed. *Contemporary Idealism in America.* New York: Russell and Russell, 1964, pp. 1–9.

PERRY, RALPH BARTON. "Two American Philosophers: William James and Josiah Royce." In *In the Spirit of William James.* New Haven, Conn.: Yale University Press, 1938, pp. 1–43.

RANDALL, JOHN HERMAN, JR. "Josiah Royce and American Idealism." *The Journal of Philosophy,* Vol. 63, No. 3 (February 3, 1966), pp. 57–83.

Santayana, George. "Josiah Royce." In *Character and Opinion in the United States*. New York: Scribner's, 1920, pp. 97–138.
Smith, John E. *Royce's Social Infinite: The Community of Interpretation*. New York: Liberal Arts Press, 1950.

Chapter VII

Descartes, René, "Meditations on First Philosophy." In *The Philosophical Works of Descartes*, Vol. 1. Trans. by Elizabeth S. Haldane and G. R. T. Ross. New York: Dover Publications, 1955, pp. 132–99.
Donceel, Joseph. *Philosophical Psychology*. 2nd ed. rev. New York: Sheed & Ward, 1961.
Feuer, Lewis S. "American Philosophy Is Dead." *The New York Times*, (April 24, 1966), Sec. VI, pp. 30–31, 122–24.
Hume, David. *A Treatise of Human Nature*. Garden City, N. Y.: Doubleday, 1961.
Marcel, Gabriel. *Being and Having: An Existentialist Diary*. New York: Harper & Row, 1965.
————. *Man Against Mass Society*. Trans. by G. S. Fraser. Chicago: Regnery, 1962.
————. *The Mystery of Being*. Trans. by G. S. Fraser. Chicago: Regnery, 1960. 2 vols.
————. *The Philosophy of Existentialism*. Trans. by Manya Harari. New York: Citadel Press, 1963.
May, Rollo, ed. *Existential Psychology*. New York: Random House, 1961.
————. Ernest Angel, and Henri F. Ellenberger, eds. *Existence: A New Dimension in Psychiatry and Psychology*. New York: Basic Books, 1958.
Strasser, Stephan. *The Soul in Metaphysical and Empirical Psychology*. Pittsburgh, Pa.: Duquesne University Press, 1957.
Watson, John B. *Behaviorism*. 2nd rev. ed. New York: Norton, 1930.
————. *Psychology from the Standpoint of a Behaviorist*. 3rd ed. rev. Philadelphia: Lippincott, 1929.

INDEX

INDEX

Existential Psychology, 61n., 180, 180n.
Existentialism, 61, 174
Experience and Nature, 25n., 89

Fechner, Gustav, 57
Feuer, Lewis S., 182, 182n.
Freedom, man as source of, 17

Gilman, Daniel, 64
God, 10, 11, 14, 30, 61, 62, 186, 187; attributes of, 44; concern of, that "nothing be lost" (Whitehead), 139; "death" of, 8, 11, 187; Dewey's views on, 90, 93, 103–04, 107, 186; existence of, issue of, 5, 44, 53, 54, 72–73, 159; as finite, 132; and human suffering, 130; as immanent, 131; individual response to (Whitehead), 135–37; James's views on, 30, 31, 42, 44, 46, 47, 50–58, 59, 61; metaphysical argument for, 11; negated by American naturalism, 13, 51–52; as noncreator, 132; of process (Whitehead), 124, 127–30, 135, 138; reality of (Peirce), 70–74, 75, 76, 83; and reconciliation of extremes (Whitehead), 131–32; as redeemer, 130; scholastic proofs of, 44; and secularized religion, 4; transcendent, 131; as "ultimate irrationality" (Whitehead), 125–26; as ultimate value (Whitehead), 127; *see also* Religion; Theism; Theology
Grace, of Christianity, 172

Harper, William R., 86
Harris, William T., 16, 86
Hartshorne, Charles, 112, 114, 114n.
Hegel, G. W. F., 16, 17, 148; and Dewey, 17, 92–95; and Royce, 149, 152
Herberg, Will, 3, 3n., 4, 5, 6, 6n., 7, 8, 10; quoted, 4
History of American Philosophy, A, 18n.
Hocking, William E., 110n., 112, 112n., 113, 113n., 114, 114n.
Hofstadter, R., 16n.
Hook, Sidney, 87, 87n., 89n., 104, 104n.
Howison, George H., 148n., 149, 149n., 150
Human personality, 21–22, 69, 75, 108, 161, 186; and dualism of "secular" and "spiritual," 99–101
Human purpose, 17, 25
Humanism, secular, 6
"Humanist Manifesto," 3, 3n.
Hume, David, 11, 182, 183, 183n.
Huxley, Thomas, 91

Idealism, rationalistic, 12, 17, 21, 30, 45, 56, 58, 153, 176; Hegel's, 17, 92–95; Royce's, 146, 147, 150, 154, 159, 171, 173; *see also* Rationalism
In the Spirit of William James, 148n., 151n.
Inquiry, theory of, 23
Interpretation of Christian Ethics, An, 2, 2n.
Introduction to the Philosophy of Religion, 25n.
Introspectionism, 176, 177, 182
Irrational Man, 61n.

"Is Life Worth Living?" 32n., 39–40

James, Henry, 78
James, William, 12, 13, 14, 15, 18, 20, 27–62, 63, 114, 141, 142, 175, 187; on empiricism, 53–54, 58, 59, 84; *Essays in Radical Empiricism*, 30, 60n.; faith defined, 55; and God, views on, 30, 31, 42, 44, 46, 47, 50–58, 59, 61; "Is Life Worth Living?" 32n., 39–40; on limitations of science, 43, 46, 58, 141, 176; *Meaning of Truth*, 54n., 56, 56n.; naturalism of, 58–60; and Peirce, 63, 64, 65, 72, 77–84, 184; personalism of, 176; philosophy, teaching of, 28; *Pluralistic Universe*, 56, 57n., 58n., 80; *Pragmatism*, 29n., 30, 41, 44, 47–55, 56, 57n., 59n., 79, 81–82, 84, 84n., 176; as psychologist, 28, 30, 41, 43, 52; quoted, 29, 30, 32, 36, 38, 39–40, 42, 43, 44–45, 47, 49, 51, 52, 55, 56; "Reflex Action and Theism," 32n., 38–39, 50n., 57n.; on religious experience, 40–46, 141, 142; and Royce, 146, 149, 150, 151, 153, 154, 159, 162, 163; "Sentiment of Rationality," 32n., 35–38, 39, 41, 52, 54n., 55n., 82n., 84n.; spiritual crisis of, 50; style of, 31; and theism, 13, 14, 30, 31, 37, 38, 39, 40, 41, 47, 50–58, 59, 82, 141; *Varieties of Religious Experience*, 30, 40–46, 51, 51n., 55, 57n., 58n., 59, 163; "Will to Be-

lieve," 32–35, 37, 38, 39, 53n., 54n., 176
John Dewey: A Centennial Bibliography, 85n.
John Dewey: His Thought and Influence, 87n.
John the Evangelist, 129, 130
Journal of Philosophy, The, 61n., 103n., 110, 148n.
Judaism, 3

Kant, Immanuel, 11, 16, 17, 148, 149, 152

Lamont, C., 103n.
Laplace, Pierre de, 16
Larrabee, Harold A., 14, 14n.
Leclerc, I., 110n.
Leibniz, Gottfried W., 56–57
Linguistic analysis, 182
Logic, symbolic (Peirce), 65
Lotze, Rudolph H., 149, 152
Love, as example of mystery (Marcel), 178
Lowe, Victor, 110n., 111n., 114, 114n., 115, 115n., 133n., 134n.
Lubac, Henri de, 53, 53n.

McGiffert, Arthur C., 10
Man Against Mass Society, 179n.
Marcel, Gabriel, 174, 174n., 178, 178n., 179, 179n.; quoted, 178
Maslow, A. H., 180n.
Materialism, 17, 30, 37, 51, 92, 120, 121
Mathematics and philosophy, 182, 183
Matter, importance of, 17, 18–22
Mayeroff, Milton, 61, 61n.
Mead, George H., 153
Meaning of Truth, The, 54n., 56, 56n.

Mechanistic determinism, 16, 17, 21, 59, 121
Meditations on First Philosophy, 183n.
Melancholy, religious (James), 52
Men and Movements in American Philosophy, 14n.
Metaphysics, defined, 141
Modes of Thought, 110, 115n., 116n., 119n., 120n., 121n., 123n., 125n., 126n.
Monism, religious, 47
Moral Man and Immoral Society, 2, 2n.
Moral Philosopher and the Moral Life, The," 52n., 53n., 82n.
Morris, George S., 17, 92
Murphey, Murray, 65, 65n., 66n., 78
Mystery and problem, distinction between (Marcel), 178
Mystery of Being, 179n.
Mysticism, 41

Naturalism, 9, 20, 21, 146, 148, 180; of Dewey, 95, 98, 101, 107, 108; God negated by, 13, 51–52; of James, 58–60; and liberal Christianity, 3, 6, 7; method of, 22–26; and religious view, 11–16; rise of, 16–18; of Whitehead, 143, 144
Naturalism and the Human Spirit, 14n.
Newman, John H., 133
Niebuhr, Reinhold, 2, 2n., 3, 4, 5, 6, 8, 10
Nietzsche, Friedrich, 11
Novelty: in developing universe, 21, 23, 59, 118; Whitehead's emphasis on, 117, 118, 129

Ontological wonder (James), 36, 82
Origin of Dewey's Instrumentalism, The, 92n.
Outlines of a Critical Theory of Ethics, The, 95, 102n.

Palmer, G. H., 148n., 150, 150n., 151, 151n.
Pantheism, 57, 131
Papini, Giovanni, 79
Patriotism, 160
Paul (Apostle), 130, 167, 168, 169
Peirce, Benjamin, 66
Peirce, Charles Sanders, 12, 13, 14, 18, 26, 63–84, 96, 114, 141, 142, 146, 153, 187; *Collected Papers*, 65n., 80, 184n.; and James, 63, 64, 65, 72, 77–84, 184; on love of neighbor, 75, 76; on man's relation to nature, 66–70; and mathematical analysis, 65; and pragmatism, 63, 64, 78, 79; quoted, 71; on reality of God, 70–74, 75, 76, 83; on religion, 65–66, 70–77, 83, 84, 142; on science, 67, 68, 70, 142, 176, 183–84; and symbolic logic, 65; *Will to Believe*, criticism of, 80
Perry, Ralph B., 50n., 53, 53n., 55, 55n., 64n., 78, 78n., 148n., 149n., 151n.
Personal Knowledge, 61n.
Personalism (James), 176
Personality, human, *see* Human personality
Pessimism of European existentialism, 174
Peter (Apostle), 139
Philosophical Psychology, 181n.

125n., 129n., 130n., 133n., 134n., 135n., 136n., 137, 137n., 138n., 140n., 141n., 143n.

Religious Aspect of Philosophy, The, 152, 154, 155, 155n., 158, 159, 164

Religious experience: Dewey's views on, 101–07, 142; James's views on, 40–46, 141, 142

Religious melancholy (James), 52

Roodkowsky, N. D., 87n.

Roth, R. J., 13n.

Royce, Josiah, 12, 17, 18, 26, 30, 58, 63, 81, 145–74, 185; on Christianity, 165–72, 173; and community, Christian teaching about, 166–68; *Conception of God*, 152, 159; in Germany, 149, 152; on grace, 172, 173; and Hegel, 149, 152; idealism of, rationalistic, 146, 147, 150, 154, 159, 171, 173; and individualism, 157; and James, 146, 149, 150, 151, 153, 154, 159, 162, 163; on Lost Individual, 168–69; on loyalty, 159–63, 164, 165, 173; *Philosophy of Loyalty*, 154, 159, 160n., 164, 164n., 172; and pragmatism, 146, 147, 159; *Primer of Logical Analysis*, 149n.; *Problem of Christianity*, 154, 164n., 165, 169n., 173; *Religious Aspect of Philosophy*, 152, 154, 155, 155n., 158, 159, 164; and religion, 151, 154–73; on salvation, 155, 163–65, 174; on sin and atonement, 169–72; *Sources of Religious Insight*, 154, 163, 163n., 164, 164n., 172, 174n.; *Spirit of Modern Philosophy*, 147n.; *World and*

the Individual, 152, 154, 159, 172

Royce's Metaphysics, 174

Russell, Bertrand, 87, 110n., 112, 112n., 115, 115n., 133, 133n., 134n.; *Principia Mathematica*, 111

St. Louis Movement, 16

Saintliness, 41

Salvation, Royce on, 155, 163–65, 174

Santayana, George, 14, 152, 152n., 153

Schiller, Ferdinand, 79

Schneider, Herbert W., quoted, 18

Schopenhauer, Arthur, 149, 152

Science, 12, 13, 24, 25, 29, 39, 179, 182; and Christianity, traditional, 95; determinism in, 16; Dewey's views on, 95, 97, 98–99, 142; limitations of (James), 43, 46, 58, 141, 176; limitations of (Whitehead), 120–22, 140; Peirce's views on, 67, 68, 70, 142, 176, 183–84; philosophy of (Peirce), 65; physical, 23; and religion (James), 46–47, 54; and religion (Whitehead), 140, 141; revolutionary effect of, 98–99; theoretical, distinguished from practical (Peirce), 184

Science and Philosophy, 110, 110n., 116n., 117n., 133n.

Science and the Modern World, 109, 110, 112, 118n., 119n., 120, 120n., 121n., 123, 124, 124n., 125n., 132, 132n., 134, 134n., 135n., 136n., 137n., 139n., 140n., 141n.

7
8
9
0
1
2
3
4
5
6